READERS' GUIDES TO E$

CONSULTANT EDITOR: ℩

Readers' Guides to Essential Criticism
Series Standing Order ISBN 978–1–4039–0108–8
(outside North America only)

You can receive future titles in this series as they are published by placing a standing order. Please contact your bookseller or, in the case of difficulty, write to us at the address below with your name and address, the title of the series and the ISBN quoted above.

Customer Services Department, Macmillan Distribution Ltd, Houndmills, Basingstoke, Hampshire, RG21 6XS, UK

Contemporary British Poetry

DAVID WHEATLEY

Consultant editor: Nicolas Tredell

No portion of this publication may be reproduced, copied or transmitted
save with written permission or in accordance with the provisions of the
Copyright, Designs and Patents Act 1988, or under the terms of any licence
permitting limited copying issued by the Copyright Licensing Agency,
Saffron House, 6–10 Kirby Street, London EC1N 8TS.

Any person who does any unauthorized act in relation to this publication
may be liable to criminal prosecution and civil claims for damages.

The author has asserted his right to be identified as the author of this work
in accordance with the Copyright, Designs and Patents Act 1988.

First published 2015 by
PALGRAVE

Palgrave in the UK is an imprint of Macmillan Publishers Limited,
registered in England, company number 785998, of 4 Crinan Street,
London N1 9XW.

Palgrave Macmillan in the US is a division of St Martin's Press LLC,
175 Fifth Avenue, New York, NY 10010.

Palgrave is a global imprint of the above companies and is represented
throughout the world.

Palgrave® and Macmillan® are registered trademarks in the United States,
the United Kingdom, Europe and other countries.

ISBN 978–0–230–36252–9   hardback
ISBN 978–0–230–36253–6   paperback

This book is printed on paper suitable for recycling and made from fully
managed and sustained forest sources. Logging, pulping and manufacturing
processes are expected to conform to the environmental regulations of the
country of origin.

A catalogue record for this book is available from the British Library.

A catalog record for this book is available from the Library of Congress.

Typeset by MPS Limited, Chennai, India.

Printed in China.

CONTENTS

are tested against the work of poets engaging with the postcolonial in a wide variety of ways, from Vahni Capildeo and Fred D'Aguiar to W. N. Herbert.

The intersections of gender, sexuality and class and the poem form the focus for this chapter. Responses to the work of Medbh McGuckian and Vona Groarke illustrate a tension between identity politics and more formalist approaches drawing on theories of intertextuality, while maleness and the sexing (or queering) of the lyric poem are also examined. Questions of voice and class in the work of Tom Leonard, Douglas Dunn and others are discussed, as is the often fractious debate they stage with the politics of the lyric.

This chapter looks at the experimental tradition, and the critique of language and the self in which critics locate its differences from more mainstream styles; background and context on publishers and movements are provided. Veronica Forrest-Thomson and her theory of 'naturalisation' offer a powerful anti-realist template, whose effects can be traced in the work of poets and critics such as Peter Manson and Andrew Duncan. While experimental poetry addresses itself to questions of language, it does not do so at the expense of questions of politics, as shown in the radical agenda of Keston Sutherland, and his imbuing of experimental poetry with a new sense of transformative possibility.

This chapter looks at the new domains explored by ecopoetry. Jonathan Bate's Song of the Earth makes the neo-Romantic case for poetry as a force of mediation and salvation, but closer analysis shows how the ecocritic must strike a balance between the detached imagination and ideological wish-fulfilment. These positions are explored in relation to a range of poets including Kathleen Jamie, Helen Macdonald, and R. F. Langley, and the debates they have inspired.

CONCLUSION

Criticism Today

Looking at the public face of poetry in Britain today, this chapter
considers the difficulty of 'making it new' in ways that go beyond
commodification and the selling short of the art in today's market
economy. Despite deep anxieties about the future of poetry and the
relationship of writer and reader and the general public, criticism
nevertheless manages to find fresh and resilient ways of 'keeping
going'.

In memory of Dennis O'Driscoll

Introduction

' The recent past', observes Theodor Adorno in *Minima Moralia* (1951), 'always likes to present itself as if destroyed by catastrophes.'[1] Where poetry is concerned, the twentieth century and its aftermath have been a history of contestation and counter-contestation, each generation theatrically forswearing its precursor. The 1950s and the Movement reject the windy rhetoric of the 1940s, relegating a whole generation of writers to the limbo of the lost and sending the lonely genius of W. S. Graham into years of internal exile; the 1960s swap bicycle clips and ration-book common sense for the excitement of Sylvia Plath's *Ariel*, Allen Ginsberg in the Albert Hall and Basil Bunting's *Briggflatts*; poetry in England implodes into rival factions at *Poetry Review* in the 1970s even as it erupts scarifyingly into life in Northern Ireland; the sophisticates of the Martian school fine-tune their metaphors in Thatcher's Britain while Peter Reading and Tony Harrison pick over the scraps of a junked and polarised nation in the 1980s; a new populism is born in the 1990s with the New Generation, freeing up a demotic style hailed and argued over in equal measure today, as British and Irish poetry passes its millennial moment and enters the twenty-first century. As thumbnail sketches of recent poetic history go, the above too can be contested at every step.

Where definitions are concerned, the 'contemporary' is an often elusive commodity. In 'Annus Mirabilis' Philip Larkin situated his adult awakening between the end of the *Lady Chatterley* ban and the Beatles' first LP,[2] and as Chapter 1 will dwell on the overlap between Ian Hamilton's *Oxford Companion to Twentieth-Century Poetry* and the New Generation issue of *Poetry Review*, both of 1994, that year might be floated as a convenient starting point. Poetic generations do not simply begin and end, or line up one after another like railway carriages, however, and 'reference back' (to use another Larkin allusion) is frequently made to the period before this watershed, all the way back to the defining power struggles of the 1960s centred on A. Alvarez's *The New Poetry* (1962). Where the Britishness of contemporary poetry is concerned, this book was written in a period when the continued existence of the United Kingdom has been subject to discussion as never before in recent history, with first the establishment of devolved assemblies and parliaments in Belfast, Cardiff and Edinburgh in the late 1990s, and in 2014 a vote on Scottish independence. Just as Scottish poetry would not suddenly forfeit its British dimension in the context of an independent new (or restored) nation north of the border, other historical shadows linger too, as in the case of Irish poetry and Irishness. Seamus Heaney wrote one of his most pugnacious poems in protest at inclusion in Blake Morrison and Andrew Motion's 1982 *Penguin Book of Contemporary British Poetry*.[3] Heaney was reminding the editors of his cultural Irishness, but as experienced by someone born to British citizenship. Where the binary remains strongly felt (and argued over) in Northern Ireland, it has not entirely vanished south of the border either, and some reference will accordingly be made in this book to poets from the Irish Republic, many of whom continue to publish in and make their careers in Britain.

Where other territories are concerned, the work of decolonisation was well under way before the period under consideration in this book, with India achieving independence in 1947, the Suez crisis (as registered in Larkin's 'Homage to a Government') occurring in 1956, and Ghana, Nigeria, Uganda and Jamaica all winning freedom from British rule in quick succession in the late 1950s and early 1960s. Enoch Powell's 'rivers of blood' speech, delivered in 1968 and precipitating Powell's dismissal from the Conservative shadow cabinet, marked the moment when expressions of open racism become unacceptable in mainstream British politics. Poetry was slow to respond to the new reality of multi-cultural Britain, however, and many anthologies published in the 1970s and 1980s would blithely ignore the existence of Black British and non-UK-born poets. It is one of the ironies of British identity that it should have been embraced by poets of African or Jamaican ethnicity at a time when the poets of the United Kingdom's home nations largely traded Britishness for Irishness, Welshness, Scottishness and Englishness, but the history of contemporary poetry follows no single linear narrative.

The historian E. P. Thompson wrote of rescuing the radical past from the 'enormous condescension of posterity',[4] but even the era closest to ours can easily slip out of focus without due critical care. Pondering the suggestion that the poets of the past seem remote to us because we know so much more than they did, T. S. Eliot answered, 'Precisely, and they are that which we know.'[5] This leaves the critic of the contemporary in a difficult and exposed position. We 'know' the poets of the past through our distance from them, and the canonical sifting that previous generations have performed on our behalf. The critical attention received by contemporary poets is often of an ephemeral kind, with even prize-winning status conferring no guarantee of a reputation's survival. Critics of contemporary poetry are also, however, in the uniquely favourable position of responding to a literature-in-progress, with all the chances this affords to shape reputations and poetic generations. Critics such as Christopher Ricks, Helen Vendler, Edna Longley and Jahan Ramazani have exercised enormous influence, not just on which poets are read, but on how we read, and how the study of poetry has reinvented itself in the face of new and competing academic discourses such as literary and postcolonial theory.

This book is organised around a number of themes and genres in which we see this reinvention most clearly at work. In Chapter 1, we consider the role of anthologies. The first English anthology was *Tottel's Miscellany*, published in 1557. In Greek the word originally meant a collection of flowers, but anthological roses seldom come without thorns. Anthologies have played a large part in shaping the canon, marking the rise and fall of generations and forming chain reactions between them, as one volume proves itself by attacking its predecessor. The anthology introduction is a critical genre unto itself, and depending on its surroundings the same poem can carry very different meanings in different anthologies. Anthologies can be centripetal or centrifugal, concerned to shore up or dismantle narratives of cultural power. How many poets constitute a poetic generation? Current trends show numbers rising, with Roddy Lumsden's *Identity Parade* (2010) featuring more than four times as many poets as are included in Motion and Morrison's *Penguin Book of Contemporary British Poetry* (1982). Other factors shaping the evolution of anthologies include small versus large, commercial versus independent publishers, and gender and race. On the invasion of Iraq in 2003 a number of anthologies were compiled at speed as a protest gesture, prompting debate on the role and efficacy of poetry in a time of conflict. The premise of a good anthology is the conversion of an assembly of poems into a movement or critical climate. The intermediary space it occupies between the creative and the critical makes the anthology an ideal starting point for a look at the life of poetry today.

In Chapter 2, I discuss the critical frameworks within which the conversation about poetry is carried on. An important subset of the critic is the poet-critic. Some poet-critics do and others do not draw on their personal experiences. The most distinguished critic of our time, Christopher Ricks, is not a practising poet, and while Ezra Pound suggested we should pay no attention to the opinions of those who have not themselves 'produced notable work',[6] it would be grossly foolish to discounts Ricks's judgements on these grounds. Ricks has also been a key figure in the debates in our period on literary theory. From its rise in the 1970s, theory treated with scepticism notions of the lyric self and individual judgement. Theory aspired to a specialised vocabulary, which would mark it off from the genteel amateur chatter of the books pages, but also imbue the discussion of poems with the same excitement as developments in structuralist and post-structuralist thought. At its worst this became an exercise in the doctrinaire application of ill-fitting philosophical readings to poems. There are exceptions: Veronica Forrest-Thomson's *Poetic Artifice* (1979) could not have been written without the hothouse influence of theory, and (another example of the poet-critic) the poetics sketched out in that book bear further fruit in her quirkily important poems. A standard accusation against theory is that it over-interprets texts, substituting preposterous critical invention for authorial intention. To W. K. Wimsatt and Monroe C. Beardsley's New Critical attack on the 'intentional fallacy' was added Roland Barthes's critique of the 'death of the author', transferring the power to generate meanings within the text to the reader. A poet who strongly matches this mood is Paul Muldoon, whose work is 'packed to the gunwales with further education', in the words of John Carey,[7] and who delights in unanswered riddles at the reader's expense. Reading a Muldoon poem we are aware that it might be an allegory for the Northern Irish Troubles – or it might be an innocuous poem about a car ticking over by the side of the road. How do we tell the difference?

In Chapter 3 I consider British poetry in a postcolonial context. Michael Hofmann's political satire 'Campaign Fever' features an incontinent dog 'who confuses home and the world', with unfortunate consequences. For many decades now, British poetry has experienced a blurring of the lines between home and abroad, in ways that have been disorienting but exhilarating too. In his study *Devolving English Literature* (1992), Robert Crawford unpicks the assumptions of centralised cultural authority that have traditionally underlain the study of English literature. This interrogation has multiple fronts. Language will frequently be to the fore, and the question of standard versus non-standard English. While the work of Caribbean, Guyanese or Asian British writers such as Vahni Capildeo, Fred D'Aguiar and Daljit Nagra represents one departure from narrow canons of poetic Britishness, the poetry of the Northern Irish Troubles has produced a domestic test-case for postcolonialism and British poetry. The poetry of Seamus Heaney has provoked wars of interpretation redolent of the territorial skirmishes that inspired the original poems. To one critic Heaney's work becomes poetry to the extent that it leaves the sordidness of political violence behind; to another it invests unhealthily in that violence, succumbing to voyeurism and martyrology; and to another again it deviates into dubious sectarian mythology rather than serve up the radical postcolonial critique of injustice the Northern Irish situation demands. On the 'mainland' of Albion itself, immigrant voices such as Michael Hofmann have performed subtle excavations of the colonial heritage. 'Native'-born writers are no less involved in the same critique. While Geoffrey Hill might be many people's idea of a conservative poet, he has used his work of recent years to articulate a radical conservative assault on the mediocrities and failings of British life (political as much as poetic) unprecedented in modern British writing.

Much contemporary criticism has approached poetry through the prisms of gender, sexuality and class, the themes explored in Chapter 4. As the demographics of British poetry change, so too do styles of reading.

The default neutral position under which texts are assumed to be spoken by white male heterosexuals no longer fits the contemporary poem, nor is this a useful model for reading poems in a heteroglossic society. Philip Larkin misleadingly speculated that being a novelist required an interest in others whereas being a poet required only an interest in himself, but in reality the voice of a poem – even the short lyric poem – is defined by a synthesis of competing voices and social registers. Often a Larkin poem such as 'Mr Bleaney' will trade on the presumed familiarity of the speaker and the world that it creates before springing the trap of defamiliarisation, forcing a realisation that our assumptions are not so well founded after all. Sexuality too has proved a fertile territory for defamiliarisation: the worlds of strangeness conjured in the work of Denise Riley and Medbh McGuckian are startlingly sensual yet lyrically available. Larkin's contemporary Thom Gunn spent his early years struggling to reconcile his gay identity with the normative sexual politics of 1950s Britain, but in *The Man with Night Sweats* (1992) and other collections he articulates a gay poetics that is also a searching poetics of the sexually desiring self. Where class is concerned, the work of Douglas Dunn and Tony Harrison – and in subsequent generations, of Sean O'Brien and Don Paterson – has challenged cultural authority and rigid hierarchies of high and low. It also focuses on the poet's access to authority, and the ways in which the poem alternately resists and colludes with the respectability of the lyric voice; class becomes a question of rhetoric and self-interrogation as much as of subject matter.

Chapter 5 addresses the experimental tradition. Terminology varies from poet to poet, with some preferring the 'innovative' label. The alternative tradition in British poetry has tended to see itself in opposition to a lazy or decadent mainstream, identifying a number of key moments in literary history where the chance for a radical transformation of public taste was lost. The oppositional model of modernist or neo-modernist poetics can be overdone, however, and may not be an accurate reflection of how its practitioners relate to the way they write. 'As far as I'm concerned', Peter Riley has told Keith Tuma, 'where I am is a normal and proper place to be, is where people like me always have been, and mainstream and avant-garde are way out on a limb, really nowhere.'[8] It is a paradox of critical writing that labels impose themselves even as we dispute their accuracy, but one good reason for their persistence is the frequency with which accounts of British poetry screen out writers who have not published with large commercial presses and whose reception has bypassed the prize-lists and festival circuit. The previously-mentioned Morrison/Motion *Penguin Book* referred to the 1960s and 1970s as a period 'when very little [...] seemed to be happening',[9] despite the striking work produced during this period by Basil Bunting, Roy Fisher, Tom Raworth, and many others, none of whom features in their anthology.

The presence in the UK at the time of Ed Dorn had a profound effect on many of these writers, but for those who looked to Robert Lowell, John Berryman and Sylvia Plath for their American poetry (not that a choice is necessary) other kinds of poetry often remained invisible. Groups and camps are only one among many factors. However they choose to self-identify, writers such as Keston Sutherland, Peter Manson and Helen Macdonald work in styles that radically honour Pound's prescription to make it new. Manson's translations from Mallarmé turn the energies of the original text back on the English versions, interrogating questions of originality and textual fidelity. Macdonald renovates traditions of nature writing with her poems on birds of prey, and Sutherland brings a rampaging Marxist sensibility to his critiques of language and society. Sutherland is also a prolific commentator, helping to define the critical terms in which this work can be properly understood and absorbed.

Macdonald's work has much to say too to a student of ecopoetics, the subject of Chapter 6. Much new poetry engages with nature in ways that rethink the Romantic legacy. Jonathan Bate's *The Song of the Earth* (2000) mixes John Clare, Edward Thomas and the deep ecological thinking of Martin Heidegger to update the Shelleyan idea of the poet as unacknowledged legislator, creatively saving the world. The work of Ted Hughes crossed the English nature lyric with an interest in non-Western and shamanic approaches to the natural world, often with violent results. Nevertheless, Hughes has left a clear legacy for contemporary poets such as Alice Oswald. The challenge of nature is, among other things, a challenge of form. For some critics, the lyric line traceable from Edward Thomas is the natural form for the British tradition, an identification that would doubly confirm the alienness of modernism. The Scottish poet, artist and *avant*-gardener Ian Hamilton Finlay gives the lie to the equation of the nature lyric with a peaceable native tradition: his work is full of classical violence, experiments in concrete poetry, and demands of its readers a new relationship to the environments of art. Beyond the natural world, poetry today has explored new publishing environments too. A Sunday newspaper feature on young poets will speak lazily of a 'facebook generation', but writers have engaged with new media creatively as well as for self-promotion. The poems of Sam Riviere's *81 Austerities* (2012) began life as postings on tumblr – an ideal medium for dispatches on the harried state of austerity Britain.

The Conclusion hazards a speculative look into the future. Democratisation and diversity have transformed British poetry, but who are the major figures today? How do contemporary poetry and criticism compare in ambition and quality to those of previous generations? Reviewing the *Collected Poems* (2012) of Peter Redgrove for the *Times Literary Supplement* (*TLS*), Graeme Richardson began in confrontational style: 'In the second half of the twentieth century, British poetry criticism lost its bite.'[10] Tracing the decline of poetry back 60 years to the Movement, Richardson offers the frequently-heard lament of poetry's disconnection from a popular audience, as subsidised modern poetry was force-fed to a public that 'preferred Philip Larkin'. In the absence of this sustaining readership, the fate of the modern poet would appear to be oblivion: Richardson cites the example of Ian Hamilton, whose posthumously-published *Against Oblivion* (2002) was a gloomy stock-taking of the reputations of the seeming-Titans of the twentieth century. The death of poetry is a familiar jeremiad among critics: American poet-critic Dana Gioia published an essay collection, *Can Poetry Matter?* in 1991, and Vernon Shetley a study, *After the Death of Poetry*, in 1993 (so familiar did the theme become that Donald Hall was moved to a rejoinder, 'Death to the Death of Poetry'); but a counterargument is easily made too. Anthony Thwaite's satirical poem 'On Consulting *Contemporary Poets of the English Language*' takes the form of a long list of poets' names, arranged as rhyming couplets, and ending with a quotation from Yeats:

■ No one can tell who has talent, if any.
Only one thing is certain. We are too many.[11] □

Read by anyone with a concern for modern poetry, Thwaite's satire cannot help backfiring, since the large majority of the writers cited continue to command critical respect, and in many cases their anthology berths too. A corollary of laments for the death of poetry is laments for the death of criticism, a criticism that could take up Yeats's challenge and bring order to our contemporary chaos. To some, Richardson's 'failure of nerve' finds expression in a bland submission to the promotions and prizes through which poetry tries to recapture public attention. For John Redmond, contemporary poetry exists in a world from which the more high-brow pursuits of modernist art have been almost eradicated: 'Although exceptions like the so-called "Cambridge School" exist, the dominant culture of contemporary poetry is promotional in outlook and anti-intellectual in spirit.'[12] Observing British poetry from a transatlantic distance, Keith Tuma finds an art unable to project itself on a world stage: 'In the United States, British poetry is dead.'[13] Irish poetry has had the totemic figure of Seamus Heaney, but since the death of Larkin in 1985 it is debatable whether any British poet has commanded a global audience.

Literary history will often project importance onto periods by declaring them 'transitional'. The 1930s are proverbially transitional, with poets writing in the shadow of an all-consuming but unborn apocalypse. Judged only on its externals, the present age is also one of transition. Where the 1970s witnessed intense levels of small-press and magazine activity, and old Oxbridge publishing cartels were broken up by competition from

Bloodaxe and Carcanet, the story today is one of economic uncertainty and decline. The internet has created new (self-)publishing opportunities, but its rise has coincided with the shrinking of the poetry market and the disappearance of established lists such as Oxford's and those of independent publishers such as Salt. In his humorous poem 'The Poetry Promise', Roy Fisher makes a series of promises to the reader in the language of customer service relations ('Ensuring Quality', 'Maintaining Quality', 'Observing Guidelines'), ending with the slogan 'Poetry You Can Count On'.[14] The dark side of Fisher's satire is not how inimical the world he conjures is to the imagination, but how closely it resembles today's world of higher education and the literary arts as branches of the service economy – a world in which the audience at a poetry reading today will routinely be asked to fill out questionnaires detailing their customer satisfaction and offering information on their gender and ethnicity.

Defeatism is tempting but offers a less than complete picture of the current state of the art. Another rejoinder to the 'death of poetry' argument is the abundance of fine critics at work today, pessimistic though some might be about the future (or present). A list of intelligent critics who have written with distinction on poetry would include Denis Donoghue, Barbara Everett, Neil Corcoran, Edna Longley, Angela Leighton, Peter McDonald, Justin Quinn, Fran Brearton, Tim Kendall, John Redmond, Jeremy Noel-Tod and Maria Johnston. The relationship between poetry and criticism is not always harmonious, but their spheres are far from mutually exclusive. The special case of poet-critics has been noted, but it is also a central tenet of this book that poems are their own first readers and, as such, perform a critique of themselves and their period. Donald Davie's 'Remembering the 'Thirties' condenses into a short lyric what many a book about the Movement fails to say, while another Roy Fisher poem, 'On the Neglect of Figure Composition', could stand in for any number of articles on the internecine struggles of the British *avant-garde*.

The founder of twelve-tone music in the early twentieth century, Arnold Schoenberg, once declared that there was still plenty of good music to be written in the key of C major. The advent of gender studies or postcolonialism no more renders the art of close reading poems redundant than a Schoenberg string quartet replaces our favourite folk songs. While making no claims to address the full spectrum of contemporary British poets, this book aims to give a meaningful sense of the larger whole. It does this by moving between poets, critics, and debates, maintaining at all times a primary focus on the poem itself. As noted, Eliot thought we knew more than the poets of the past, because *they* are what we know, and by finding a critical language for the poetry of the present we begin the process of transforming its qualities from hypotheses to something closer to values and facts. We place the present and posterity in conversation, gaining a clearer understanding of both.

CHAPTER ONE

Anthologies and Canon Formation

F ew forms of literary production are simultaneously more revealing and more concealing of the nature of contemporary poetry than the anthology. Revealing, in the sense that a phalanx of rival anthologies crowds the market, promising vibrant newcomers, reassuringly familiar names and laurelled elders; and concealing, in the sense that any given anthology will necessarily present a skewed and partial survey of what is happening in poetry today. The anthology can be a textbook or a battle cry; many have been both. Assessing the role of the anthology in turn-of-the-century surveys of British poetry, Edna Longley writes:

■ While anthologies survive, the idea of poetic tradition survives. They house intricate conversations between poets and between poems, between the living and the dead, between the present and the future. In more polemical converse with one another, some anthologies dramatise the contest over aesthetic terms and values; all, as time goes by, betray the hidden forces that also shape canons.[1] □

The anthology played a central part in the rise of modernism, notably in the hands of Ezra Pound, and the changing generations of post-war poetry too were shaped by decisive anthological interventions such as Robert Conquest's *New Lines* (1956) and A. Alvarez's *The New Poetry* (1962). The first enthroned the lyric empiricism for which 'the Movement' (a label coined by a reviewer in 1954) became the enduring shorthand,[2] while the second retaliated with a critique of the 'gentility principle', introducing audiences to the American Confessional poets and championing the work of Sylvia Plath, while also finding room on the 'home' team for poets as different as Philip Larkin, Ted Hughes and Thom Gunn. Alvarez's playing off of Americans against British was not without an element of artificiality or Machiavellianism, and a reader of Donald Allen's *The New American Poetry* (1960) might find Alvarez's American line-up trading on a gentility principle of its own. Such slogans, in other words, are often little more than rhetorical conveniences, but good for a rallying call in the pages of an anthology introduction.

Entire movements, most notably the Movement itself, can be built on impressionistic slogans of this kind, with the knock-on effects visible in the criticism they generate too. Sifting good from bad, the anthologist does the hands-on work for the academic critic who upgrades opinion into scholarly authority; the anthologist's provisional gathering hardens into canonical fact. While Larkin was publicly sceptical of the Movement, the boost he received from its saleable brand of plain-speaking rationalism is unarguable, and the dialectic of group-identity and individual diffidence is one that has continued to the present day, notably with the Poetry Society's New Generation and Next Generation promotions in 1994, 2004 and 2014, featuring three cohorts of twenty poets. Asked on a New Generation questionnaire whether 'talk of movements should be discouraged', Michael Donaghy replied: 'Yes. "Movements" are dreamt up by publicists to help us sell poetry or by journalists and academic bores to help us understand it.'[3] Donaghy's cheery scepticism does not cancel the ironies of its occasion; nor does it prevent Fiona Sampson from describing Donaghy and his associates as having 'sometimes appeared to be the only community within British poetry'.[4] The use of 'community' avoids the self-promoting and academic overtones of 'movement' and 'school', while conjuring the close-knit intimacies of village life. Where anthologies once paraded their ambitions to stage literary take-overs, a more conciliatory tone is often now preferred, as the faux-naturalism of a 'community' would suggest. How many communities can contemporary poetry support, though, and how are peaceful relations maintained?

Revisiting *The New Poetry* in its second edition, Alvarez conceded that the inflammatory rhetoric of its introduction was not fully borne out by the contents, but an anthologist who restricted him or herself to a businesslike response to the work assembled would gravely have misunderstood the nature of the beast. Posterity is kinder to the dramatically wrong in an anthology than to the unassuming and meekly correct, and even in his wrongness there remains much to admire in Alvarez's editorial will-to-power. Anthologies can be comprehensive or exclusive: where Douglas Dunn's *Faber Book of Twentieth-Century Scottish Poetry* (1992) is encyclopaedic in range, Paul Muldoon's *Faber Book of Contemporary Irish Poetry* (1986) is a swingeingly restrictive selection of modern Irish poets, almost all of them drawn from his Northern Irish contemporaries. Among the factors in the mix dictating an editor's approach will be: a sense of the national tradition; the urgency of its renovation in the face of decadence or exhaustion; its opening up to foreign influence or vindication in the face of the same thing; the rise of new movements and schools; the influence of changing critical trends; and the recognition of new or previously under-represented groups. An anthologist keen to opt out of these Freudian tussles might call his or her book *A Selection of Some Poets Offered on a Non-Committal Basis and Without Reference to Larger Questions of Nation, Gender, or Tradition*, but in practice such anthologists tend not to exist, or to succeed in finding publishers who share their vision.

Contexts: Magazines, Editors

If nation and language are the larger nexus from which a tradition is built, anthologies are often the concretisation of the power blocs (or power grabs) represented by small magazines. 'The little magazine is the natural home of the deranged, the talentless and the bitterly disenfranchised', wrote Tim Kendall in his editorial for the last issue of *Thumbscrew* (1994–2002), one of the most important magazines of the turn-of-the-century period.[5] Dylan Thomas joked in the 1930s of those who had turned the Paris review *transition* (1927–1938) into a permanent resting place, and for Kendall's 'deranged' bards too the question is whether the bolt-hole of the magazine represents a form of day-care or something more long-term. As its name would suggest, the Oxford-based *Thumbscrew* was oppositional in flavour, and took great delight in attacking New Gen favourites. If the magazine had any mission, it had more than carried it out by the time of its final issue in 2002. With the death in 2003 of William Cookson, who had edited the modernist-leaning journal *Agenda* for forty-four years, *P. N. Review* (1977–) became the outstanding example of editorial continuity among contemporary British magazines. Other journals have reinvented themselves under different editors, with varying degrees of success. As the journal of the Poetry Society, *Poetry Review* (founded 1909) might be expected to play a central role in poetic debate, but has at various stages in its history threatened to be the 'organisational mouthpiece' of its vested interests;[6] it effectively sat out High Modernism, for instance, much as the Irish Free State sat out the Second World War. In recent times it has reflected (sometimes turbulently) a number of strongly differentiated strands in contemporary poetry. The editorship of Eric Mottram (1971–7) precipitated a near-terminal crisis for the Poetry Society, as Mottram's radical tastes provoked a backlash and institutional civil war.[7] Peter Forbes (1986–2002) by contrast was a dynamic populariser, whose tenure overlapped with the New Generation promotion of 1994. If not traumatic enough the first time round, this pendulum swing was duplicated in recent years by the innovative-friendly tenure of David Herd and Robert Potts, who were replaced in turn in 2005 by Fiona Sampson, who then excluded any work from Herd and Potts's reign from her anthology *A Century of Poetry Review*, before Sampson was duly replaced in 2012, after a period of in-fighting comparable in unpleasantness to that of the 1970s. The editor might hope that doing his or her job conscientiously is the 'best insurance that the next thing, whatever it will be, can emerge undistorted',[8] but the 'next thing' has a habit of taking us violently by surprise. Magazines that have done more than most to divine for and foster this 'next thing' during our period would include *Honest Ulsterman* (1968–2003), *P. N. Review, Stand* (1952–), *Poetry Wales* (1965–), *The English Intelligencer* (1966–68), *Gairfish* (1983–95, originally *The Gairfish*), *The North* (1986–), *Verse* (1984–), *Angel Exhaust* (1979–), and *Magma* (1994–).[9]

The relationship between small magazines and more established public prints has rarely been harmonious, however. To jaundiced outsiders such as Hugh Kenner in *A Sinking Island* (1988), Britain's journalistic old-boy network has long acted as a draught-excluder against the modernist storms threatening to blow in from the outside world or from the pages of Britain's literary underground. To Kenner, the critical astringency displayed by Ian Hamilton in the pages of *The Observer*, the *TLS*, and his journal *The Review* (1962–72) was an entirely rear-guard action devoted to maintaining the post-Movement Little Englander hegemony and freezing out neo-modernists such as Basil Bunting. On this reading, a book such as Blake Morrison and Andrew Motion's *Penguin Book of Contemporary British Poetry* (1982) grows naturally out of such a consensus. Hamilton's poetic career, conducted as though clandestinely under the nose of Hamilton the critic, bears out the strains of his position: endlessly productive as a critic and reviewer, Hamilton the poet produced little over fifty poems, imagistically precise and painfully short in the main. The element of masochism involved has not been lost on one of his chief acolytes, Michael Hofmann, a prolific critic who appears to approach his own poetry with something resembling acute hostility. Yet Hamilton was never less than a shrewd editor and, as he showed in his final critical book *Against Oblivion* (2002), entirely undeceived over the capacity of the promotion machine to keep the reputational grim reaper at bay. Hamilton's career ended before the eclipse of the print journal by the internet, and with it the all-but-impossibility of any one critic ever wielding such power again.

This development brings gains in its wake but losses too, if the only alternative to Hamilton's knowing metropolitanism turns out to be a pluralised blandness. It is interesting that Hamilton never attempted a generation-defining anthology himself, treading with circumspection for once, though Peter Forbes devotes considerable space in his introduction to the New Generation issue of *Poetry Review* in 1994 to attacking Hamilton's *Oxford Companion to Twentieth-Century Poetry* (1994). To Forbes it represents 'a map of a lost empire' (by which Forbes did not mean a commitment to postcolonial poetry), falling from the press with 'instant obsolescence'; a 'less timely publication' could 'scarcely be imagined'.[10] To Forbes, this is canon-making as Oxbridge patronage system, blind to all beyond the Oxbridge triangle and hopelessly sexist (when a *Festschrift* was organised for Hamilton in 1999, not one contributor was female).[11] The centre represented by Hamilton–Morrison/ Motion could not hold, and into the vacuum they left, or created, any number of aspirant hegemonies were about to step. Yet if the tottering orthodoxy in need of overthrow is one stereotype of anthologising, the over-ripe epitomes of what 'the age demanded', in Pound's words, is another, and Forbes does little to advance his case by praising Carol Ann Duffy at the expense of Alan Jenkins by describing the former as 'ha[ving] merely won all the prizes going and [being ...] on the way to becoming "the representative poet of our times"'.[12] Timeliness is a powerful metaphor, but one that can be overplayed: the representative poet of Victorian Britain was probably Felicia Hemans rather than Browning or Hopkins, but being the representative poet of one age may be a shortcut to being an unremembered curiosity for the next. When an older rhetoric of excellence comes up against newer imperatives of inclusion and diversity, the encounter can be bruising on both sides. The challenge then becomes to short-circuit this opposition with an anthology that provides enough of each to make the stand-off seem staged and false. Striking this balance has been, in many ways, the great challenge of contemporary poetry.

Against Anthologies?

Not everyone cares for anthologies, however, or wants to be party to their king- and queen-making campaigns. Laura Riding and Robert Graves co-authored a *Pamphlet Against Anthologies* in 1928, and in more recent times Paul Durcan has expressed trenchant views on the pernicious effects of anthologising:

■ Normally, there is no class of book more slipshod, more boring, more prejudiced, more snobbish, more exclusive, more incestuous, more narrow-minded, more arid, more ignorant, more canonical, more soulless, more soul-destroying, more anti-poetic than a poetry anthology.[13] □

The reasons behind his dislike are easily guessed at. While *Palgrave's Golden Treasury* (1861), the Victorians' anthology of choice and a *bête noire* of Ezra Pound's, was a fireside favourite, a more twentieth-century production such as *The Norton Anthology* represents canonicity as commercial juggernaut. Inclusion versus exclusion can be a determining factor in a poet's career, and smooth the path to prizes and academic honours. Described in such blunt terms, the anthology highlights one of the most notable trends in contemporary poetry: the rise of creative writing, following the establishment of the University of East Anglia's Master's Degree in the subject in 1970,[14] the institutionalisation of the art of poetry, and the professionalisation of its practitioners. An appearance in a contemporary poetry anthology will typically be accompanied by at least some of the following: an author photograph; a biographical note detailing degree credentials and teaching affiliation; a list of prizes and shortlist appearances; an author's statement. With its commitment to what it calls 'the pluralist now', Roddy Lumsden's *Identity Parade* (2010) is among the least academic of anthologies, yet almost exactly half its 85 poets came up through or now teach in the creative writing system. Selection for an anthology that will be taught on undergraduate poetry courses signals group membership of a different kind from that of signing an *avant-garde* manifesto in the early twentieth century, but while the contemporary anthologist may have impure designs on the canon, the poetic ecosystem is more than capable of fighting back. Nothing is more defunct than a failed anthology and the deflated superlatives of promotions past. Yet even as their poets fade or disappear entirely, anthologies allow us a unique entry-point into the moments in literary history they represent. It is therefore not entirely perverse of Patrick McGuinness to suggest an 'anthology of anthology introductions',[15] by way of a distillation of this most front-loaded of literary genres. Such a volume would illustrate perfectly the process by which opinionation and the vagaries of literary fashion harden slowly into something as close to certainty as the process of canon-making comes.

The rise of creative writing as an academic discipline has not taken place without misgivings and resistance, but to study the profiles of younger writers in anthologies such as Clare Pollard and James Byrne's *Voice Recognition* (2009) is to witness a new form of professionalisation. The young writer today will tend to have a web presence, whether a dedicated site or social networking page, and use it for a mixture of creative and self-promotion purposes. More than an adjunct to publication proper, an online presence of this kind may even have become a prerequisite for it. In the era of university 'impact' statements and an anxiety about the audience for academic and artistic activity, the poetry anthology will frequently commend itself to the public as anything but a product of the belles-lettrism of Palgrave's *Golden Treasury*. At its most dramatic, it may even declare that it wants to save our lives. Neil Astley's trilogy of anthologies *Staying Alive* (2002), *Being Alive* (2004) and *Being Human* (2011) make a full-throated pitch for an audience beyond the usual small market for slim volumes of verse. This provoked some disdain among reviewers, with Mark Ford diagnosing a case of art-as-therapy, and accusing Astley of selling short the classic poems he includes by making them cohabit with undistinguished contemporary examples, a juxtaposition he finds 'simply cruel'.[16] *Staying Alive* bristled with signs of what a marketing department would call a 'breakout' publication, attempting to reposition poetry in the marketplace (a strategy that paid off richly where the volume's sales were concerned). Its pre-publication blurbs came not just from poets but from film stars and other celebrities. Its sections were divided on an entirely thematic, rather than generational or formal basis (sample section titles included 'Body and Soul' and 'Me, the Earth, the Universe'). Ford spoke of the 'appallingly written [...] boosterisms of jacket copy', unthinkable even in the sedate early 1970s, never mind the days of T. S. Eliot's minimalist copy for new Faber books.

Astley replied to Ford and other nay-sayers in a caustic lecture at the StAnza Festival, the online text of which was heavily redacted for legal reasons, suggesting the tendency of this intractable debate to descend all too soon into a poetry Punch and Judy match. This standoff can be compared to the American case of the long and fulminating review published in *Poetry* by August Kleinzahler of Garrison Keillor's anthology *Good Poems* (2002). The logic of Keillor's position, as Kleinzahler explains it, is that readable middlebrow poems will help create the audience currently lacking for more demanding, higher-brow work. Kleinzahler refuses to accept this, and accuses Keillor of reducing the anthology to social work by another name, the *trahison des clercs* of accessibility and good intentions. The promised challenge to the middlebrow reader never comes: 'Everything Keillor does is about reassurance, containment, continuity. He makes no demands on his audiences, none whatsoever. To do so would only be bad manners.'[17] Underneath these debates simmers an age-old unease over the therapeutic role of art. Astley and Keilor perpetuate the Arnoldian model of poetry as a cultural panacea, making us better moral beings, while a sceptic such as John Ashbery sees in the therapeutic model only grandiose self-delusion: 'There is the view that poetry should improve your life. I think people confuse it with the Salvation Army.'[18]

'Great Hatred, Little Room'

In their introduction to *Voice Recognition*, Pollard and Byrne make the connection between burgeoning poetic numbers and the supply-side economics of creative writing: 'Outside of poetry gigs, the first generation to benefit from studying Creative Writing has also emerged. Almost every university going seems to have a poetry course.' Creative writing has a much longer history than this would suggest, but the sense of urgent novelty here is driven by a territorial imperative:

> ■ For many years the poetry world has belonged to older writers. Few young poets were published and fewer were nominated for the major prizes. An invitation to a poetry reading conjured thoughts of warm white wine in a pokey bookshop or plodding recitals in a half empty village hall. Being a poet was uncool.[19] □

Given *Voice Recognition*'s overt focus on *ingénus* (its youngest contributor was born in 1991), it may be churlish to apply excessive critical force to its editors' rhetoric. Yet even in so short a passage, tell-tale signs are apparent: a new poet will be a young poet (all the New Generation poets of 1994 were under forty); poets make their mark by winning prizes, which older poets have unjustly withheld from young poets; a 'pokey bookshop' is not somewhere a young poet will feel comfortable (as borne out by the threatened status of independent bookshops today); and coolness or 'buzz' (another term used by Byrne and Pollard) is the quality by which the talented poets of our time will make themselves known. Looking back on the New Gen as he introduced its sequel, the Next Generation promotion in 2004, Simon Armitage remembers the hard sell with which its poets had been marketed to the public:

> ■ Poetry, apparently, was about to replace stand-up comedy as the new rock'n'roll. Poetry was Britpop. Poetry was New Labour. Poetry was outselling hardback fiction. Poetry was sexy, and suddenly there we were, the 20 newest, poppiest, wittiest, most saleable and sexiest of them all.[20] □

Just as Larkin both deprecated and benefited from the Movement half a century before, Armitage displays a palpable ambivalence, undercutting the reductive sound bites to which journalists unused to dealing with poetry resort ('the new rock'n'roll'), but repeating them with only a stray 'apparently' by way of qualification. Pollard and Byrne's generalisations are not born of entryist anxiety alone, in other words, but form a part even of the established writer's self-image. Armitage is writing about a poetry promotion as one of its chosen writers, an activity leaving little room for critical distance or manoeuvre. When he came to coedit *The Penguin Book of Poetry from Britain and Ireland since 1945* (1998) with Robert Crawford, he suffered no such awkwardness, taking the wise decision not to include his own work (not an option exercised by all poet-editors). Debates over contemporary poetry often exhibit 'great hatred, little room', in Yeats's words, but for all its imperfections the anthology remains the least worst option available for rising above the fray, for surveying the deforming imperatives of poetry marketing, even as these shape the genre of the anthology itself, and restoring a middle ground between the rough-and-tumble of the latest Forward Prize or Poetry Society promotion and the would-be timelessness of inclusion in the canon, as represented at the Olympian end of the market by the *Oxford Book of English Verse*.

The question of poetic territory is fraught with cultural politics. When former Tory Secretary of State for Education Kenneth Baker published his *Faber Book of Landscape Poetry* in 2000, the volume came decked out in endpapers mapping its poets onto the landscape: Marvell in Hull, Wordsworth in the Lakes, Betjeman in Cornwall. This is landscape as birthright, with no place for meditations on the matter of Albion from interlopers or birds of passage such as Pound, Lowell or Ed Dorn, to list only Anglophone visitors. It does not take a Tory grandee to write poets out of the landscape, however. Owen Sheers's *Poet's Guide to Britain* (2010), a tie-in for a BBC television series, offered a poetic map of the territory that finds room for first-collection debutants but none for Geoffrey Hill or Basil Bunting. If Baker's appropriation of Albion bespeaks one kind of cultural capitalism, so does the front-cover boast 'As seen on BBC', and the absence from the series in question of anyone unlikely to oblige with an affable fireside chat. Nothing could be more ideological than the unexamined view of the landscape to be found in these volumes, and which Harriet Tarlo combats in her 2011 anthology, *The Ground Aslant*, which she subtitles *An Anthology of Radical Landscape Poetry*, and whose writers are as likely to approach the matter of nature through scientific field work, cultural anthropology or performance art as through the expected 'other' route of poetic experiment.

'English' and Other

A select few anthologies have become populist successes, synonymous with their time while also outliving it: the previously mentioned Palgrave's *Golden Treasury* remains in print, an indomitably pre-modernist world preserved in sepia. A reprint of the former Irish schools anthology *Soundings* (1969) achieved unexpected best-seller status long after the curriculum it served had vanished. Both these examples trade on nostalgia for a wholeness beyond confusion, to paraphrase Robert Frost, and the sense that where consensus once held, cacophony now reigns. Different anthologies have their own strategies for imposing order on the field. The question of territory is again a primary consideration. *The Oxford Book of English Verse*, most recently edited by Christopher Ricks (1999), continues to apply the epithet 'English' to all poetry produced in Britain and Ireland, but few other anthologies would dare to subsume national and regional differences so confidently. The youngest poet in Ricks's book is Seamus Heaney (b. 1939), and explaining his reluctance to venture beyond this, Ricks writes of 'the experienced conviction that most of us are not good at appreciating the poetry of those appreciably younger than we are'.[21] Besides, he adds, since younger poets are 'presently before the public eye' they 'stand in no need of reinstatement'.[22] Ricks is not in the business of compiling a contemporary anthology, but even so this is a striking refusal of a punt on posterity by one ideally placed to indulge in such a wager. A similarly canonical volume, Patrick Crotty's *Penguin Book of Irish Poetry* (2010), is more audacious with younger poets; but while this led to the usual post-anthology fallout from reviewers, it is worth pointing out that the contemporary section, addressing the period 1971–2009, is still longer than the section devoted to the entirety of the seventeenth and eighteenth centuries.

'English', British and Irish poetry are not alone in this dilemma. The reception of Rita Dove's *Penguin Book of Twentieth-Century American Poetry* (2011) revealed the sensitivity of the fault line between the canonical-exclusive and more permissive approaches to the art of the anthology. Dove affords more than twice as much space to Harlem Renaissance poet Melvin B. Tolson as she does to Wallace Stevens, triggering a furious review by the eminent conservative critic Helen Vendler.[23] The ensuing fracas attracted high levels of media exposure by poetry standards, while cementing the association in the public mind between canonicity and inflexibility on the one hand (the case against Vendler often shading into implied racism) and blandly anti-literary multi-cultural inclusiveness on the other. (The work of Sylvia Plath was excluded altogether, allegedly for reasons of prohibitive copyright costs: the cheque book is an important shaping influence on anthologies too.) It should be possible to object to an overly inclusive anthology without triggering accusations of right-wing bias (Dove's anthology was also notably light on experimental poets), and possible too to promote the work of writers from ethnic minorities without race being the defining or only context for debate. In the fractured landscape of British poetry, editorial statesmanship of an exceptional kind is required to negotiate these dangers. One volume that does manage this feat is Paul Keegan's *New Penguin Book of English Verse* (2000), even with the all-encompassing 'English' of its title. Keegan takes the bold decision to organise his book by year rather than author, requiring recourse to the index for those concerned to measure relative levels of author representation (in his *Chatto Book of Love Poetry* (1990) John Fuller took the more extreme step of printing poems without authors' names in the main body of the text, arranging the poems ingeniously to form a single composite narrative of the course of a love affair).

Anthologies, then, can be broadly divided into the dynamic-exclusive and the democratic-representative – democratic-representative in ambition at least, if not always in practice. The introduction to a Faber or Oxford anthology is unlikely to be an extended attack on the entire apparatus of mainstream verse and a plea for its replacement with the poets of the unregarded fringe, though Patrick McGuinness notes 'the obligatory side-swipes at London and Oxbridge, most often made by people who publish their poetry with Faber, Cape and Oxford and their anthologies with Penguin and Picador'.[24] Where such an anthology does occur, it may enter the market from a consciously oblique angle, as with Richard Caddel and Peter Quartermain's *Other: British and Irish Poetry since 1970* (1999), published by an American university press, or be the product of a self-advertised maverick in the system, as with Iain Sinclair's Picador anthology, *Conductors of Chaos* (1996), both of which will be discussed in Chapter 5. When an established British press publishes a more freewheeling anthology, such as Faber's *Emergency Kit* (1996) or Bloodaxe's *Making for Planet Alice* (1997), the absence of canonical rigidity will typically be accompanied by a vocabulary of transgression (*Emergency Kit* 'values [...] the outlandish and the playful above ideology and sententiousness', *Making for Planet Alice* draws on 'subject-matter previously thought "inappropriate" [...] a train of glorious transgressions', and its writers 'pay no attention to the restrictions of this universe').[25] Controversy-stirring introductions to restrictive-canonical anthologies are not unknown, however, and most frequently emanate from editors self-consciously on the defensive. An unusual case of this occurs in Don Paterson and Charles Simic's US-published *New British Poetry* (2004), which offers American readers a post-New Gen canon of British and Irish poetry complete with fire-breathing denunciations of 'postmodern' poets, none of whom is named in the introduction let alone represented in the book. Without the benefit of familiarity with these squabbles (sometimes likened to a knife-fight in a phone booth), the American reader's response can only be guessed at. Peter Howarth has suggested that 'these enemies were actually parts of Paterson's own poetic line-up being ticked off for imagining they could go solo',[26] which makes excellent sense as a reading of the artistic tensions within Paterson's *oeuvre*, but a less excellent excuse for the baffled American undergraduate confronting British poetry for the first time. Yet for many poet anthologists, the chance to self-define against the backdrop of one's peers is high or even chief among the attractions of the genre.

Counting the Generations

Just far enough apart, chronologically, to represent different poetic generations, Blake Morrison and Andrew Motion's *Penguin Book of*

Contemporary British Poetry (1982), Michael Hulse, David Kennedy and David Morley's *The New Poetry* (1993), and Roddy Lumsden's *Identity Parade: New British and Irish Poets* (2010) demonstrate revealingly different approaches to the demographics of the anthology. Most tellingly, the number of contributors grows significantly from one to the next. Morrison/Motion include 20 poets, Hulse/Kennedy/Morley 55, and Lumsden 85. On any simple analysis, the anthologist is reflecting inflationary tendencies. The reductive inference at this point would be that more means worse, or watering down, but this is to presume that Morrison/Motion's exclusivism (comparatively speaking) represents a vision of British poetry recognisably the same as that of Roddy Lumsden three decades later but applied with more discriminating vigour. Yet even by the time of the Hulse/Kennedy/Morley volume, Morrison/Motion's landscape had come to seem painfully antiquated. The Martian school, represented by Craig Raine and Christopher Reid and taking its name from Raine's hyper-descriptive *A Martian Sends a Postcard Home* (1979), had achieved its zenith in Reid's *Katerina Brac* (1985), but by 1993 the Soviet Union and the world of dissident poetry it spawned (as gently satirised by Reid) were no more. The Northern Irish poets provided Morrison/Motion's Oxbridge-heavy home (counties) team with a whiff of conflict closer to home, but Peter Reading's dark Thatcherite visions and Michael Hofmann's sophisticated nihilism found 1990s England in a state of self-laceration undreamt of a decade before. Conversely, it is just as true to point out that merely topical poetry from this period is not at any advantage over more rarefied-seeming work (Paul Durcan's satirical poems, which feature in *The New Poetry*, signal their sociological dimensions to the point of disappearing into them). In her survey of anthologies Edna Longley identifies what she terms the 'culturalist fallacy', under which sociological change or political piety do duty for the harder business of poetic discrimination – the unpleasantness to contemporary ears of the very word 'discrimination' hinting at a deep-lying malaise. Her examples include the formulation from Hulse/Kennedy/Morley that 'plurality has replaced monocentric totemism' and the ubiquity on back-cover blurbs of the words 'confident' and 'representative'.[27]

Representativeness, it is worth repeating, is not in itself conclusive proof of anything: a Northern English poet is not a synecdoche for a whole region, a woman poet is not all women's poetry. Shifting the focus away from the collective, Carol Rumens categorised her 1985 anthology *Making for the Open* as a book of 'post-feminist poetry', to critical misunderstanding and ire, where 'post-' was read as 'anti-'.[28] Scepticism towards 'representativeness' does not preclude a commitment to representation, however, and poetry by women (Pauline Stainer, Maggie Hannan, Kathleen Jamie) receives a much-needed acknowledgement in *The New Poetry*. The prevailing narrative for these changes is one of the 'marginal becoming central'; the editors speak of the new poetry 'emphasis[ing] accessibility, democracy and responsiveness', and being 'risk-taking' and 'plural'.[29] While this vocabulary has subsequently been degraded through over-familiarity, it was new enough in 1993 for the editors to balance their good intentions with reference to a *Poetry London* editorial bewailing the 'hectic pluralism' and 'special interest serving' that would water down artistic autonomy. (Deploring the fragmentation of the canon into competing special-interest groups, Edna Longley has wondered whether Shelley could have written a *'Defence of Poetries'*.) Who though would not wish to be described as 'risk-taking'? Yet if all are 'risk-taking' no one is, and the term is fit for nothing but the graveyard of blurb-speak; and one of the editors of *The New Poetry*, David Kennedy, has compiled a checklist of the assumptions and slogans, reminiscent of Myles na gCopaleen's 'Catechism of Cliché', on which the encounter of poetry and the language of blurb-writers and arts administration typically comes to grief.[30]

A paradox of Bloodaxe's intervention into British publishing at this time, and one lurking below the surface of words like 'risk-taking', was the extent to which their prime discoveries (Armitage, O'Brien, Duhig) were subsequently picked up by the metropolitan presses Bloodaxe had been established to bypass. It could even be suggested that its ethic of decentralisation and challenge to an addled establishment showed common traits with the Thatcherism which, as the publisher of Tony Harrison's *'v.'*, it simultaneously did so much to oppose – as Sean O'Brien has argued.[31] The foregrounding of inclusiveness in *The New Poetry* has become a less conspicuous anxiety for Lumsden in 2010, though he is keen to stress the presence in his pages of a majority of female contributors. Despite its generous headcount, *Identity Parade* assigns all its writers almost exactly the same number of pages, making it hard to establish who it considers the dominant figures of its generation. Lumsden positively repudiates sweeping claims for the writers he has assembled ('A common temptation for earlier anthologists was the making of great claims for the generation'). The purpose of an anthology 'is *not* to act as a canonical document of an era, but to spread the word'. As a meremost modicum of sloganeering would seem to be in order, he settles on the term 'plural' in the final sentence of his introduction, devoid of a finite verb:

■ Plural in its register – monologue, memoir, satire, comedy, complaint; plural in its regional and ethnic diversity; plural in its subject-matter and – moving from traditional metrics to fractured syntax, from dialect to diatribe, mirror poem to prose poem – satisfyingly plural in its form and style.[32] □

It is salutary that Lumsden makes the poetic forms he collects ('monologue, memoir ...') the bearers of pluralism as much as the ethnicity or gender of their authors. Other ways in which *Identity Parade* does this include its generous representation of publishers typically overlooked by prize committees, including Salt, Shearsman, Egg Box and Smith/Doorstop; a calculated indifference to the mainstream/experimental stand-off, amidst a proliferation of writers of a recognisably innovative stamp (Peter Manson, Vahni Capildeo, Matthew Welton); hospitality to non-standard forms, such as the prose poem; and a commitment to reintroducing ('naturalising' would be the wrong word) British-born writers such as D. S. Marriott who have spent long periods overseas and whose work is better known in their new domiciles than back at home.

Millennial Perspectives

Coming between the second and third of my last examples but addressing an entirely different need and occasion is the rash of anthologies published to coincide with the new millennium, of which I wish to consider three instances: Sean O'Brien's *The Firebox: Poetry from Britain and Ireland After 1945* (1998), Michael Schmidt's *Harvill Book of Twentieth-Century Poetry in English* (1999) and Simon Armitage and Robert Crawford's *Penguin Book of Poetry from Britain and Ireland from 1945* (1998). More so than the books we have just considered, these are anthologies which must justify their choices of contemporary poets in the light of tradition. Schmidt's longer timeframe (beginning with Thomas Hardy) sets a different tone from that of the O'Brien and Armitage/Crawford volumes, but equally distinctive is his belief that modernism retains the centre ground after the war: 'Modernism in its various forms is the defining movement of the twentieth century.'[33] By modernism, Schmidt means those pre-war heavyweights Yeats, Eliot and Pound, whose obscurity and sprawling forms the Movement generation believed they had cut down to size. Schmidt circumvents arguments about the nativeness or otherwise of modernism in British poetry by blanking the national question altogether, including poetry by Americans, Australians and New Zealanders alongside writers from these islands. The list of featured poets born since 1945 reads, in its entirety: Wendy Cope, Bill Manhire, Veronica Forrest-Thomson, John Ash, James Fenton, Jorie Graham, Paul Muldoon, Mark Doty, Andrew Motion, Robert Minhinnick, Carol Ann Duffy, Sujata Bhatt, Michael Hofmann, Gwyneth Lewis, Glyn Maxwell, Simon Armitage and Sophie Hannah. By standards of archipelagic inclusiveness this is, on some fronts, not a bad trawl, with its numerous Welsh choices. However, the downplaying of the second generation of Northern Irish poets (no Medbh McGuckian or Ciaran Carson) gives succour to Thomas

Kinsella's complaint that that grouping represented a mere 'journalistic entity', while Scotland has vanished entirely. England, meanwhile, is represented by two poet laureates and two writers best known for their light verse, or three if we count the recent work of James Fenton, alongside the more cosmopolitan cases of John Ash, the German-born Michael Hofmann and the German-based Sujata Bhatt, the much-heralded Armitage and Maxwell, and the unjustly neglected Veronica Forrest-Thomson.

Warming to his modernist theme, Schmidt insists that the poetry of the twentieth century has remained largely true to the 'metropolitan' in setting, and exhibited consistently high levels of concern with language itself, as manifested in 'poetry about poetry'.[34] There is, in arguments over the modernist inheritance, a persistent problem with questions of lineage and nativism. To their detractors Pound and early Eliot represent a stage-managed moment of attempted rupture and takeover, invoking which is a sterile appeal to *avant-gardes* past, whereas writing in the lyric mode is to demonstrate continuity with the organic lyric tradition. Schmidt devotes an inordinate amount of his introduction to Eliot and Pound, rather than later twentieth-century elaborations of the *avant-garde*, but ends with an ambitious binary distinction. Spurning mandatory inclusiveness ('Anthologies of modern poetry often aim to be representative [...] The net effect of such efforts is that nothing is represented'),[35] he divides poetry into the 'popular' and the 'communal'. The first is 'immediately political and deeply wedded to what it takes to be its community of concern', the prime example of such work being performance poetry. The second type is poetry which seeks to elicit a 'communal' response, 'a poetry to which each reader responds in an individual way and which is sufficiently capacious to admit a variety of responses'.[36] This is a persuasive thesis, but not one borne out by the anthology that follows. Insisting that performance poets carry the can for issue-driven populism fudges the question of kind of public poetry written by Andrew Motion and Carol Ann Duffy, whose work somehow transcends its themes and issues in a way that performance poetry does not. Equally, the religious overtones to the term 'communal' in Schmidt's second strain of poetry are not just implicit but vocally explicit in some of the work he champions, such as that of Australian Les Murray, which rejects with venom the elitist misanthropy, to Murray's mind, of the modernist project so dear to Schmidt's heart.

To a critic sceptical of Schmidt's internationalism, such as Edna Longley, the subsuming of these differences into the modernist narrative unhelpfully edits out whole local and national traditions. Comparing Schmidt's anthology to Andrew Crozier and Tim Longville's *A Various Art*, she writes:

■ Crozier and Schmidt subscribe to different types of collusive Anglo-American narrative, each of which gives England a role, even if it has lost the poetic empire that [Robert] Conquest implicitly mourns. Both narratives pretend to transcend nationality (that very transcendentalism being culturally and imperially specific), yet ignore Yeats's dialectic with modernist forms.[37] □

There is an appreciable level of internal conflict towards the strictly contemporary end of Schmidt's *Harvill Book*. The stony path of Poundian modernism, as championed in the pages of *P. N. Review* down the decades by Donald Davie, has not, on the evidence of Schmidt's own anthology, led to a paradise of heteroglossia and parataxis. Keepers of this flame are represented by Schmidt, but chiefly among older writers (John Peck, Michael Palmer – Americans, rather than their UK counterparts). The implication is that the modernist legacy is now something writers mature into, rather than proclaim with the brashness of youth, as happened a hundred years ago. This is not to accuse Schmidt of bad faith, since Carcanet Press, of which he is director, has continued to support innovative young writers such as Oli Hazzard, Matthew Welton and Jeremy Over, but to suggest a certain drift among the national traditions notionally unified under the banner of the *Harvill Book*. Without the masking effect of non-UK and Irish poets, the tensions and territorial disputes discernible under the surface (modern Scottish poetry with no Tom Leonard) would rise more fractiously to the surface. Schmidt's project thus offers a transcendence of the 'little room' of which Yeats complained, without quite reaching the utopia of a fully integrated internationalism.

Modernism is not the same thing as progressivism, despite Fiona Sampson's odd claim in her study *Beyond the Lyric* (2012) that 'As the term suggests, [modernism] has faith in progress.'[38] There is no reason why today's modernism need take its bearings slavishly from a manifesto written in 1915. Where rhetoric of the *avant-garde* translates into praising, as new and alternative, work that was tired and second-hand when it was written decades ago, lazy literary history will result. But the alternative, of relegating modernism to the first half of the century, and blocking or policing its percolations into the post-Movement dispensation carries risks of its own, and remains a strong influence on much contemporary anthologising. A rather different approach from Schmidt's to this problem can be found in Sean O'Brien's *The Firebox*. With its foreshortened span, *The Firebox* includes many more poets born since 1945 than Schmidt, while almost invariably restricting them to one or two poems each.

I have alluded to O'Brien's sceptical view of the *avant-garde*, but different editors will use critical terminology in different ways. Thus, to O'Brien postmodernism is represented by John Fuller and Paul Muldoon, a labelling that in Fuller's case at least makes little sense. Attempting to flesh out the condition of postmodernity, O'Brien writes:

■ Of postmodernism's numerous features, the most relevant and prominent include a renewed interest in the use of narrative; a sceptical view of the fixity of meaning; and the tendency to use various historical literary forms as an ironic pattern-book, so that a postmodernist poem may often seem partly a parody and writing is construed as rewriting. Some of these features were noted by Blake Morrison and Andrew Motion in the introduction to the important 1982 anthology *The Penguin Book of Contemporary British Poetry* and seen as evidence of a new spirit of adventure.[39] □

To O'Brien, J. H. Prynne and Geoffrey Hill, two poets with many differences, are late or neo-modernists for whom the innovations of the early twentieth century have yet to tip into the self-conscious parody and simulacrum they become in the hands of his preferred postmodernists. The insistence on irony is also significant: O'Brien's canon will be more savvy and streetwise than Schmidt's, with its residual Anglican–Arnoldian high seriousness. There are limits, however, to the radicalism of this strain of postmodernity, as indicated by the circling back to Morrison/Motion, an anthology whose Martian/Oxbridge focus cannot be plausibly connected with the strains of poetry that might pass for postmodernist today. There will always be figures who cross party lines: O'Brien is warmly disposed towards Roy Fisher, an innovative poet whose long poems *City* (1961), *The Cut Pages* (1971), and *A Furnace* (1986) are among the outstanding works of the post-war period. Fisher was born in the midlands in 1930, just eight years after Larkin, yet for all his similarities to the author of *The Whitsun Weddings* (their aversion to London, love of jazz, and signature urban pastorals), Fisher's appearance in non-experimental anthologies cannot conceal the radically different context in which his work has been received. Once again it would appear that seniority confers acceptance withheld from more unruly juniors: an anthology that accommodated both Armitage and Keston Sutherland, Andrea Brady and Sophie Hannah is difficult if not impossible to conceive, under current conditions.

Class is a topic to which O'Brien frequently returns, but *The Firebox* exhibits a tension between reformist and radical impulses where the canon and its traditional *droits de seigneur* are concerned. Rather than reject the Movement narrative of post-war poetry outright as other radical critics and editors have done (his debts to his fellow Hull poet Larkin are too salient for that), O'Brien synthesises its better self with the work of its contemporary rival, the Group – a self-consciously oppositional reaction to the Movement, centred on Cambridge, rejecting 'gentility' and numbering Peter Porter and Peter Redgrove among its members. By eschewing more linguistically innovative poetry, O'Brien places a heavy burden on political protest as an agent of renovation, and the work of Douglas Dunn and Tony Harrison features prominently. Yet where larger trends and movements are concerned, O'Brien typically overhauls rather than rejects previous orthodoxies: the Movement's negative view of the 'hysterical irrationalism' of the 1940s, for instance, is not really questioned. Movement sexual orthodoxies are 'subverted' by Thom Gunn's writing of gay love poems. The conceptual framework inherited from Conquest and Morrison/Motion emerges from the fire-box singed but not remade.

Armitage and Crawford's *Penguin Book* has much in common with O'Brien's anthology, but is of special interest for its greater effort to look beyond Anglophone British poetry. British poetry, even of the native kind, is not just poetry in English, but while anthologies have begun to respond to this fact such inclusiveness carries fresh risks. Patrick McGuinness notes with dismay the rationale offered by Armitage and Crawford for not publishing original texts alongside translations from the Welsh, given the presence in their anthology of texts in Irish and Scots-Gaelic: because of the 'friendlier relationship between English and Gaelic than exists in Wales between English and the Welsh language', they write, 'we have had difficulty in finding English versions of some Welsh poets which convinced us that they demanded inclusion'.[40] As McGuinness further observes, there is a 'centralising pull' and a 'normative facility' to Armitage and Crawford's devolutionary language, offering an implied rebuke to the Welsh tradition for its inadequately 'friendly' demeanour.[41] This is all the more surprising coming from Crawford, author of the influential *Devolving English Literature*, but the reader with some background knowledge of the Irish, Gaelic or Welsh-language traditions may decide that what is going on here constitutes tokenism. If Irish-language poetry is represented in anthologies of British and Irish poetry today, it will almost inevitably be in the person of the widely-translated Nuala Ní Dhomhnaill, leaving the Anglophone reader as effectively in the dark as ever about the wider corpus of Irish-language poetry. The presumption that the language of inclusivity will be enough to overcome the massive and structural imbalance between a majority and minority language has even attracted gestures of protest from Irish-language poets such as Biddy Jenkinson, who refuses to have her work translated into English.

A more genuinely inclusive approach can be found in Menna Elfyn and John Rowlands' *Bloodaxe Book of Modern Welsh Poetry* (2003), which assembles almost a hundred poets, few of whom (with the exceptions of Gwyneth Lewis or, as a translator, R. S. Thomas) will be known to an Anglophone readership. In their introduction Elfyn and Rowlands chart the ability of succeeding generations of Welsh poets, in their evolution from the stricter cultural nationalism of Saunders Lewis, to reinvigorate *cynghanedd* and other traditional verse forms. Equally, the rediscovery of the forgotten Welsh modernist Lynette Roberts, whose 1951 long poem *Gods with stainless ears* was republished in 2005, is a reminder of the Welsh dimension of modernism, and not just in the writings of David Jones. Yet it is in the category of older but still contemporary poets that Armitage/Crawford's book excels – poets sufficiently 'before the public eye' to make their 'reinstatement' otiose, but still in need of advocacy (e.g. Elizabeth Bartlett, Richard Murphy, Bobi Jones, Elaine Feinstein).

The American View

Published by the American wing of the Oxford University Press in 2001, Keith Tuma's *Anthology of Twentieth-Century British and Irish Poetry* is in many ways an anomalous text. It is an American's view of the British and Irish scene, and its eccentric inclusions may have been a factor in the publisher's decision not to follow its usual practice and use the word 'Oxford' in the title, with all its attendant prestige. Some latitude should be permitted, however, to the outsider's perspective, which in the twentieth century gave British culture T. S. Eliot, who as a young man in London was in the habit of signing his letters *'metoikos'*, 'resident alien'. As mentioned in my introduction, Hugh Kenner attracted much opprobrium for the snobbery of *A Sinking Island*, which painted English literary life as dominated by the Edwardianism attacked in Ezra Pound's *Hugh Selwyn Mauberley* (1920), and English poetry as a quaint old boys' network blind to neo-modernist heroes such as Basil Bunting. Up to a point Keith Tuma would agree, though his capacity to see past Movement-derived stereotypes is considerably greater than Kenner's. The eccentricity of his anthology is partly but not exclusively down to its commitment to innovative poetry: Peter Riley, Bill Griffiths, Brian Catling, John Wilkinson and Allen Fisher are here, among numerous other experimenters not often seen outside niche anthologies, but a peculiar gender divide can be seen in its choice of mainstream figures: while Shapcott, Duffy and Kay feature, O'Brien, Armitage and Maxwell do not, to take three comparable male writers. Reaction to the book in Britain was often furious, with Sean O'Brien delivering a withering tirade on its 'bizarre' and 'humourless' qualities.[42] While questions of territory militate strongly against a favourable reception for an anthology of cis-Atlantic poetry compiled by an American, the very eccentricity of Tuma's perspective has illuminating things to say about how the subject is normally handled. He describes the insidious equation of citizenship with 'authentic experience' as having had a 'devastating effect' on British literary history,[43] and is keen to stress reciprocities and exchanges between the British-Irish and other (but not exclusively) American traditions. While Thom Gunn and Sylvia Plath are the obvious exemplars of this in post-war poetry, other figures have suffered rather than benefited from their biculturality (the often-overlooked Asa Benveniste, Gael Turnbull and Caroline Bergvall, born respectively in the Bronx, Canada and Germany, and all included by Tuma).

Where Tuma wishes to contest rather than expand the nativist tradition is in his explicitly formalist turn. He confesses that he is 'less interested in history than [...] in the history of poetry'.[44] Tuma's vision is unequivocally one in which poems are made out of other poems rather than out of life. While this rules out the sub-genres, still favoured by many publishers, of anthologies for weddings, funerals and other occasions on which poetry obtrudes into the life of the non-formalist general reader, Tuma has a larger target in sight. It is the narrow-track tradition under which poems are written on a shared assumption of the naturalness of a certain kind of lyric and the alien inauthenticity of another. This argument has a long pedigree, and some of Tuma's examples highlight it unflatteringly. Among these is Edward Lucie-Smith's *British Poetry Since 1945*, whose first edition in 1970 made a plea for receptiveness to the British Poetry Revival then underway. By the time of the anthology's second edition in 1985, Lucie-Smith had recanted and decided the modernist 'adjustment' to native traditions had not really occurred. Tradition, in the absorptive way described in Eliot's 'Tradition and the Individual Talent', had neutralised the foreign body. It is a peculiar paradox that in the name of modernity Tuma wishes to retreat from 1985 to 1970, but his anthology struggles with the concept of what Marxist historiography might term 'unequal development'. (A comparable version of this can be found in the work of Donald Davie, whose *Thomas Hardy and British Poetry* (1972) shows him passionately urging British poetry to follow American poetry down the path of Black Mountain experiment while feeling instinctively that this will not or cannot happen; in America yes, but Britain no.) Tuma's unease at the gap between the unfinished business of modernism and the monumental proportions of the book he is editing drives him into a position of anti-canonical face-saving to offset his omissions, but in ways that cannot help but appear uneasy or self-defeating. His anthology aspires to drive 'younger readers' (why only younger?) 'to search out poetry as it lives beyond this book' and regrets not being 'twice its current size',[45] but devotes too little energy to bridging the gap between its mourning for a lost modernism and the patently less-than-modernist contemporaries such as Shapcott, Duffy and Kay in whom it culminates. In this sense its preface more accurately belongs to an as-yet unpublished book in which all these divisions might be made whole.

Anthology Wars and War Anthologies

In an essay on anthologies (2012), William Wootten describes the shift from the dynamic-exclusive to the democratic-representative style of

anthologising as part of 'a colossal failure of nerve'.[46] The debates of
the 1960s may have been played out against the backdrop of 'English
poetry breaking up' (that Yeatsian loose-bottomed 'centre' again), but
attempts to put it back together again have simply not delivered.
A sticking point for Wootten, as he grapples with the popularising arguments of Neil Astley's anthologies, is that such volumes cater for an
existing concept of taste but cannot move beyond it – cannot create
the taste by which new poetry could hope to be enjoyed, to paraphrase
Wordsworth's hopes for *Lyrical Ballads*. Where previous generations
might have devoted their critical energies to dethroning their elders, on
the principle of Yeats's declaration that 'We are too many', today they
are likelier to be professionalising themselves as workshop facilitators,
and positioning themselves in a cultural economy disproportionately
slanted towards supply over demand. The lust for poetic glory is not
new, but the pervasiveness of our culture of inclusive over agonistic
anthologising and reviewing is, with all the pressure on canonical space
this entails.

Generational showcasing is not the only occasion for contemporary
anthologies, however. Conflicts in the Middle East have provided poets
with a challenge, but also an opportunity to experience the adrenalin of
poetry activism. The outbreak of the Iraq War in 2003 saw a large and
rapidly mobilised response from British and Irish poets. Faber published
an anthology of *101 Poems Against War* which, on closer inspection,
contained several poems not vocally against war at all, such as Keith
Douglas's 'How to Kill', a chilling and breezy account of a sniper at
work in North Africa. Part of the brilliance of Douglas's poem is its shock
value for readers accustomed to First World War poetry and Wilfred
Owen's claim that 'The poetry is in the pity.' There is pity aplenty in
the horrors of war but not always in war poets' pronouncements on
their theme, most classically in the case of Douglas. The comparative
absence of contemporary poets with first-hand experience of combat is
a factor in changing perceptions of the war poet (though the American
Iraq veteran Brian Turner has published in the UK, and Simon Armitage
has been 'embedded' with a British unit in Afghanistan), but in posit-
ing poetry and war as incompatibles rather than forming a troubling
overlap anthologists of war poetry are at risk of appearing naive and disingenuous. In the original version of 'September 1, 1939' Auden wrote
'We must love one another or die', which he later amended to 'We
must love one another and die', since, as he noted, we die anyway.[47]
Unsurprisingly, it is the former version of the poem that is preferred in
101 Poems Against War.

Another anthology of war poetry was assembled for the online journal *nthposition* by Todd Swift and Val Stevenson, and which attracted
notably sceptical criticism from Tim Kendall in his study *Modern English*

War Poetry (2006). Citing Wilfred Owen via Anthony Hecht, Kendall insists that a war poem should be a *'matter of experience'*.[48] In the absence of such experience, Swift falls back on activist rallying-cries. Unable to ignore Auden's insistence that 'poetry makes nothing happen', Swift decides in the face of much evidence to the contrary that these words are 'ironic'. Kendall contrasts this political forcing with the behaviour of Anthony Hecht, who insisted his resistance to the Vietnam War should not find expression in 'public poetry readings on the subject', which he felt would have represented 'only a kind of self-promotion'.[49] Political doggerel was written in favour of, as well as against the war, Kendall reminds us, but where art is forced to operate in emergency conditions opposites will often meet. Commenting on 'the dismissive reaction of "anti-war poet Adrian Mitchell"' to a collection of pro-war poetry, as reported by the BBC, Kendall writes:

> ■ If the reading of poetry promises more than a lazy pleasure in having pub talk rhymed, there is no reason to praise Mitchell above the pro-war poets. War poetry which advertises its opinions with a prefix is likely to be more interested in those opinions than in poetry.[50] □

The most interesting case among anti-war poets is Harold Pinter, who found his own way of addressing the inefficacy of well-intentioned opinionation in the service of art. Pinter's solution was the heavy use of obscenity and desperate sarcasm ('We blew the shit right back up their own ass').[51] His poems take out on literary decorum the violence they absorb from the field of politics, but to succeed as poems require us to find Pinter's technique genuinely shocking rather than melodramatic and juvenile. If we are shocked, our disappointed expectations of the poem might then become a microcosm of the political critique required to resist the Iraq war. In practice this is more analysis than Pinter's poems can bear, and his overheated rhetoric cannot conceal the aesthetic emptiness at its heart. Picking up on a comparison by Swift of his project to the Blitz spirit, Kendall compares anti-war poetry to war profiteering, 'finding it a blessing to live in interesting times'.[52]

Ian Brinton compares another war poem, Tony Harrison's *A Cold Coming*, to the Objectivist George Oppen's cold war-era 'Time of the Missile'; but no less strongly than Auden, Oppen took a strong stand against the recruitment of his poetry to a political cause, choosing to take a stance instead by *not* publishing any poetry for 28 years while he pursued the life of a political activist.[53] In Harrison's '*v.*', the polarisation of the Thatcher years is represented in a series of oppositions, whether social, political or racial, which as the poem progresses it attempts to resolve in images of the speaker's marriage, the conjugal union filling in for the togetherness sorely lacking elsewhere.[54] Writing of an Iraqi soldier incinerated on the road to Basra, Harrison cannot resist the temptation to repeat his familial metaphor, imagining the dead man's 'longing to be beside / my wife in bed before I died', and his hopes of fathering a child 'untouched by war's despair'.[55] On what authority can Harrison know what the dead soldier wanted? War obliterates the voices of its victims, but Harrison's ventriloquising of the victim's words falls some way short of solving the problems we have identified with contemporary war poetry. Harrison's is not the only possible response to contemporary wars, however, and as Brinton reminds us, Prynne's *To Pollen* is a powerful anti-war gesture, as in a different way is David Harsent's *Legion*.

Responding to Kendall, Swift vigorously disputed the claim that poet-bystanders risked nothing in opposing the war, while conceding the point that the anthology had included 'weaker, homely poems by amateurs'.[56] Detecting an 'anti-anti-war' bias, Swift raises the possibility of a Christopher Hitchens-style backlash against liberal anti-war orthodoxy. While no poet of significant reputation took to writing pro-war poems, the example of W. B. Yeats refusing to contribute to an anthology of protest poetry during World War One ('I think it better that in times like these / A poet's mouth be silent, for in truth / We have no gift to set a statesman right')[57] remains as valid today as a hundred years ago. No poet could be less of a political quietist than Yeats, reminding us that his reluctance stemmed from a desire to respond to the challenge of the war poem on his own terms and in his own way. Asked what the influence of the French Revolution had been, Zhou Enlai supposedly joked that it was too early to say. Looking beyond the activist pay-off of immediate response and validation, we might suggest the same is no less true of contemporary war poetry. It is a feature of the quarrels and campaigns that drive all anthology wars that they should mistake short-term response and validation for the qualities that define more durable victories. There is no shortcut to posterity, however, and if the follies and failings of the poetry anthology often seem effort expended in vain, it is still to the anthology that we look to sift all this confusion and house the conversations 'between the living and the dead, between the present and the future'.[58]

CHAPTER TWO

Approaches to Contemporary British Poetry

Poet as Critic

Since at least the time of T. S. Eliot and Ezra Pound a central contribution to the criticism of our times has come from poets themselves. While many poets have written criticism, historically, the poet-critic acquired a new dimension in the nineteenth century with Matthew Arnold, a writer whose evolution into the presiding critic of his age coincided with his abandonment of poetry. Arnold had great ambitions for culture as a force that might fill the vacuum left by the collapse of religious belief, but found his own poetry deficient in the requisite weight or authority. For the contemporary poet-critic, the temptation can be strong to lay down in criticism the narrative by which one's own poetry can then be read. Do we look to poet-critics for what they have to tell us about poetry in general, or for insight into their own work? Does the creative identity of a poet-critic offer an exemption from the impersonal argument we might expect from other critics? Why should the life-story of this or that poet-critic be thrust centre-stage? These questions bring into focus the shared space between genres in which many poet-critics operate, while reminding us of the spectrum of possibilities the role allows too.

A related issue is the leniency granted to poet-critics, historically, when their critical judgement is shown to have been faulty. When Arnold is wrong, as in his description of Pope and Dryden as 'classics of our prose' rather than 'our poetry', posterity has tended to find his error of judgement intriguing, as an index of how the Augustans were read in the nineteenth century. If a contemporary poet-critic appears to get it wrong, as Seamus Heaney appears to do in his hostile and controversial reading of Larkin's pessimistic 'Aubade', do we grant him the same licence? 'Our interest in poets' criticism ought to be a *critical* interest', Peter McDonald has written, 'and not an aspect of our veneration for the poets concerned.'[1] The case of Heaney on Larkin is revealing in other ways too: Heaney's critical prose is overwhelmingly affirmative in tone, and the overlap of negativity and arguable judgement where Larkin is concerned compels further investigation.[2] Poets' prose can be the danger zone where the tensions underlying their work flare most vividly into life.

Another aspect of poet-critics' style is where they place themselves along the scale from the programmatic to the improvisatory, stylistically speaking. Tom Paulin is a programmatic critic, in the sense of returning frequently to the same themes (Puritanism, Britishness, Protestant identity), and possessing a fixed agenda which obtrudes into his writing regardless of the subject, as when he unexpectedly compares Stevie Smith to the Protestant preacher Ian Paisley. Ian Hamilton and Barbara Everett by contrast are quintessential improvisers, writing to commission and deploying an urbane wit in the absence of any controlling obsessions. This distinction shapes the books poet-critics write too: a Hamilton or Everett volume will tend to be a round-up of reviews and essays, whereas a Paulin volume will have a more through-composed feel. A Seamus Heaney volume may arise from a lecture series, such as the Oxford lectures that provide the occasion for *The Redress of Poetry*, whereas Robert Crawford or Peter McDonald, though also reviewers, are equally at home with the academic monograph.

Manifestoes were much in vogue in the Modernist period, from the Vorticist manifesto in Wyndham Lewis's *Blast* to Ezra Pound's 'A Few Don'ts by an Imagiste', but are less common in post-Movement times, as we find in W. N. Herbert and Matthew Hollis's *Strong Words* (2000), an anthology of poets' prose discussions of their art. The revolutionary rallying-cries of a century ago have given way to more utilitarian advice on getting started and how to get published. Where, one might ask, are the manifestoes of Andrew Motion, Simon Armitage and Carol Ann Duffy? The role of Robert Conquest's *New Lines* (1956) is historically important, with its essentially negative view of poetics: for Conquest, the aesthetic shared by his poets amounts to 'little more than a negative determination to avoid bad principles', a platform whose vindication of 'genuine and healthy poetry' leaves sceptics in the implied role of deviants and decadents.[3] The adage 'never apologise, never explain' is variously ascribed to the Duke of Wellington or Disraeli, and for these sceptics post-Movement poetry can seem to inhabit a state in which aesthetic correctness is a condition of self-evident common sense, not in need of any theoretical elaboration or defence.[4] Whether they range themselves for or against literary theory, however, poet-critics place themselves in a position of close and sometimes uncomfortable proximity to the first principles from which they work – principles they cannot help but reinvigorate as they write.

Geoffrey Hill: from Poetry as 'Atonement' to 'Alienated Majesty'

Among poets who are also critics, there are those who harness their prose to the service of their poetry, splicing criticism and memoir in an implicit defence of their art. As a consideration of the woman poet in Irish tradition, Eavan Boland's *Object Lessons* (1995) is just such an apologia for her own work. In a slightly different category is the critical prose of Seamus Heaney, which presents at carefully selected moments episodes in the poet's life to illustrate a striking cultural contrast or clash. The factors that make the critic what he is are part of the drama, but for the most part only one element in a larger orchestrated whole. Geoffrey Hill's criticism is different again since, as he insists, the authority with which he speaks in the primary act of creation escapes from the artist into the art, forcing the critic to fall back on alternative resources. Like Eliot before him, Hill is not at all interested in narrating the tale of his own writing life, but when he mockingly quotes Eliot's 'recurring commonplace phrase "the enjoyment of poetry"' in his essay 'A Postscript on Modernist Poetics' (2005),[5] he signals that the poet-critic who rejects autobiographical testimony is not resigning himself to desiccated *politesse*. An example to the contrary occurs in the same essay, as Hill discusses the placing of the word 'savour' in a line of Keats's (Hill is adept at extracting larger critical points from single lines, phrases or even words). The physicality of Hill's description recalls A. E. Housman's description of poetry raising the hairs on the back of his neck while he shaved: 'Whatever strange relationship we have with the poem, it is not one of enjoyment. It is more like being brushed past, or aside, by an alien being.'[6]

When Hill was named Oxford Professor of Poetry in 2010, he announced that he would give no readings from his work during his time of office: he would serve the art of poetry without any self-advancing distractions. Hill's work as a critic has never been without an intensely personal quality, but one he wishes to distance from false notions of accessibility and the pseudo-democratic. Hill's passionate defence of the right of poetry to be difficult cannot help recalling Eliot's belief that modern poetry 'at present, must be *difficult*',[7] raising the dark suspicion of a critical method programmed to prefer the difficult and the obscurantist to the simple and transparent. While Hill finds nothing more congenial than expounding a lesser-known passage of Milton or Hopkins, how might his elevated critical style adapt to reading a Robert Burns song? Hill has foreseen this objection, and protests that his ambition for his work is to write poems that (in Milton's words) are 'simple, sensuous, and passionate'.[8] The *Collected Critical Writings* he published in

2008 is bookended by two lectures from opposite ends of Hill's career, 'Poetry as "Menace" and "Atonement"' and 'A Postscript on Modernist Poetics', which exemplify this tendency, amounting almost to personal manifestoes. In 'Poetry as "Menace" and "Atonement"' Hill articulates his sense of the forces from which poetry arises. Hill is highly sensitive to the potential for critical language to descend into jargon and cant, and raises the possibility at the outset that his 'real challenge' may be 'resisting the attraction of terminology itself',[9] and the glib answers criticism offers to questions that should remain intractable. He is fond of returning key critical terms to their etymological origins, and explains that by 'atonement' he means an 'act of at-one-ment, a setting at one, a bringing into concord'.[10] What prevents the poet or critic from achieving this state of at-one-ment is the fallen condition of language and the radical taint of guilt that attaches to our attempts, in words, to go beyond the fallenness they represent. There is in any critical act a degree of performative contradiction. Hill is a highly rhetorical critic, full or ornate and rococo flourishes, but more often to self-flagellating than self-applauding ends. W. B. Yeats features strongly in both of the Hill essays I consider here, and of a resonant and guilt-ridden passage in 'The Circus Animals' Desertion' he asks, 'How it is possible, though, to revoke "masterful images" in images that are themselves masterful?'[11] Eloquence and guilt are fatally intertwined. First comes the desire for verbal mastery, followed by a recoil from the falseness of rhetoric and an embrace of humility; this is followed by the awareness that humility too is a form of rhetoric, and that only an honest reckoning with the imperfections of language can lift the writer's burden of guilt. To achieve a true picture of the relationship of language and guilt one must go beyond mere thought to '"the mind's self-experience in the act of thinking"', Hill writes, quoting Coleridge.[12] The poet-critic is required to think to the power of two. Poetry is an atoning agent, but one whose path leads the writer by way of affliction and purgation to whatever redemption is in store.

Turning to the more recent essay, we find Hill in essentially the same predicament, of needing to incorporate self-consciously within our judgement the 'condition of the judgement' too.[13] What prevents us from achieving proper self-awareness within language is the alienation at the centre of the creative act. Hill takes his cue here from Emerson: 'In every work of genius we recognise our own rejected thoughts: they come back to us with a certain alienated majesty.'[14] Hill extends this proposition to the works we make ourselves, and the shock of separation that accompanies the moment of creation: 'In the act of creation we alienate ourselves from that which we have created, or, conversely, the genius of language alienates us from itself.'[15] This alienation is not in itself a bad thing. Hill's example is from the correspondence of Yeats and the young actress Margot Ruddock, who chafed at the older poet's harsh treatment of her poems and his insistence on poetry as 'technique'. Yeats would have been familiar with Ezra Pound's declaration 'I believe in technique as the test of a man's sincerity', with its inspired refusal of the opposition between self-expression and the impersonal requirements of art. Hill takes up the theme enthusiastically:

■ It is the being forced down under the surface by the resistance of technique that inaugurates a self-alienating process which, as it drives down into strata that are not normally encountered, may produce alien objects [...] In what Yeats says to Margot Ruddock we may find yet another vindication of the Bradleian axiom: the 'condition of the judgement' in this case would be the blade of the plough driving under the surface together with the soil's resistance itself; obedience to the mechanical principle would be – would have been – the essential transformation of Ruddock's judgement; either a finer poem or the realization that she was no poet and there was no poem there.[16] □

Like guilt, difficulty is an essential part of the wrestle with language. Advanced as an overcoming of difficulty, the argument to sincerity is one that Hill resists with force. There is a Yeats poem titled 'The Fascination of What's Difficult', and when Hill introduces the phrase 'the eros of technique', he is displacing the passionate element of poetry from Ruddock's belief in sincerity onto the field of poetic form itself. Here again we have a type of performative contradiction at work. Hill quotes the mid-century critic Charles Williams on Milton as an example of the same drive: how is it, Williams asks, that a poem can be 'raised to its height' to deny something – the sensual glory of humanity in all its fallenness and disobedience – which the 'tremulous power of the verse continually expresses'?[17] This sounds like an updated version of Blake's argument that Milton was 'of the devil's party without knowing it', but is also an argument for how renunciation and what Barthes would call 'the pleasure of the text' can coexist. Freedom is not possible without constraint, nor constraint without freedom, and the wisdom that this is so is not acquired lightly; a true expression of this paradox may require an artist as great as Milton or Yeats.

In the conclusion to his essay Hill takes what might have seemed a random collection of *aperçus* on this or that line from Yeats and Eliot and builds to a searching verdict on these great modernist poets. Yeats concludes his poem of carefully stage-managed resignation, 'The Circus Animals' Desertion', with the lines 'I must lie down where all the ladders start / In the foul rag and bone shop of the heart.' Hill has made it clear that artistic redemption will have to pass by way of shabbiness first, but is troubled by these lines. They are too full for his liking of their 'claim to some supposed majestic right of his own characteristic jargon to ennoble humiliation'.[18] They break Hill's rules by spelling them out, too programmatically and pre-emptively; the revocation of mastery is not quite masterful enough, the shabbiness too puffed up and self-conscious. This is the risk Yeats runs by introducing more earthy material as a counterweight to his usual rhetoric of 'the pleasure that harnessed recalcitrance gives him', or wisdom through renunciation. The instability of Yeats's later rhetoric results in poetic unevenness, but where late Eliot is concerned the elimination of tonal risk leads to an altogether more gloomy result: choosing the Christian platitudes of *The Rock* over the abandoned uncertainties of his poem *Coriolan* represents a 'savage defeat' of Eliot's imagination, Hill damningly pronounces.[19]

As we will see, the grounds of Hill's theories of early versus late Eliot, of what he calls the 'pitch' of the former versus the 'tone' of the latter, have not passed without challenge, but this verdict leads to a stirring conclusion on poetry and posterity. Auden enters the argument tangentially with his much-quoted declaration that 'poetry makes nothing happen', which Hill resists as he tries to arrive at a true estimate of how a poem shapes its posterity. Hill has been haunted throughout his career by the legislative power of poetry, or the Romantic and Modernist delusions of executive power (Shelley's 'unacknowledged legislators', Pound's 'yearning for identity between saying and doing'),[20] and finds a fleeting embodiment of this principle in the moment of the poem's self-composure 'even when it is discord that is composed'. A poem enters history either 'as an effective agent, or hostage'.[21] While misreadings will denature it, the true poem is not exhausted by them but instead becomes 'alienated from its existence as historical event'.[22] Yeats's poems of the 1920s and 1930s on the great political themes of the day alternately embrace and reject their political dimension, but circle tragically round the moment of daring and loss that will overcome them as they enter history. As Hill writes in conclusion:

■ The act of composing itself is itself the instant of composure, even when it is discord that is composed. The magnificent composure is nonetheless an alienated majesty; the alienated majesty is in itself unstinting.[23] □

Intensely personal and impersonal at once, this passage combines huge critical authority with an unguarded, spontaneous quality, telescoping the poem's afterlife to the instant of its entering the 'living stream' of posterity. It is one of the great moments in contemporary criticism, and one that above all communicates a sense of lived engagement, of grappling with the text, of (to repeat Hill's description of reading Keats) 'being brushed past or aside, by an alien being'.

Christopher Ricks: 'Literary Principles as Against Theory'

The encounter of traditional scholarship with literary theory in the 1970s and 1980s was a bruising affair, with the latter mounting a concerted assault on the post-Leavisite canon and its philosophical underpinnings, or assumed lack of such things. Exposing the ideological self-masking of anti-theory rhetoric in English Studies became something of a rite of passage for young theorists of the time.[24] The Cambridge English Faculty witnessed particularly fierce skirmishes, with Christopher Ricks in the vanguard of the traditionalists. As a poetry critic of magisterial authority, Ricks polemicised in defence of the canon at a time when the notion of the canon, never mind its constituent parts, had come under severe strain. Opposition to theory would often be gathered under the umbrella of 'close reading', as practised by adherents of 'New Criticism', and an activity whose close attention to the words on the page was seen as exclusive of wider considerations of politics or philosophy. This terminology is less than exact, however. The five critics identified by John Crowe Ransom in *The New Criticism* (1941) as central to that movement were I. A. Richards, William Empson, T. S. Eliot, R. P. Blackmur and Yvor Winters, but surprisingly little of T. S. Eliot's criticism consists of close readings, while William Empson's strong commitment to biographical readings of poetry is directly opposed to Wimsatt and Beardsley's line in their anti-biographical essay of 1954 'The Intentional Fallacy'. F. R. Leavis, so often touted as a patriarch of New Criticism, has little in common with the methods and findings of Cleanth Brooks. Another fallacy of the broad-brush interpretation of 'new criticism' is that such critics refuse an engagement with poetry's political dimension. Helen Vendler, it is true, strongly asserts the primacy of poetry over politics in ways that, where Yeats or Heaney are concerned, over-hastily elide the political contexts from which art is forged. Reading Vendler, Peter McDonald (a critic with deep misgivings about theory) argues that in 'taking for granted poetry's ability to transcend its circumstances, such an attitude forgets how real poetry also answers to its circumstances'.[25] What we think of as traditional ways of reading poetry have a varied and evolving history, in other words. It may even have been a beneficial effect of the 'theory wars' to encourage traditional critics to revisit the aesthetic basis for the value judgements we make as readers, and spell out explicitly what we normally prefer to take on trust.

While many critics of traditional sympathies preferred not to engage with theory in the 1980s and 1990s, Christopher Ricks was more inclined to answers its claims *in extenso*, as in his 1996 essay 'Literary Principles as Against Theory'. Beginning with a letter of Gerard Manley Hopkins, Ricks argues for rhetoric, an experiential art based in teaching, over the abstraction that is theory. Literature is 'principled rhetoric'[26] (the implication being that theory, with its promiscuous proliferation of meanings, is intellectually unprincipled). The resistance to the very word 'theory' has an institutional dimension too, as Ricks resists the advance of those who would dilute literary studies into a new academic discipline. Ricks insists on a distinction between 'intelligence and intellectuality', with French theory guilty of the latter. The subtext is that anti-theoretical, empirical responses to poetry more exactly meet the national character; or, as Yves Bonnefoy wrote, contrasting the Gallic imagination with that of John Donne: 'People often repeat that English poetry "begins with a flea and ends with God." To that I reply that French poetry reverses the process, beginning with God, when it can, to end with love of no matter what.'[27]

Ricks denies that his argument opposes thought and feeling (his hero Eliot had pilloried the Victorians for succumbing to just such an opposition), arguing instead that the slickness of theory and of its ready-made deconstructions is equally untrue to thought *and* feeling. The theorist wishes to place the study of literature on a scientific basis and tends to distrust the subjective element as 'personal values' which constitute an 'interference' or 'prejudice', in the example quoted by Ricks:

■ The assumption that 'personal values' constitute an 'interference', like the longing for a 'guarantee' that all such interferences would be avoided, entails the extirpation not merely of prejudice but of judgement and therefore of literature. It is the peril of literature, but also its glory, that values, convictions, beliefs and profound enduring agreement constitute not only its nature but its medium, language.[28] □

It is important, in these debates, to maintain an awareness of the historical nature of our critical terminology, and not just terms such as 'structuralism' or 'postcolonialism' but 'creative' or 'imagination'. The theoretical premise attacked by Ricks is that a scientific model renders all previous modes of reading, in their groundless impressionism, redundant. An odd moment intrudes, however, when a quotation from Eliot casts that critic in a negative rather than positive light. Eliot attacked E. M. Forster for praising D. H. Lawrence as the 'greatest imaginative novelist of our generation': 'unless we know exactly what Mr Forster means by *greatest, imaginative* and *novelist*, I submit that this judgement is meaningless'.[29] Here it is Eliot's turn to deride 'personal values' as hopelessly prejudiced. Refusing to engage with a literary conversation conducted on these terms, he deflects the argument away from practical engagement into abstraction. This is not Ricks's idea of meaningful debate: 'Those who stall or forestall the reading of a poem by first asking combatively what it is to *read* can themselves be asked the prior question of what it is to *to*.'[30]

Ricks rails against the simplifying power of abstraction, but the division he applies of engagement versus abstraction has had many noticeably simplifying effects on the discussion of contemporary poetry, not least of the kind excluded from the Ricks canon. The work of Ricks's sometime Cambridge contemporary J. H. Prynne has no obvious affinities with the French theory against which Ricks does battle, but to its opponents (and not just Ricks) its apparent abstraction and intellectualism is evidence of its loyalty to the alien gods of theory and rejection of the organic, home-grown tradition. Yet in his longest critical work, *Field Notes* (2007), Prynne devotes 134 pages to a close reading of a single short Wordsworth poem, 'The Solitary Reaper'. There are parallel but separate traditions at work here, and close reading and native intelligence are not the exclusive property of either. As the 'theory wars' recede into intellectual history, it becomes easier to see the local and territorial issues at stake in 'Literary Principles as Against Theory', not least in the evolution of English as an academic discipline. Reviewing *Essays in Appreciation* (1998), Marilyn Butler characterised Ricks's polemical style as 'a form of underworld activity reminiscent of bear-baiting', sinking its teeth into a procession of biteable bodies one after the other. For the onlooker rather than the participant, however, the mêlée becomes 'strictly impossible to follow'.[31] Twenty years on, the theory boom that so enraged Ricks has largely dissipated, and critics uninterested in close readings have moved on to a more historicist and contextualising approach, leaving the number of close-reading critics probably about the same as it was in 1996 or at any other time in Ricks's career – which is to say, small. While the burden of Ricks's essay is to vindicate close reading over theory as a form of attention to the text, we would be failing as readers if we assumed that the act of close reading is a disengaged, merely private activity. Among the wonders of close reading, even after decades of theory, is its capacity to generate intense disagreement over what is going on in any given short lyric poem, who is right, who is wrong, and how we tell the difference.

'A Trifle': Paul Muldoon and Close Reading

A poet who has spent much of his career refusing to explain himself in prose is Paul Muldoon. Few poets are more learned than Muldoon, and to his detractors the Muldoon poem is typically a confection of riddles designed to attract academic critics. Samuel Beckett's novel *Watt* (1953) ends with the cryptic pronouncement 'no symbols where none intended', revealing everything and nothing at once, and in a short poem such as 'Ireland' Muldoon too both solicits and disables interpretation.

A car 'ticking over' in a gap induces doubt as to whether it might mean 'lovers' or men 'hurrying back / Across two fields and a river':[32] whether, in other words, it represents an innocuous everyday scene or something more sinister. Yet without that all-inclusive title, 'Ireland', or the Ulster provenance of its author, the poem might seem entirely inconsequential. The poem is both knowingly evasive and evasively knowing. An argument between Sean O'Brien and Tim Kendall over the interpretation of another Muldoon poem, 'A Trifle', shows how cannily Muldoon leads us to the point of almost-revelation before performing his strategic vanishing act. A building in Belfast has been evacuated during a bomb scare, and a woman walks outside carrying a 'blue-pink trifle / (...) with a dollop of whipped cream on top'.[33] To Kendall, the point of the poem is to assert the persistence of the everyday amidst the Troubles' state of emergency; he also favourably contrasts it with a more self-centred account of the poet and the Troubles that he finds in Seamus Heaney's *The Government of the Tongue* (1998), where the consequences of a bomb going off are all about the poet, and his presumed centrality to what is going on. To Sean O'Brien, keen to see a postcolonial subtext to this humdrum detail, Kendall is being disingenuous and the sugary dessert has been colour-coded to represent the British flag. Given how quickly the disagreement escalates from a wobbling trifle to invocations of genocide, O'Brien is worth quoting at length:

■ Kendall appears to be so concerned with Muldoon's disinclination to make a drama out of a crisis that he himself neglects the crisis altogether; yet the poem would be merely a stylish display of *sang-froid* without the historical and political dimension. To quarrel over a flag is a 'trifling' act in one sense; but it is costly in terms of lives. To quarrel over a territorial claim is equally 'trifling', but equally expensive. While complaining that the Irish are obsessed with ancient history, at the same time the British defend the expensive fruits of imperial and intermittently genocidal conquest. The British also complain about the cost of paying for Northern Ireland while offering the province the sustaining or (according to taste) unwanted tit of imperial subsidy parodically sketched in the poem.[34] □

It is a classic rank-pulling moment, with O'Brien overtaking Kendall's formalist reading on a turbo-charge of postcolonial indignation. The only problem is the absence of any guarantee whatever that O'Brien's is the correct reading of the poem, as pointed out by John Lyon in his own intervention in the debate. Sensing the difficult position in which he had placed his readers, Beckett insisted that 'the key word in my plays is "perhaps"',[35] and a deconstructive reading of Muldoon might easily proceed by way of the stand-off between everyday trifles and tragic politics – everywhere and nowhere at once in the Northern Ireland drawn in Muldoon's work. Yet as chance would have it, Muldoon has pronounced on the meaning of this poem in a 2000 interview with Neil Corcoran. The fourth-last line of the poem reads 'and on the tray the remains of her dessert', and for Muldoon 'Somewhere between that word "her" and "dessert" the poem resides,'[36] showing a careful awareness, on his part, of the line between reticence and explicitness (the 'remains' to which the woman would have been reduced had the bomb gone off, rather than just the 'remains of her dessert'). O'Brien's reading appears to go too far for him:

> ■ I'm not persuaded by the extent to which one can pursue such a reading. You know? That's not to say – and these ... of course, the colours are politicised – but I don't find that as fruitful an avenue as just the simple, fairly, one-dimensional, in a sense, reading of it.[37] □

Muldoon is such a skilful manipulator of the reader (he is fond of quoting Robert Frost's lines from 'Directive', 'If you'll let a guide direct you / Who only has at heart your getting lost') that we should not rule out another possibility again: that O'Brien's reading is all too accurate, and that Muldoon is attempting to put his interlocutor off the scent. Yet even if this were the case, there remains a world of difference between a Muldoon poem with a vaguely nationalist whiff to it and O'Brien's far blunter cultural politics.

Muldoon confronts these problems with, for him, revealing directness in his 1998 lecture 'Getting Round: Notes Towards an *Ars Poetica*'. He begins with metaphysical poetry, whose central device of the 'conceit' was defined by Samuel Johnson as 'heterogeneous ideas yoked by violence together'.[38] Muldoon too specialises in both his poetry and prose in yoking the heterogeneous together, in his case with the instantaneousness of an internet search engine. When he developed his theories of intertextuality in *The Anxiety of Influence* (1973), Harold Bloom did not require one poet to have read another for influence to have occurred, but Muldoon insists on crediting his poets with an intimate knowledge of the works to which they allude: Robert Frost is 'as likely as not' to have had an allusion in mind, and other details are 'likely to have been known by Frost' (in his Oxford lectures, *The End of the Poem* (2006), Muldoon carries this habit to near self-parodic levels).[39] Key to Muldoon's argument is the question of interpretation and (or shading into) over-interpretation, as when he finds a sexual subtext to the Frost sonnet 'The Silken Tent'. Is the meaning really there or not? Muldoon returns to that other Frost poem, 'Directive', in which a goblet lies hidden 'like the Grail / Under a spell so the wrong ones can't find it, / So can't get saved, as Saint Mark says they mustn't'.[40] The act of leading the reader in can also be a form of leading the reader on, and distracting attention from something else the poem would rather keep hidden, from some readers at least. This is to make of the poem a semi-mystical, or Gnostic text, speaking its truth only to initiates.

A contradiction Muldoon identifies in his position is the insistence that the poet should create out of the 'unknowing' of inspiration yet be possessed of 'almost total knowingness' as the poem's first reader.[41] Like Ricks, Muldoon expresses deep scepticism about the deconstructive theorist's power to overcome the author, but is wary of placing the poet in the role of a spokesperson for the poem, always on tap to manage its critical afterlife. The solution to this problem is to shift the emphasis from the poet to where it more properly belongs, on the poem itself:

■ [W]hat must be determined is the intent of the poem. For it is the *poem*, to continue in the film or dramatic lingo, that 'creates the role' of the first reader, and all subsequent readings must take that into account. [...] When I write that the poet must 'take into account, as best he or she is able, all possible readings', I'm well aware that no writer can allow for *every* reading.[42] □

Consistent with this is Muldoon's vision of the poem as a confluence of its shaping influences ('a product of its time') even as he reserves the poet's right 'not to espouse directly any political position'[43] and not to feel beholden to the larger community, as community representative or shaman. This is not a collapse into the apoliticism decried by O'Brien, since Muldoon has engaged so memorably with not just the Northern Irish Troubles but more recent conflicts too, but an honest statement of the competing motives, conscious and unconscious, that go to make the poem, and a refusal to equate the political poem with a simple 'espousal' of one position. The political poem today will often be better served by obliquity than directness, not for reasons of cowardice but the better to clarify what constitutes direct, effective, political speech, and the better to reject the cheapened substitutes that take its place.

Tradition and the Individual Talent: Poetry and Community

Muldoon's 'Getting Round' and the debate over his 'A Trifle' situate the poem at a contested zone between individual and community, whether the community of readers or the shaping force of history. In a conflict situation, such as shaped Muldoon in Northern Ireland, the community will make claims on the individual artist which it may take courage to resist, but for art to lack any engagement with community is to run the risk of dilettantish inefficacy. In his *Keywords* (1976) the Marxist critic Raymond Williams stressed how a small number of abstract terms have shadowed and shaped modern society, and 'community' is strongly among that number for present-day politics and literary debate. When Margaret Thatcher proclaimed in 1987 that there is 'no such thing as society' she voiced a worldview that spurred many poets into defiantly communitarian stances, as in Tony Harrison's 'School of Eloquence' sonnets.

In communitarian mode in her *Beyond the Lyric*, Fiona Sampson applies T. S. Eliot's essay 'Tradition and the Individual Talent' to the shepherding of like-minded individuals into the movements by which contemporary poetry is judged and anthologised:

■ Ultimately, then, this is a book about the great web of tradition. Within that web the poems themselves create a series of dialectics. When I read a poem by Colette Bryce it reminds me equally of Jo Shapcott and of Fleur Adcock – though for different reasons – and thus, in reading Bryce, I reawaken both older poets. All three are held together in my reading experience. This kind of overlapped differentiation [...] isn't a sign of the exhaustion of invention but, on the contrary, of how unexhausted the resources within contemporary poetry are. At its most radical, it is a kind of co-creation.[44] □

Poetry is a collaborative art, Sampson argues, co-created by practitioners and audience, a folk tradition preserving the bond to the organic community we had long thought lost. As William Wootten has pointed out, however, Sampson misunderstands Eliot's essay. While the Latin *traditio* means handing down over time, it also denotes a surrender of possession or the handing over of prisoners. Where Sampson sees only benign continuities, tradition carries within it antagonistic and divisive energies too. As Eliot wrote:

■ [I]f the only form of tradition, of handing down, consisted in following the ways of the immediate generation before us in a blind or timid adherence to its successes, 'tradition' should positively be discouraged.[45] □

Or as David Gervais wrote, considering Anthony Thwaite's claim that John Betjeman exhibited 'awareness of the Tradition': 'as if we all still knew what that was [...] Which tradition?'[46] The invocation of the thing should not be taken for the thing itself, in the absence of the meaningful conversation by which 'tradition' is sustained. 'A poem is a little church, remember, / you, its congregation, I, its cantor', wrote Don Paterson in 'Prologue'.[47] If a poem contains a congregation, an anthology might be an entire community. With its connotations of cosy belonging, 'community' is a handy political shibboleth, though sometimes deployed in ways that cannot conceal the hard times on which it has currently fallen, as when psychiatric patients are released into 'care in the community'. Sometimes, however, an accurate picture of a poetic generation can involve resistance to the ersatz 'communities' in which it appears to have come to rest. For Sampson, the term appears entirely unproblematic: Michael Longley possesses a 'dignified and also modest role as a communal spokesman', staging 'communal truths' in 'images or stories that will be universally understood'; the Serbian Vasko Popa and Palestinian Mahmoud Darwish come from 'socially and culturally unified communities'; 'enthusiasms are shared and junior colleagues helped along', we are told of the 'Oxford elegists', a spectacle that is 'always encouraging'; by the time of his death in 2004, the group centred on Michael Donaghy 'sometimes appeared to be the only community within British poetry'; and the author herself is also a 'community artist'.[48]

Donaghy's influence on contemporary poets has been considerable, but to refer to Donaghy and his friends as forming 'the only community within British poetry' is hyperbolic, obscuring among much else the energetic debate Donaghy carried on with other 'communities' within British poetry. Where Longley is concerned, casting the poet as shaman renders problematic not just the backdrop of sectarian difference and injustice against which he writes (the associations of the phrase 'community spokesman', in a Northern Irish context, are not always savoury), but the reality of difference within any 'community' of writers themselves, who will usually have their own ideas about the accuracy or otherwise of group labels. As critics such as Fran Brearton and Heather Clark have shown, the creative tensions among the Northern Irish poets are at least as important as any shared aesthetic.[49] In a revealing example cited by Brearton, Longley published a verse letter to Derek Mahon in *The New Statesman* in 1971 only for Mahon to write to that journal the following week taking vigorous issue with Longley's use of the first-person plural. 'Poetically, the only ways are separate ways', Mahon declared.[50] Yet over the decades that followed, Longley and Mahon's work would remain mutually shadowing and informing in ways that belie Sampson's sloganeering sense of 'community'. Few shared aesthetics could survive a definition of poetry as 'the hum of neighbourly voices in a meeting-hall. To be welcomed in, all you need do is open the door',[51] but the rejection of pseudo-communitarian newspeak (cf. David Cameron's 'Big Society') is not the same thing as a surrender to fragmentation and solipsism. To adapt one of Maurice Blanchot's book titles, *La communauté inavouable* (1983), poetic community may be truest where it is most unspeakable, or most irreducible to the simplifications waiting to ambush the dialogues that poems conduct among themselves.

Longley and Mahon's friendly disagreement is one version of the larger narrative of group versus individual identity, and the pressure that the former exerts on the latter in the name of community, class or nation, as we shall see in later chapters. To push back against group identity is not the same as political quietism, and on the contrary may be essential to the carving out of the imaginative freedom in which political poetry can most meaningfully do its work.

Pitch and Tone: Hill, Ricks and Critical Lineage

One of the most charged critical debates of recent times has been Geoffrey Hill's revaluation of T. S. Eliot. Hill's closeness to Eliot has long been an article of critical faith (he has been denounced by Tom Paulin as a 'parasite on Eliot's imagination'),[52] but in a review of Eliot's *Varieties of Metaphysical Poetry* (1994) Hill outlined a contentious theory of Eliot's poetic development from the 'pitch' of *Prufrock and Other Observations* (1917) to the 'tone' of *Four Quartets* (1945). For Hill, the tone of later Eliot marks a decline that corresponds uncomfortably with his elevation to the godlike authority he acquired in post-war times: 'It was the pitch of *Prufrock and Other Observations* that disturbed and alienated readers; it was the tone of *Four Quartets* that assuaged and consoled them.'[53] A prime indicator of this decline is Eliot's use of 'you' in *Four Quartets*, interpellating the reader with suggestions of shared patrimony, faith, and obedience ('You are here to kneel / Where prayer has been valid'). Hill objects to this not because of its religiosity *per se* but for its collusive, wheedling tone, which substitutes religious cliché for lived religious experience; religion becomes the form of religion, belief for belief's sake. He includes in his dismissal a defence of *Four Quartets* by Christopher Ricks, who had praised Eliot for a recognition of 'generous common humanity', which Hill takes to be another cliché. His conclusion expands the point into a blanket condemnation of a whole line of British poetry since Eliot:

■ The residual beneficiaries of *Four Quartets* have been Larkin and Anglican literary 'spirituality', two seeming incompatibles fostered by a common species of torpor. If I were to ask Ricks how it is that, against all the evidence his own unrivalled critical intelligence could bring to the process, he is pleased to be numbered among Larkin's advocates, I anticipate that he might answer, 'Because he speaks to the human condition.'[54] □

There are few moments in modern criticism comparable to this, in which one major critic so publicly arraigns another (Hill continues the attack in an oversized and stinging endnote). As Hill would be well aware, the word 'anticipate' means not just to foresee but to take preventative measures too. Hill wants nothing to do with the easygoing assumptions about the 'human condition' he finds in Larkin and his acolytes, and violently rejects the literary history that elevates this line of British poetry to its mainstream.

Perhaps because of how much time it spends in the seventeenth century, Hill's criticism thrives on such civil-war-style ambushes. As we read Hill it can seem he is fighting a one-man battle against modern literary history, but in Ricks he chose an adversary fully capable of defending himself, as he does in his book *True Friendship* (2010), a study of the influence of Eliot and Pound on younger poets (Hill, Anthony Hecht and Robert Lowell). There is an element of the hall of mirrors involved in reading Ricks on Hill on Ricks, but this exchange is as far as possible from critical incestuousness. Eliot has a habit of occasionally confessing to incomprehension in his criticism, where a reader might infer that he understands very well but prefers to affect the contrary, and Ricks flatly confesses to a failure of understanding before Hill's terms: 'I am unable to fathom just what Hill means by "pitch".'[55] Hill finds *Four Quartets* defective in their style of assuaging and consoling, but is this because Eliot has imperfectly phrased his consolations or because consolation is in every instance wrong? Does this expose Hill to charges of reverse-sentimentality, a fetishising of the rebarbative? Ricks's remonstration is patient and reasoned:

■ What is wrong with assuaging and consoling? This is left, no less conveniently, in the vague. True, there can be corrupt and sentimental forms of these, but that would not mean that there is no honorable place for them in literature. Frank Kermode memorably observed that a particular evocation may be too consolatory to console, but this does not constitute a disparagement in itself. What are the grounds for believing that *disturbing* and *alienating* readers are intrinsically the good or the better things to do? I think we should be told.[56] □

The gravamen of Ricks's response to Hill, developed over seventy pages, is the disjunction between the ingratitude Hill the critic has shown to Eliot in his recent work and the debts of gratitude his poetry continues to show to the American's work; better (or worse) still, he suggests ways in which Hill's poetry is directly beholden to Larkin's. Antagonism can be a source of influence, and where it finds merely antagonistic voice in Hill's prose it may find more harmonious expression in his poetry, without thereby discrediting the doubts expressed in the prose. Ricks draws attention to Hill's exaltation of the mode of '*Laus / et vituperatio*' in the 1998 sequence *The Triumph of Love*, a sequence that ends with Hill's defining a poet as 'a sad and angry consolation',[57] which may go some way to answer Ricks's question as to the role of the consolatory in art.

There is another way in which Hill's relationship with Eliot can be configured, however. How different is the dyad of pitch and tone from Eliot's 'dissociation of sensibility', as a seductive but highly personal response to literary history, and not one we should confuse with objective fact (whatever that might be in these questions)? One might suggest that in the very wilfulness of his terms, Hill proves himself an eminently Eliotian critic, following the earlier poet at the same time as he discredits him. This would be wholly in keeping with the 'unreconciled' nature of Hill's critical practice. Reading an attack by his former devotee Randall Jarrell, Auden announced 'I think Jarrell must be in love with me',[58] which is one way to make sense of the extremes of *odi et amo*, love and hate, at stake in the great critical disputes from Hazlitt on Coleridge, to Larkin and Jarrell on Auden, to Heaney on Larkin, and Hill on Eliot. All personal investment aside, these are debates that speak most passionately to what British poetry is today, how it traces its lines of influence, and how it expects to shape its own legacy.

Serious Poetry: the Fate of Authority

Few contemporary writers have combined the roles of poet and critic with more distinction than Peter McDonald. His critical work has addressed the Victorians, Louis MacNeice, Geoffrey Hill and contemporary Northern Irish poetry, but is also marked by scepticism of the drift in contemporary poetry away from traditional frameworks of authority and judgement towards a more inclusive and democratised aesthetic – or at least towards the critical vocabulary that proclaims this shift as a *fait accompli*. In his *Serious Poetry: Form and Authority from Yeats to Hill* (2002), McDonald notes the chilly connotations of the word 'authority', and its implied hostility to most of the values we have learned to cherish in literature in recent times. In Armitage and Crawford's *Penguin Book of Poetry from Britain and Ireland since 1945*, he finds a literary map of 'local accents, dialects, languages attaining their own authority, at the same time as ideas of absolute central authority dissolve'.[59] Yet canons continue to be formed, reputations made and broken, and prizes awarded. If not on the basis of an 'absolute central authority', then on whose say-so? In 2012, a defensive David Cameron claimed that he wanted 'privilege for all', a statement undermined by the fact that privilege can by definition only be for the few. Poetic authority cannot realistically be for all either, and saying so carries uncomfortable undertones of privilege and resistance to further discussion. Eliot insisted that tradition cannot be inherited, but only acquired with great labour. Is poetic authority any different?

A strong feature of the theory wars of the 1980s was the invocation of a natural way of reading poems uncontaminated by deconstruction and other foreign arts. Allied to this is the belief that ever since modernism poetry has been hijacked by the academy, whose investment in the difficult poetry of Eliot and Pound is a ploy to divorce the art from the common reader. Among the most succinct statements of this narrative is the introduction to Philip Larkin's *All What Jazz* (1970), where he announces that Louis Armstrong played for a popular audience while his modernist successors (Miles Davis, Charlie Parker and John Coltrane) turned their backs on this audience and made music for themselves. Modernism is a series of 'irresponsible exploitations of technique in contradiction of human life as we know it'.[60] (This argument is somewhat compromised by the fact that as a jazz musician Armstrong was *already* a modernist, raising questions as to how 'natural' a critical state of nature can ever be.) It would be easy to paint McDonald as a reactionary, harking back to a state of pre-theoretical bliss, but even as he worries about authority he is fully conscious of the historicity of the debate. He draws a contrast between the language of commonality in Samuel Johnson and the latter-day modernist-baitings of John Carey, author of *The Intellectuals and the Masses* (1992). When Johnson wishes to enshrine Thomas Gray's great 'Elegy Written in a Country Churchyard' (1751) as a popular classic, he 'rejoice[s] to concur with the common reader', whereas when Carey defends Larkin he superimposes a populist 'we' on the 'I', rather than bringing them into agreement in the manner of Johnson. The 'personality' projected by Larkin's poems, Carey claims, 'gains our trust [...] he is a didactic poet, teaching us how to survive'.[61] For McDonald, the equation of these two examples as defences of the common reader is a grave mistake.

Where the shift is at its most pronounced is in the emphasis placed by Carey on the poet as 'personality' rather than crafter of forms. For Ezra Pound, technique is the test of sincerity, but for Carey the two have become sundered and it is the extra-poetic aura of Larkin the icon that 'teach[es] us how to survive.' It was also the extra-poetic supplement of Larkin's personal life that caused such damage to his reputation, and personality-based readings such as this are a less than effective means of fighting back against the misreading suffered by that poet since his death. For McDonald, the *malaise* goes deeper than this, however, as he finds traces of the same pseudo-populism at work in Larkin himself. The difference here is that McDonald does so strictly in the arena of Larkin's work, in 'Church Going', whose conclusion could be a parody of Gray's 'Elegy' and makes use of the first-person plural as a way of boosting its authority ('A serious house on serious earth it is, / In whose blent air all our compulsions meet').[62] Applying Poundian standards of impersonality, McDonald finds Larkin seriously wanting:

> ■ The poem's 'I' has been so convincingly (and winningly) presented that to resist the conclusion, and the assumptions in 'our', seems either churlish or tone-deaf. Yet there is another telling moment in the stanza, when Larkin's voice prepares for the conclusion, in the flat-footed iambics of 'And that much never can be obsolete': at this point, metrical regularity trammels the speaking voice into a cadence that rings false, protesting too much [...] the regular tramp of metrical progress becomes too audible, and form is not the poem's rationale but the mode of enforcement for its thought.[63] □

We would seem to have returned to Hill's disagreement with Ricks over 'generous common humanity' and the 'human condition'. The ending of 'Church Going' shows an unmistakable wobble or loss of nerve on Larkin's part, as reflected in its mock-Augustan phrasing. The poet confronts the church's empty shell and reflects on the community it once housed. His attitude towards religious faith is one of sceptical belatedness, but he is reluctant to condemn the church and what it stands for altogether. In the absence of faith, the church becomes symbolic of continuity and tradition in the abstract, as reflected by the poem's progressive attunement to the style of an eighteenth-century pastoral. A sceptical reader might read this as an outbreak of involuntary parody as Larkin struggles to justify his attachment to a tradition in which he no longer appears to believe. This reader might also see here an encoding of Larkin's doubts about a rhetoric of our 'common humanity', where a more credulous reader saw only a successful resolution, hammered home with appropriate emphasis. Larkin makes an especially good test-case, given his history of being appropriated for conservative readings at the expense of more radical but unauthorised interpretations.[64] A certain kind of poetry will always crave mass approval, McDonald writes in conclusion, and 'authority' can help, but authority of the kind foisted on Larkin during his lifetime can become a distortion and a prison. The poem can work against abusive authority from within, in the engagement with form that constitutes the true poetic occasion, not least because 'creative fascination with form is so often combined with a sceptical attitude to the received shapes of authority in the literary, cultural, and political spheres'.[65]

'The timeless flux / that cannot help but practice / materialisation': On Poetic Form

The intrinsic authority of the poem, McDonald argues, may be a very different thing from the authority it acquires through the accidents of reputation. The same can be argued for poetic form, a concept underlying many discussions of the merits of close reading versus theory but which, paradoxically for this most concrete of entities, easily acquires the status of an abstraction. When the Beat poets began to publish in the late 1950s, they used free verse rather than the more formal style of their immediate forebears. Thus, one might argue for the politically conservative aspect of formal verse versus the uninhibited spontaneity of Ginsberg's *Howl*. The problem with this argument is the large number of examples where the relationship of politics and form is just the opposite: Byron, Burns, John Clare and Hugh MacDiarmid are just some of the poets who have turned to traditional forms to express radical politics. Despite his reputation for conservatism, Geoffrey Hill has written a poem in rhyming quatrains about the revolutionary French socialist Charles Péguy. Writing on form in 1917, Ezra Pound proposed that 'there is a "fluid" as well as a "solid" content, that some poems may have form as a tree has form, some as water poured into a vase'.[66] It is not that experimental poems of the kind we will examine in Chapter 5 are lacking form, but that the vocabulary to discuss their form has yet to evolve to the same level as the critical discourse on the sonnet or the villanelle. Even where traditional forms are concerned, there remains much scope for 'fluidity'. Paul Muldoon's sonnets are as different from Keats's as a Schoenberg string quartet from Schubert's. Consequently, there is no meaningful discussion of poetic form that is not a discussion of specific poems and their individual forms. Proper attention to this fact would show up much critical debate as based on the false opposition of a tradition as stasis and innovation as deviation from a lifeless formula.

In *On Form* (2007), Angela Leighton considers the legacy in critical discourse of this complex word. For Coleridge, via Kant and Schiller, there is a distinction between 'forming form' and 'formed form', the first an agent of creative intelligence, the second inanimate and dead. Leighton quotes a passage from Coleridge's notebooks in which the poet feels himself possessed by the form of a mountain: 'Poems. – Ghost of a mountain I the forms seizing my body, as I passed, became realities – I, a Ghost, till I had reconquered my Substance. I'[67] The Romantic poem finds its form through an interpenetration of poet and natural world rather than an act of intellectual calculation. At its most inflated the Romantic vision confers godlike powers on the poet, which William Empson saw as dangerously self-justifying ('*Form* is its own justification; it sustains itself, like God, by the fact that it exists'). How does one achieve critical distance from such a circular vision? Reading Shelley's 'The Triumph of Life', Leighton argues that:

■ [Empson] also perhaps misses the fact that Shelley's forms are not God-sustained at all, but self-sustaining, and thus skim across an epistemological void. The combination of two near-tautologies: the phantom of a form, and moving on motion, almost defies sight, gravity (and sense) altogether. The lines do not explain or name the form, and do not offer it as a metaphor of the mind; instead, they set it afloat on a stream of language which carries it on its own momentum.[68] □

Form is forever in motion, and cannot meaningfully be grasped except kinetically. This is the genius but also the fragility of defences of poetry on the grounds of form alone. It is not that the true poem excludes questions of class or gender, but that the streams of language in which they meet may not always mix harmoniously: the 'gendered poem', the 'political poem' can just as easily be a shorthand for creative tension as for a desired set of attitudes and beliefs.

Tracing this formalist line from Oscar Wilde and Walter Pater to contemporary theorists, Leighton dwells on that 'epistemological void' to connect art for art's sake (Pater's aesthetic *credo*) with modern theories of semiotics. For Barthes, 'form is what is *between* the thing and its name, form is what delays its name'.[69] This echoes the deconstructive belief in the signifier as an agent of semantic deferment (Jacques Derrida's *différance*), but more importantly it imbues this delay with the qualities of drama rather than emptiness, just as Beckett makes drama from non-event in *Waiting for Godot* (1953). Leighton pursues this theme in a number of quotations on art's disavowal of practical purpose, and its insistence on pursuing its aims 'for nothing'. In French the words *pour rien* designate silence – silent bars are *mesures pour rien* – so when Beckett publishes a volume of *Textes pour rien*, the *Texts for Nothing*, he is rejecting any use value for words beyond themselves, but also inscribing their active dimension, the element of forward motion in their apparent paralysis.

Among the contemporary poets that Leighton chooses to exemplify her theories of form is Roy Fisher. Fisher's early affiliation to American poets and publishers hampered his reception in Movement-dominated circles. Where Larkin often writes in rhyming quatrains Fisher favours a more open-field approach, but the achievement of his major sequences *City* and *A Furnace* is as much one of form as of symbolism or narrative. *A Furnace* is a meditation on the Birmingham of Fisher's childhood, much of it destroyed by the war, and Leighton notes the congeniality to Fisher of the genre of 'furtive elegy'.[70] Elegy is among the most flexible of forms, its one requirement being an (absent) human body, and in his cityscapes Fisher traces the elusive and indeterminate forms of the urban poor and the factories and graveyards that become their stage. In 'Diversions' Fisher describes the work of a foundry patternmaker:

■ His work fulfils the conditions for myth:
it celebrates origin,
it fixes forms for endless recurrence.[71] □

The factory patterns occupy the intermediary state assigned by Barthes to artistic form. Fisher is not given to emotive declarations of belonging: the factory 'fulfils the conditions for myth', but the poem does not take up its own invitation and supply the myth in question. The worker produces the patterns that determine others' labours, and is not named or otherwise individuated. Picking up on the elegiac theme in the sequence, Clair Wills finds Fisher 'reluctant to offer consolation' at the same time as he 'often eschews lyrical forms altogether'.[72] Because the form of the sequence remains provisional or embryonic, waiting to emerge properly into focus, the moment for consolation too has yet to arrive.

The effects of this on Fisher's style are marked. Larkin's poem 'Here', which features its own cityscapes, begins with a long, grammatically ambiguous sentence ('Swerving east, from rich industrial shadows') in which we look in vain for a named subject until we realise that the subject is in fact the participle 'swerving'. The shift from an observer moving through the landscape to the process of observation itself as the focus of the poem is a favourite Fisher device too. The narrator of *A Furnace* defers to a principle of anonymity: 'Something's decided / to narrate / in more dimensions than I can know.'[73] Combining social realism with modernist collage, Fisher is able to use the quasi-religious word 'apparitions' for the appearance of an ironworks from a bus window. The materialisation of the dead takes place in a series of cinematic fade-ups, assembling the materials of perception out of original chaos. Intra- and extra-diagetically, form is a matter of decanting between states of flux. Form for Fisher is a vehicle not merely of knowledge, but of discovery; hence the tropes of touch and exploration, the rich architectural detail, and teeming ghostly presences we find in such abundance in *A Furnace*. The intricate nature of Fisher's quest, excavating layers of historical memory, makes for rewarding but difficult poetry. For critics who engage with Fisher's work, the mysteriousness of his forms becomes an ideal entry-point for the connections he makes with the larger historical worlds beyond the scope of the usual short lyric poem.[74] Bad poetry and criticism can be parasitic on each other, but the best poetry and criticism practise a form of symbiosis in search of a common goal. As Leighton writes in conclusion:

■ Form is a word which gives writers a figure for something essential to literary work: for that obliqueness of style and matter, music and meaning, which demands attention, and becomes, in its way, a new kind of knowledge.[75] □

CHAPTER THREE

Postcolonialism

Devolving English Literature and 'Cosmopolibackofbeyondism'

As the twentieth century came to an end, a report of the Commission into the Future of Multi-Ethnic Britain found that 'to be English, as the term is in practice used, is to be white'. While Britishness was marginally less exclusive, allowing for hybrid identities such as Black British, Indian British and so on, 'Britishness, as much as Englishness, has systematic largely unspoken, racial connotations [...] It is widely understood that Englishness, and therefore by extension Britishness is racially coded.'[1] The misfit between Englishness and Britishness is not lost on Robert Crawford, who has devoted several studies to the origins of 'English literature', tracing its roots persuasively to the Scottish Enlightenment.[2] When we democratise 'English literature' today we are breaking up not a timeless monolith but an entity whose roots lie in archipelagic pluralism. Reviewing Crawford's *Devolving English Literature*, Donald Davie nevertheless found the attention given to a metropolitan English culture centred on London and Oxbridge disproportionate. Finding only Kingsley Amis and John Betjeman to embody the Anglocentric smugness denounced by Crawford, Davie observes: 'The ramparts so frailly manned should have given way long ago to the armies massed against them. What Crawford doesn't realise is that this indeed has happened; he is sounding the bugle for an assault on a fortress that surrendered years ago.'[3] In his defence Crawford points to his coverage of Leeds-born Tony Harrison as an opponent of the London–Oxbridge monopoly on Englishness, but more fundamentally he rejects the implication of static national categories:

■ There is no fixed, unchanging entity called Englishness, or Britishness, or Jamaicanness. Each of these cultural identities, like that of Scotland, is in constant evolution, continually re-manufacturing itself.[4] □

In one of Harrison's 'School of Eloquence' sonnets the young poet reads a Keats poem aloud before being interrupted by his teacher, who bristles at this high-cultural artefact being tainted with a Yorkshire accent. The irony is that Keats was of lower-class Cockney origins, but the teacher's proprietorial assumptions win out: linguistic imperialism presumes or imposes a standardisation even where none existed. Among the key theses of Crawford's study is the provincial origins of Modernism: Yeats, Joyce, Hardy, Lawrence, Ezra Pound and many others began their careers as awkward young parvenus, able to turn the demotic vigour of their speech to advantage in the literary marketplace. Writers who chose not to live or publish in London, such as Hugh MacDiarmid, still found the jadedness of standard English an essential article of faith, joining battle with the patronising metropolis the better to uphold the newly assertive cultural fringe. Crawford places T. S. Eliot in this category too, though Eliot's acquired hyper-Englishness obscures the extent of his once-outsider status, and draws on Deleuze and Guattari, whose theories of the minor writer employ the concepts of 'deterritorialisation' and 'reterritorialisation'.[5] Unseating old Georgian certainties, the deterritorialising modernist revolution led by Eliot and Pound was followed by a strong retrenching, or reterritorialising phase of which Eliot's conservatism is one symptom (still very much a live issue, as we see from Geoffrey Hill) and Pound's marginalisation in the UK is another. More recently, Crawford has expounded 'Cosmopolibackofbeyondism' as the defining quality of a poetry which can be both central and marginal at once.[6] Jahan Ramazani has stressed the importance of place to postcolonial poetry in ways that resist reduction to what he terms the 'Aeolian' model of airy dislocation and the 'Antaean' model of rootedness in the native soil; rather, the postcolonial poet produces 'a poetry of multiple and mobile "positionings"', in Stuart Hall's term.[7] American blues are influenced by the music of West Africa, yet when the Malian musician Ali Farka Touré learned the guitar he found himself mimicking Otis Redding and American blues artists; similarly, when Nigerian poet Christopher Okigbo draws on the rituals of Igbo polytheism he does so within the framework of 'Western modernist syncretism and free verse'.[8] As with the Möbius strip, in which a strip of paper is twisted into a loop, allowing movement in a straight line to turn one's position upside down, inside and outside become reversed, or doubled up, as postcolonialism reconfigures home and elsewhere into complex new relationships.

Crawford's critique complicates the post-war tendency to set Modernism up in opposition to the local or provincial: radical art can happen not only in Paris or New York but in Auchtermuchty or Llareggub. The opaque aspects of modernist art (Ezra Pound's polyglot quotations, the Babelian language of Joyce's *Finnegans Wake* (1939)) are the obverse of its reconnection with the vernacular. While Pound's worst excesses can 'overcome him and his readers', as Crawford concedes,[9] for every authoritarian follower of Pound and Eliot we also have the contemporary example of Ciaran Carson or W. N. Herbert, who fuse the highbrow and the vernacular, the classical and the anarchic. All of these writers have found humour an important tool in crossing linguistic lines of demarcation. Another of Crawford's examples, Edwin Morgan's 'The First Men on Mercury', takes this to the absurdist level of inter-planetary communication. Accommodation theory describes the alteration of one's accent to make one's speech acceptable to one's audience, and after an initial stand-off between standard English and gobbledegook Morgan's poem 'accommodates' English and Mercurian. Human–alien relations are established on a solid foundation of linguistic hybridity. As Craig Raine has said, 'All great poetry is written in dialect';[10] our mistake is to think of this as a cramping condition, rather than the gateway to untold worlds of poetic possibility.

The Colony Within, or, Postcolonialism Begins at Home

Postcolonialism begins at home, or more specifically in the spaces where home shades into 'abroad'. One such territory for British poetry is Ireland, annexed under the Act of Union of 1800 and separated in 1921 into the Irish Free State and Northern Ireland. Northern Ireland is a contested political territory, and the poetry written in the shadow of the Northern Irish Troubles has lent itself eloquently to the postcolonial debate. In Seamus Heaney's *North*, published at the height of the Troubles in 1975, the poet agonises between the poles of belonging and detachment, the intimacies of the tribe versus the 'civilised outrage' of the liberal outsider. For one of his keenest admirers, Helen Vendler, the merit of Seamus Heaney's work is to transcend the sound and fury of the Troubles, and make a world figure of its author to the extent that he leaves the squabbles of his province behind. To Vendler, the local poetic contexts underpinning Heaney are of secondary interest and the Troubles a thematic backdrop rather than a shaping discursive framework:

■ With 'Punishment', Heaney's archaeology of persons becomes an anthropology of the present: dig however deep, the person who rises to the surface is one you recognize from your own life. The situations of the past are replicated at the railings of Belfast. The cast of the imagination [...] is one for which Heaney has been condemned. But no poem is a poem unless, as Yeats said, it is about a quarrel within oneself.[11] □

Vendler wards off overly political readings by closing down the political altogether:

■ Can it be, Heaney proposes, that what we are seeing is not Catholics against Protestants, or rich against poor, or loyalist against nationalist, but rather a generalized cultural approval of violence, dating back many centuries?[12] □

There is a poem in *North* titled 'Strange Fruit', taking its title from the Billie Holiday song inspired by lynchings in the American South. One has only to imagine the grim outrages of which Billie Holiday sang described as a 'generalized cultural approval of violence' to see the shortcomings of Vendler's approach. Instinctively seeing politics as antipathetic to poetry, she issues an impartial condemnation that cannot account for the state-sanctioned agency of one side and the disenfranchisement of the other. The sanitised Heaney that Vendler offers her readers has a politicising effect on Edna Longley, a critic who once began an essay with the declaration that 'Poetry and politics, like church and state, should be separated.'[13] For all her keenness to uphold poetry criticism as a buffer zone against the depredations of bad politics, and the bad readings of poetry they bring in their wake, Longley is sharply impatient of a critic so dismissive of the contexts in which poems are read. Vendler urges American readers to look past commendations of Heaney as an 'Irish poet', because the 'beauty and significance' of his work are 'as germane to our lives as any other poet'. '"Beauty and significance", it would seem, bypass small countries', Longley tartly comments.[14]

Longley's reading of *North* is one of the great interventions in contemporary poetic debate (nor was she alone in her hostility to the book at the time of its publication: Heaney's younger contemporary Ciaran Carson published a highly sceptical review of *North* in *The Honest Ulsterman*). As Longley writes, judging Heaney's attempts at balancing condemnation and understanding of violent, tribal belonging:

■ He excludes the intersectarian issue, warfare *between* tribes, by concentrating on the Catholic psyche as bound to immolation, and within that immolation to savage tribal loyalties. This is what he means by 'slaughter / for the common good' ('Kinship'), and by 'granting the religious intensity of the violence its deplorable authenticity and complexity' – and, of course, no apologia for the 'male cult' of imperial power. 'Kinship' defines the battlefield in astonishingly introverted Catholic and Nationalist terms.[15] □

Negative responses to Longley's position tend to overplay her apoliticism, seeing an outright refusal rather than a scepticism of political readings, and assume this reduces her own position to one of insipid neo-Arnoldianism. For Mark Patrick Hederman, the logic of Longley's stance is 'to cordon poetry off into an anodyne, detached and insulated cocoon where it loses all its essential meaning and force'.[16] Longley's position is paradoxical: attacked by Hederman for her depoliticising of Heaney but suspicious of Vendler for *her* depoliticising reading of Heaney. Longley contests Heaney's politics and the Catholic nationalist analysis of conflict she finds in *North*, but to Hederman this is to give up on politics altogether.

It is instructive to compare the scepticism towards *North* we encounter in Longley and Carson with that of David Lloyd, whose trenchantly-worded critique of Heaney in *Anomalous States* (1993) comes from a radically different perspective, that of the postcolonial Marxist left. Deploying the language of Frankfurt School Marxism with a heavy hand, Lloyd sees in Heaney's 'major' status evidence only of the false consciousness of late capitalism and the simulacra of choice and individualism to which it condemns cultural consumers. Despite his nationalist sympathies, Heaney succeeds in appealing to the middle-brow British reader by eviscerating his work of any real politics, Lloyd argues, and placing a compromised Romantic aesthetic in their place. Reading 'Punishment', Lloyd finds theatrical posing licensed by identity politics and a refusal to swap its sectarian categories for a critique better equipped to make moral choices. His rhetoric escalates to a high, almost apocalyptic pitch:

■ The seeming coherence between this scenario of the elevation of a minor Irish poet to a touchstone of contemporary taste and a discourse whose most canonical proponent argued for the Celtic literature as a means to the integration of Ireland with Anglo-Saxon industrial civilisation is appropriate and pre-programmed. It is, for all that, profoundly symptomatic of the continued meshing of Irish cultural nationalism with the imperial ideology which frames it.[17] □

Lloyd links Heaney and Matthew Arnold, whose interest in Celtic literature was paternalistic and anti-nationalist, seeing literature as a balm for the wounds inflicted by politics. Heaney's political conservatism feeds his readers a comforting mirage of community and belonging just as the actuality of these concepts is being erased. Heaney has sold the political power of poetry short, yet Lloyd does this too by collapsing poetry so definitively into its ideological underpinnings (the 'pre-programmed' meshing of an Irish poet into the project of imperialism).

Like Robert Crawford, Lloyd frequently draws on the concept of 'deterritorialisation'. The poetry of which he approves refuses the consensual spaces of the nation and the post-Romantic aesthetic, as found in *The Field Day Anthology of Irish Writing* (1991) no less than in the canonical husbandry of Edna Longley. In practice, however, Lloyd's radical postcolonialism fails to identify a credible counter-canon, and appears to lack any kind of critical vocabulary for poets that do not meet its entry-requirements – poets such as Michael Longley, Derek Mahon, Paul Durcan and Paul Muldoon, to name but four, let alone Seamus Heaney. The great literary ideologue of post-independence Ireland, Daniel Corkery, articulated his theory of a decolonised aesthetic in *The Hidden Ireland* (1924) and *Synge and Anglo-Irish Literature* (1931). His critical values were protectionist and anti-modernist, and escaping from his grasp has been a test for generations of Irish writers. His influence can be seen in the work of Thomas Kinsella (b. 1928), whose interventions in Northern Irish politics, in his poem on Bloody Sunday, 'Butcher's Dozen', and critical deprecation of the Northern Irish poets as a 'journalistic entity',[18] have borne a distinctly nationalist stripe. One result of this has been the steep decline in Kinsella's reputation in the UK after a promising start in the 1960s. Younger poets who publish in the Irish Republic are often as little visible in the UK as non-Anglophone poets on mainland Europe. The reception of Irish poetry in Britain becomes a microcosm of the encounter between Britishness and postcolonialism, as manifested in questions of decolonisation, border-crossings, the power of metropolitan publishers, and critical visibility. Nor within the British archipelago are these questions confined to the Celtic fringe. Much recent poetic and critical attention has focused on bringing the debate home to the dark heart of Albion itself.

Englands 'Where Nobody Lives' and Decolonising the Motherland

In *The Triumph of Love* Geoffrey Hill calls Britain 'a nation / with so many memorials but no memory'.[19] In his *Mercian Hymns* (1971) the naming of suburban estates after long-ago battles drew satiric attention to the ways in which the narrative requires neither our understanding nor approval to shape our daily lives. Where historical understanding fails us, the distinctly modern substitute of heritage is always ready to take its place. The problematic overlap between the two is illustrated in the critical reception of Philip Larkin, whose career coincided emblematically with the post-war withering of empire. During his lifetime Larkin was taken to represent a benign and quintessential Englishness, a view that suffered a disastrous reversal with the publication of his biography and *Selected Letters* (1992), revealing his far-right political sympathies and leading Tom Paulin to attack the 'sewer under the national monument'.[20]

In the intervening years, a series of revisionist readings has retrieved Larkin's reputation, highlighting the simplifying effects of projecting the author's life onto his art, but also disputing the ways in which Larkin's Englishness was ever so quintessential or celebratory in the first place. The late poem 'Going, Going' was commissioned by a Conservative association and prompted Larkin to elegiac visions of a departed England ('And that will be England gone, / The shadows, the meadows, the lanes, / The guildhalls, the carved choirs'),[21] but its distaste for the anti-environmental effects of industry ('move / Your work to the unspoilt dales') and identification of enterprise with rapacity did not go well, and the poem was rejected. His worship of Margaret Thatcher notwithstanding, Larkin might thus be seen as harking back to an earlier and more genteel form of conservatism. A further complicating wrinkle lurks here too, however: the guildhalls and carved choirs whose disappearance he fears scarcely belong to the country he had mapped with such painstaking care in his work up to this point. They are an abstraction, a dutiful response to the expectations set up by the genre of national lament. The poem is best understood as a critique of the form of elegy itself, and of the nation as proper matter for such poems (England as a 'museum to house itself', in David Gervais's formulation).[22] As such, the nation serves its poetic purpose admirably, even if, to adapt a phrase of Sean O'Brien's for Geoffrey Hill, it is an 'England where nobody lives'.[23]

In truth, Larkin had plainly stated his unease with the matter of Albion in his 1955 poem 'The Importance of Elsewhere'. Though he was 'Lonely in Ireland' in a period spent in Belfast, 'strangeness made sense'.[24] Coming up against local difference he makes the necessary accommodations and communicates with the locals across the divide of strangeness. Back in England there exists no alibi for maladjustment, nor is he free to accept or reject local customs. He is merely stuck with them, and what had been a bicultural experience has shrivelled to sameness with no way out ('Here no elsewhere underwrites my existence'). Readers who trawl Larkin's work in search of self-assertive patriotism will be sorely disappointed; with his pull towards the nation's fringes (a run-down Welsh resort in 'Sunny Prestatyn', 'The Importance of Elsewhere', the East Yorkshire coast in 'Here'), Larkin is the bard of centrifugal Britishness, of a country slipping away from itself – as one of his most sympathetic critics, James Booth, has shown. Challenging Seamus Heaney on his reading of Larkin as 'nurtured' on Anglocentric values, Booth insists 'There was, in fact, nowhere where Larkin felt "nurtured" by being among "his own".'[25]

While the words 'confident' and 'vibrant' are much used by blurb writers to describe Black or Asian British poets, exhaustion and entropy remain the default condition of Englishness itself. Having endured the breakup of Empire, England has most to lose from the redrawing of the United Kingdom too, as Scotland, Wales and Northern Ireland (but not England) all achieved devolution within the union. For George Orwell, England was 'a family with the wrong members in control',[26] and in 'Phrasebook', Jo Shapcott dramatises the loss of this control in ways that highlight its underlying paternalist assumptions. An Englishwoman is travelling abroad during a time of conflict (the poem dates from the period of the first Gulf war in 1990–1) and conducts an amorous adventure related by the poem in military metaphors; the word 'bliss', it explains, is used by pilots as an acronym for 'Blend, Low silhouette, Irregular Shape, Small, / Secluded'.[27] Getting into trouble, the woman panics and falls back on colonial attitudes of entitlement:

> ■ What have I done? I have done
> nothing. Let me pass please. I am an Englishwoman. □

'What have I done?' is skilfully banal and grandiose at the same time. 'I have done' suggests an end to the ordeal before the appearance of 'nothing' on the next line. As well as its plea to an uncomprehending policeman, 'Let me pass please' has resonances of a schoolgirl hoping to pass an exam. In the absence of anything else to hold onto, the one field in which she trumps her tormentors is Englishness; the poem's final words powerfully evoke the speaker's desperate collapse into empty self-identification. Sean O'Brien has commented on the cultural losses involved in moving from Russian to English in 'Motherland', Shapcott's translation from Tsvetaeva, and the different valencies of that title in its two contexts. Undoubtedly, there is a sizable gap to be bridged between the experiences of Shapcott's speaker and that of Tsvetaeva's Russian original. When he argues that 'It is as though the poet has not only lost her "English" bearings but also the idioms in which to name what might once have been the case', O'Brien is making a case for the turn to linguistic self-reflexivity in Shapcott's poem as a response to this predicament.[28] The question remains, however, whether framing the argument in this self-reflexive way is the same thing as resolving it. If we grant that the narrating 'I' of 'Phrasebook' is something akin to the 'robotic ventriloquist' Keith Tuma finds in the poem,[29] we must decide whether Shapcott has chosen an easy stereotype to draw off the embarrassing residue of Englishness, and avoided the more compromising and violent mesh of identities we find in a poem such as Harrison's 'v.' (1985), in which poet and skinhead shade shockingly into the same person.

For Shapcott, Englishness is a shorthand for privilege yet strangely ineffectual and comic at the same time. 'Even / the dictionary laughs when I look up / "England", "Motherland", "Home",' she writes.[30] Like many other English poets of the 1990s, Shapcott offers amused disillusionment with received ideas of English identity. So common is this tone in 1990s poetry that amused disillusionment comes to look like a national characteristic in itself, even when deployed against empty nationalist posturing. In 'The Nation' Roy Fisher describes a 'national day' on which everything is prefaced by the adjective 'national', reducing the concept to the pleonastic exhaustion of 'national dish', 'national gesture' and 'national anthem', before a group of offenders is clapped in the 'national prison' and subjected to the 'national / method of execution' for succumbing to the 'national vice', whatever that might be.[31] It is not all a one-way descent from nationalism into the inoffensiveness of the heritage industry, however, as Simon Armitage reminds us in 'The Twang', with its 'collection box / for the National Trust. I mean the National Front.'[32] While Armitage's speaker blurs the distinction, for poets at a tangent to the charmed circle of native Britishness its harder edge is more difficult to miss.

Confusing Home with the World: Michael Hofmann

In its negotiations with abroad, British poetry juggles cosmopolitanism and linguistic imperialism, caught between the offence of exoticising the other and the worse crime of ignoring it altogether. 'Xenophobia, philistinism, censoriousness, priggishness have always been offered in loose handfuls by the English to foreign writers', Michael Hofmann has written.[33] Born in Freiburg in 1957, Hofmann is numbered among those foreigners, having lived in Britain since early childhood while retaining a strong sense of his outsider status – 'England is at the edge of my circle rather than at the centre of its own', he defiantly insists.[34] One consequence of his outsider status is that British critics have not quite known what to do with him, or how best to place his work. His greatest influence is Robert Lowell – the urbanely garrulous Lowell of the late sonnets as much as the family chronicler of *Life Studies* (1959). Hofmann's work is characterised by highbrow Middle-European chatter: piled-up lists and litanies of urban bric-a-brac delivered in a tone of side-of-the-mouth knowingness, and a half-repelled, half-fascinated addiction to the tawdry detritus of mass culture, all offset by a self-mocking detachment. 'Tales from Chekhov', from his first collection *Nights in the Iron Hotel* (1984), begins 'They are in a hotel in a foreign country',[35] setting a tone of impermanence and displacement that will remain his signature throughout his four collections to date.

Alongside his high-mindedness, Hofmann has used his outsider's gift for bypassing native pieties to write some of the sharpest political poetry of recent times. In 'From Kensal Rise to Heaven', from *Acrimony* (1983), the oppositional politics to which Harrison or Ken Smith appealed in the face of Thatcherite Conservatism have become feebly deluded: 'Old Labour slogans, *Venceremos*, dates from demonstrations / like passed deadlines – they must be disappointed / to find they still exist.'[36] Not that this version of Conservatism seems interested in conserving anything, in a city where 'Building, repair and demolition / go on simultaneously, indistinguishably.' Hofmann's addiction to ellipsis gives his work a rapidly shifting focus, while also suggesting an almost fingertip closeness to the objects of its (frequent) elegiac moods. Sean O'Brien finds a 'depressed and passive-aggressive' complex at work in Hofmann's relentless downbeat tone and its refusal of the rhetorical grandiloquence one associates with Lowell.[37] In his political poems, older-style imperial fantasies persist in senile form beneath the rapacious bustle of modern London: in the National Front's pre-election radio broadcast we are treated to the 'fiction of an all-white Albion' compared by Hofmann to 'my landlady's white-haired old bitch, who confuses home with the world, pees just inside the door, / and shits trivially in a bend in the corridor'.[38] Glimpses of the world beyond the metropolis bear out John Bull and John Barrell's claim that 'It is difficult to pretend that the English countryside is now anything more than an extension of the town,'[39] as in the scarred and blasted landscape of 'Eclogue'. Hofmann flirts with the schematism of allegory to capture the plight of contemporary pastoral. In a Hofmann poem, the dictionary would laugh if we looked up 'nature'. Private life too becomes not a refuge from stylised defeatism, but a confirmation of it. Sex in these poems is clumsy, hurried and likely to be regretted the next morning: 'One perfunctory fuck on our first night, / Then nothing for ever ...'[40] O'Brien is troubled by the distancing effect this induces, likening the poems to laboratory experiments in which 'ends and purposes' recede and vanish into extinction.[41] Thatcherism was a political philosophy of adamantine certainties, and the political poets championed by O'Brien – Harrison, Ken Smith – responded with certainties of their own. Hofmann's diffidence can, in contrast, be troubling. Political slipperiness is not the same as refusal, however, and in a consideration of Hofmann and Englishness Fred D'Aguiar has drawn attention to Hofmann's fondness for parentheses as a 'way to subtract from the notion of a main clause as the main subject of the poem and draw attention to the true subject as somehow hidden and in need of teasing out into the open'.[42] Politics in Hofmann refuse to take obvious forms, but the lack of obviousness becomes a form of politics too.

A poem from Hofmann's first book is titled 'Entropy'. It is characteristic of his work as a whole to give the appearance of living on the edge of collapse. In one of his most direct political poems, 'Masque', from

Approximately Nowhere, he turns to necrophilia as an image for Britain's terminal *ennui*: 'The government is fucking a corpse.'[43] While the government goes through the motions of infantilised sleaze, only the impassivity of the corpse preserves any authenticity ('The corpse is for real'). Hofmann offers himself up to readers as the corpsed victim-cum-observer of desensitised boredom. The use of obscenity is strategic. D'Aguiar has written on the centrality to Hofmann's work of looking – acquisitive, greedy, seductive looking, with a tendency to trail off into ellipses where romance or sex are concerned, but which here exhausts itself in the over-fullness of obscenity and the poem's pornographic tone. Would a British-born poet approach these subjects differently? D'Aguiar identifies a 'European tourist aspect' to Hofmann's work, 'and a fitting preoccupation with the meanings of a German heritage for a poet thinking in English about the meaning and extent of his Englishness'.[44]

Glossolalia: David Dabydeen and Fred D'Aguiar

As a white European, Hofmann is better placed than a West Indian or Asian poet might be to offer harsh critiques of English politics followed by an elliptical disappearing act. For the latter, the option of camouflaging oneself in the host culture is not so easy. When E. A. Markham swapped Montserrat for Britain in the 1950s 'there was no particular trauma in leaving',[45] but his sense of the welcome he could expect from the 'motherland' was subject to rapid revision in post-war Britain. As Omaar Hena reminds us, however, Markham did not respond by adopting the paradigm of the outsider artist 'writing back' to the imperial centre, or defined by what he suspected was an 'outdated idea of Englishness'.[46] Instead, his critique of identity politics prompted Markham to turn to persona: that of a black Antiguan in his 1970s collections, including *Lambchops*, and that of a white feminist in the 1986 collection *Living in Disguise*. David Dabydeen, of Caribbean-Asian background but sixteen years Markham's junior, has written of a different kind of camouflage for the Black British poet, in the frequently invisible hinterland of small-press publishing:

■ Either you drop the epithet 'black' and think of yourself as a 'writer' (a few of us foolishly embrace this position, desirous of the status of 'writing' and knowing that 'black' is blighted) – that is, you cease dwelling on the nigger/tribal/nationalistic theme, you cease *folking* up the literature, and you become 'universal' – or else you perish in the backwater of small presses.[47] □

Compare with this Fred D'Aguiar's compulsion to 'state categorically' that it is 'nonsense to pretend that what black writers are doing in Britain is so unlike what their white compatriots in craft are practising that it merits a category entirely of its own'.[48] Dabydeen's point is clearly made, however, by the slowness of larger poetry publishers to address their demographic base. While Bloodaxe, Anvil and Carcanet made significant strides in the 1980s, Faber's publication of Daljit Nagra's debut collection in 2007 made him only the second non-white poet on their list after Derek Walcott. A Bloodaxe anthology, *Ten New Poets* (2010), notes in its blurb that 'less than 1% of all poetry books published in the UK are by black or Asian poets'.[49] Sarah Broom echoes D'Aguiar's point about access and visibility by linking the 'marginalisation and invisibility' of former times with the 'appropriation and commodification' that often are the price of overcoming that invisibility today.[50] Then as now, the fate of the postcolonial poet is to end up in between, linguistically as well as geographically; and Broom is further careful to signal the ways in which her own critical discourse too might become just another tool of appropriation, 'recoding' the experiences of poets of colour rather than properly attending to their voices.

As Salman Rushdie has written, 'English, no longer an English language, now grows from many roots.'[51] 'Two Cultures', from Dabydeen's first book, *Slave Song* (1984), is written in Guyanese English and mocks the returned poet for his European airs and graces ('Hear how a baai a taak / Like BBC!').[52]As in Tom Leonard's humorous poem *Unrelated Incidents* (1976), the cultural outsider invokes the BBC as a watchword for 'civilised' but alien values. The educated poet making a return is left in no doubt that he has forfeited his intimate connection to the community. Though he may protest, the poet is sufficiently self-conscious about Guyanese speech to supply a back-of-the-book translation for the baffled. This is the dialectic of standard versus non-standard English familiar from the work of Tony Harrison, Tom Leonard and others, and in 'Coolie Odyssey' Dabydeen short-circuits the language question by writing in standard English alone. Examining the colonial experience from the Guyanese side, he admits to the 'cry for transfiguration' that underpins the Guyanese fantasy of England, a fantasy of whiteness and purity he juxtaposes with the 'imagined purity' of Guyana for Walter Raleigh as he sought to escape the 'squalor' of Elizabethan England.[53] Each of these fantasies is equally doomed to fail, or to meet on the taboo-infested middle ground of sexuality, as in 'Slave-woman's Song' and 'Brown Skin Girl'. No amount of standard English can harvest the losses of the diasporic experience, however. The emigrant's father lives on 'Albion Estate' in Guyana, where he prays that his daughters' sexual honour will be protected from 'the Negroes', while in London his son dreams nostalgically of playing cricket as a boy. Cultural signifiers connect across oceans of disabling ironies in a 'criss-cross of illusions'.[54]

Fred D'Aguiar combines standard English, creole and 'nation language' polyphonically in his debut, *Mama Dot* (1985). Slave narratives have informed D'Aguiar's fiction, and in *Bill of Rights* (1998) he recrosses the Atlantic to tell the story of Jim Jones and the 1978 mass suicide of his cult members in Guyana (homeland of D'Aguiar's parents and where the poet grew up). Jones was raised in a racist environment in Indiana but sympathised with the black community, imitating the style of black preachers in the church he founded. The charismatic but menacing black witch doctor is a staple of racist iconography, but here it is a white American and religious fanatic travelling to his Guyanese plantation who fulfils the role of sinister shaman. The oral tradition, literacy and scripture all feature: for much of the book, the lower half of each page is printed in italics, often in a nursery-rhyme-like style, suggesting the teeming glossolalia, or Pentecostalist speaking-in-tongues, of the religious imagination fermenting below the discursive surface. In a review of *Mama Dot*, Blake Morrison notes the resurgence of dialect poetry at the time, linking its use in the work of poets such as Benjamin Zephaniah, Amryl Johnson and John Agard to hard-hitting political themes (literally so, in the case of a Zephaniah poem about being assaulted by a policeman). This is to lump together writers from very different backgrounds, and with different approaches to the question of standard and non-standard English. While Brathwaite pioneered the label 'nation language' as an improvement on 'pidgin' or 'patois', Linton Kwesi Johnson introduced 'dub poetry' for his style of reggae-influenced performance, and – conscious of drawing on a diverse range of traditions – Benjamin Zephaniah has used 'black' to refer to 'more than skin colour', even extending its use to groups that are ethnically white, if they have suffered prejudice and discrimination ('My Black is profound').[55] From Morrison's point of view, however, some readjustment of old reading habits is required. He admits to unease over the loss of formalist polish in such work: 'If much of this lacks sophistication, that too seems to be a choice, as if to say: elegance is something the oppressed cannot afford.'[56] The critique of elegance is an important aspect of D'Aguiar's project. The chorus of voices in *Mama Dot* recalls John Berryman's *Dream Songs* (1964; 1968) and its interventions from his minstrel-like side-kick, who addresses him as 'Mr Bones'. The text foregrounds the tension between scripture and literature in allusions to the performance poetry circuit the disillusioned convert has left behind in London, but as the action closes in on its tragic *dénouement* the text drops its stereophonic layout and the survivor-narrator retreats into near-silence. Hybrid language is a site of conflict and violence, and the retreat to safety means taciturn anonymity in Augusta. Here Uzi-ownership is a mark of suburban normality, and the narrator's story will go untold and unsuspected ('The authorities are none the wiser').[57] Such is the price to be paid for assimilation.

Bill of Rights is a quest for meaning, but also lends itself to allegorical readings as a quest for poetic authorisation and leadership. In the 1990s, Paul Muldoon exercised a charismatic influence on British poetry, as visible in the work of Michael Donaghy, Don Paterson and Simon Armitage. In *Madoc* (1991) Muldoon had written an imaginary travelogue of Coleridge and Southey's time in Pennsylvania, where their initial utopian hopes descended into colonial banditry and murder. Coinciding with his move from Ireland to the United States, *Madoc* has been received by many critics as a meditation on colonialism and violence.[58] The combination of Romantic naivety and political power is never a good mix, Muldoon implied, and with its frequent intertextual references to Muldoon, *Bill of Rights* thinks about voice and leadership in *fin-de-siècle* British poetry. It suggests the violence that lurks in misguided visions of a return to roots, but also the no-man's-land awaiting those who would strike out on their own in an uncertain world of migration and displacement.

'A Matter of Pure Conjecture': Mother Tongue, Other Tongue

Another strand of Muldoon's *Madoc* is Southey's belief, explored in his epic poem of the same name, that a Welsh prince fleeing civil conflict sailed to America in the twelfth century and left behind a tribe of 'Welsh' Indians, whose traces he wishes to uncover. Like D'Aguiar's Jim Jones, Southey is driven by fantasies of a return to roots, to which Muldoon adds a humorous linguistic dimension. Thus, the word 'penguin' has been construed as deriving from the Welsh 'pen gwyn' ('white head'), but Southey is jolted from dreams of penguins by the realisation that 'penguins don't have white heads'.[59] Linguistic mongrelisation is matched by sexual violence towards the native American population and the utter failure of their 'Pantisocrat' project. The poem ends with artist George Catlin's 'Indian Gallery' touring Wales, as the reduction of Native American culture to the stereotypes of cowboys and Indians gets underway. As Tim Kendall has observed, Muldoon 'contrasts two methods of colonization: the brutal and the assimilatory'.[60] Though the exterminationist stage of colonisation is over, the violence underlying the assimilatory stage is no less real, in the degradation of the native Americans and travestying of their culture. Where the authentic might be located in all this is a 'matter of pure conjecture'.[61]

Describing Gwyneth Lewis's Welsh-language poetic murder mystery *Y Llofrudd Iaith,* which later became *Keeping Mum* in English translation, Patrick McGuinness identifies the attractiveness for Lewis of linguistic 'polyphony' in the poem's witness statements and the 'patterns and structures' they form, which neither 'explain or console, but [...] mystify and make strange'.[62] More so than most British poets today, Lewis is conversant with 'polyphony'. Her bilingualism (publishing poetry in both languages) makes her a rarity in Welsh poetry, or indeed any modern tradition. Her decision to work in the two languages, Deryn Rees-Jones has suggested, 'creates an interesting divergence' and 'dramatises an often painful splitting of the self'.[63] While Lewis's poetry in English has attracted international praise, her work in Welsh is unanthologised and unassimilated outside Wales. But even in English, she has argued, Lewis is writing a language inescapably ghosted by the Welsh *proest* and *cynghanedd* techniques.[64] Rees-Jones also points out the implied rejoinder, in Lewis's 'Welsh Espionage' sequence, to Shakespeare's *Henry V*, a play written as a eulogy to an English king who quashed the Welsh uprising of Owain Glyndwr.[65] The equation of language and national identity is a strong feature of Celtic nationalism, but Dylan Thomas spoke no Welsh and was scathing of Anglophobic cultural Puritanism. That other great Welsh Thomas, R. S., took the opposite route to literary Welshness, expressing 'distaste', as M. Wynn Thomas writes, 'amused and contemptuous by turns, for the jumped-up boyo who had pandered, in colonised South Walian fashion, to English stereotypes of the colourful Welsh windbag'.[66] R. S. Thomas's isolationist Welshness produced figures such as Iago Prytherch, a hill farmer living far from the decadent effects of Anglophone civilisation. Lewis's Welshness is keen to explore Welshness from within, not without, the envelope of modern culture (one of her collections is titled *Parables & Faxes* and another, *Zero Gravity*, is named after a sequence on an astronaut cousin). She is alive to the quixotic aspects of cultural authenticity: the subject of Lewis's doctorate was the eighteenth-century Welsh poet and forger Iolo Morganwg who built a career on editions of druidic manuscripts, manuscripts revealed after his death to have been forgeries, but which have achieved their own place in the 'folk' tradition (cf. the 'Ossian' poems of the eighteenth-century Scottish writer James Macpherson). In 'Welsh Espionage', Lewis describes a child growing up between an English- and a Welsh-speaking parent. The father teaches the child about her body 'by fetishist quiz', and pledges his daughter to secrecy, with uneasy echoes of sexual intimacy or abuse ('"Let's keep it from Mam, as a special surprise"'). Listening upstairs to the furious row this causes, the child asks herself 'Was it such a bad thing to be Daddy's girl?'[67] As Rees-Jones notes of Lewis's gender politics and the rival claims of father and mother, there is:

■ a rift between the 'natural' state of language of the mother tongue and the ownership of language illustrated by the father's possession of it. The mother exists in the sentence only as language, while the father exists outside of language; language is something he can own, language is something the mother *is*.[68] □

In 'The Language Murderer', Lewis dramatises language death through the medium of crime fiction. For Lewis, language death is a matter of cultural ecology. A bird in one language is not interchangeable with the same bird in another, in which it will have different cultural identifications. Thus 'Today the wagtail finally forgot / that I once called it *sigl-di-gwt*.'[69] On one level this is pure projection, since the wagtail is equally indifferent to its English and Welsh name, but Lewis tropes this awareness into a parable for the duty of care we owe to languages outside the *imperium* of English, as when the accused suspect describes her right to remain silent with the words 'I'm keeping mum'.[70] If the poet does not 'keep mum' no one else will, but Lewis counterpoints the tug of piety with the urge to stray when the young poet commits linguistic infidelity by reading other (non-Welsh) languages, again sexualising the language-learning experience ('Umlauts make me sweat').[71] Linguistic straying through mistranslation becomes an agent of discovery in 'Aphasia', its missed connections reminiscent of the creative mishearings that drive another Paul Muldoon poem, 'Errata'.

'The verb to be is irregular': Caribbean Calibans

The Europeanised poet of Dabydeen's 'Two Cultures' is mocked for talking 'like BBC', but it is not just the language of the immigrant that is modified by the diasporic experience. When the National Poetry Competition was won in 1998 by Caroline Carver for her poem 'horse underwater', it was deemed noteworthy that its Jamaican English was the work of a white Cornish woman, as though some identities are subject to a *cordon sanitaire* and their imaginative exploration is an act of appropriation or trespass. The tension between standard and creolised English hinges on the question of representation. To what tradition do postcolonial writers owe allegiance? What if they are artistically the product of one tradition but sympathise politically with another? Daljit Nagra humorously ponders the matter in 'Kabba Questions the Ontology of Representation, the Catch 22 for "Black" Writers ...'. The speaker is unimpressed by a section of '*Poems // from Udder Cultures / and Traditions*' in a GCSE anthology, and complains of 'coconut' double standards (black on the outside, white on the inside). Just as Kabba imagines the Asian poet using him as a comedy 'type' in his writing, he sees the Asian poet as a subject of exploitation in poetry anthologies, speaking with just the right degree of Asianness to seem exotic, but not so much as to put his white readers off ('so hee is uzed in British anthologies – / he hide in dis whitey "fantum" English').[72]

Representation involves questions on the micro- and macro-level: micro, in the sense of what forms the writer will choose, and macro in the sense of the larger forces at work behind the pronouns 'you', 'I', and 'we'. The simplest words become context-specific, just as 'coconut', though highly pejorative, carries a different charge coming from Kabba than it would from a white speaker. Two quotations analysed by Jahan Ramazani in his study *The Hybrid Muse* will serve to frame this dilemma. The speaker of Derek Walcott's 'The Schooner Flight' describes his racially mixed heritage in hybrid terms: 'I have Dutch, nigger, and English in me, / and either I'm a nobody, or I'm a nation.'[73] Like Walt Whitman the postcolonial poet contains multitudes, but not the authority that only a white European identity confers. My second quotation is from Fredric Jameson: 'All third-world texts are necessarily [...] allegorical, and in a very specific way: they are to be read as what I call *national allegories*.'[74] Jameson is presenting allegory not as a conscious choice on the part of postcolonial writers, but as a condition of their self-expression. The problem with this scenario is what happens when the postcolonial writer seeking self-determination experiences these categories, however well-intentioned, as forms of constraint.

This predicament finds expression in modern treatments of Shakespeare's Caliban, Prospero's animalistic servant/slave in *The Tempest*. The origins of the word 'cannibal' in 'Caribbean', and its similarity to 'Caliban', have provided a sharp provocation to Caribbean poets such as Derek Walcott and Kamau Brathwaite. In Shakespeare's play, Caliban broods on his fluency in English: 'You taught me language', he tells Prospero, 'and my profit on't / Is I know how to curse.' Appropriating the master's tongue the better to curse him does not, however, solve the Caribbean writer's problem of how to address his or her own people in their own speech. As Brathwaite writes in 'Letter: Sycorax' (Sycorax is a witch and Caliban's mother): 'not de fem / de way caliban // done // but fe we / fe a-we'.[75] Commenting on the 'irreducible density' of Brathwaite's non-standard English, Don Wellman makes the connection between vigorous demotic and modernist ambitions for language, finding unexpected common ground between the Brathwaite who writes 'a cyan get nutten // write / a cyan get nutten really // rite', with its puns on 'write' and 'rite', and the Ezra Pound of the late *Cantos* exclaiming 'I cannot make it cohere.'[76] Derek Walcott's response to Caliban is slightly different, however. Walcott has decried as 'fashionable, Marxist-evolved revisionism' the identification with Shakespeare's subaltern, and has spoken of his self-image as a young writer as 'legitimately prolonging the mighty line of Marlowe, or Milton' – Prospero, not Caliban, in other words.[77] Yet Walcott's choice of hero for his long poem *Omeros* (a reworking of Homer's Odyssey) is the Caliban-like Philoctete, a man nursing literal and metaphorical wounds eventually healed by a reconnection with African roots.

Auden's response to *The Tempest* in *The Sea and the Mirror* (1944) set the tone for contemporary reworkings of that play; its mixture of poetry and prose is also duplicated in Trinidadian poet Vahni Capildeo's island sequence, *Undraining Sea* (2009). Among the lessons of Auden's text is that, where readings of *The Tempest* traditionally opposed the earthy Caliban to the airy Prospero and scapegoated the former for the failings of the latter, we now see more clearly how much Prospero needs Caliban. Modern responses to *The Tempest* challenge the binary of high and low, smooth and rough, and do not restrict the 'sweet airs' of Prospero's island, 'that give delight and hurt not', to the cultural inheritance of the master. Vahni Capildeo is a lexicographer, and in 'Found Song' presents a cento of phrases from a seventeenth-century traveller's account of a Caribbean journey. As in Jo Shapcott's 'Phrasebook', the found text wears an appearance of painful neutrality, leaving the reader to infer the context. In the poem's closing lines we progress from '*He is yet living*' to '*He is dead*' and '*Bury him, or it; which is not said only of a man, but generally of whatsoever is put into the ground, as of a Plant.*'[78] Who is the nameless 'he'? *Undraining Sea* deals with people lacking basic identifiers, 'people who are unaware that it is night', and whose lack of self-definition is inscribed as a form of verbal stalling or aposiopesis:

■ They don't count. It's as if they exist in a time slip – those places; they're as good as –
The dilemma of the people who[79] □

In 'Being Animal Figure' a series of voices in bold type is introduced with the formula 'Being the person who'. Echoing the anonymous voice of Middle England found on online comment streams, the narrator complains about gender politics and other everyday concerns before suffering a mental crisis, decoupling her language from the world around her: '**I could no longer say the green book the green was not was not-green was not not-green** ...'[80] Capildeo's texts present identity and language as a labyrinth, and she too has her minotaur or Caliban figures. 'The Monster Scrapbook' from *No Traveller Returns* (2003) turns to *Othello* for another Shakespearean crossing of racial lines. Desdemona imagines the life she might have led with Othello somewhere 'equatorial', placing Capildeo in the tradition of anti-colonial rewritings represented classically by *Wide Sargasso Sea* (1966), Jean Rhys's revisionist Caribbean prequel to *Jane Eyre* (1847), but the fantasy miscarries: '*My skin is tight over his voice.*'[81] There is intimacy but confinement too in the hemming in of Othello's voice. This is Homi Bhabha's '*ambivalence*' of mimicry[82] as Othello's acquiring and mimicking the codes of Venetian civility is mirrored by Desdemona's mimicking of what she imagines his African homeland to be. The crossing of lines of privilege, in both directions, pluralises places into multiple lived (or imagined) experiences.

'As a Woman I Have No Country': Moniza Alvi and Patience Agbabi

To Virginia Woolf, the woman writer is essentially stateless: 'As a woman I have no country.'[83] Moniza Alvi was born in Pakistan but moved in infancy to England. Writing of her return to Pakistan after the publication of her debut collection, *The Country at My Shoulder* (1993), Alvi engages less with a 'geographical location' than with 'hidden worlds'.[84] In 'The Map' Elizabeth Bishop (another poet of displacement and multiple traditions) has dramatised the humanising touch of cartography: 'More delicate than the historians' are the map-makers' colors.'[85] Old maps can seem 'delicate' because the land-grabs and empires that underwrote them have passed into history, leaving these decorative traces alongside their political legacy. Contemplating a map of India, Alvi imagines it becoming coterminous with her skin, so that 'I can prise it off the paper, / lift it like a flap of skin',[86] perhaps in the same way that Pakistan was prised free of British India in 1947. Questions of representation and self-image link Bishop and Alvi in other ways too. In 'The Gentleman of Shalott' Bishop does more than reverse the gender of Tennyson's *Lady of Shalott* (1832; revd 1842): the Lady of Shalott was forbidden to enter the world and condemned to experience it at second-hand through a mirror, but the Gentleman has a mirror running down the middle of his body. As well as the outside world, the self becomes an object of treacherous uncertainty as it enters the coils of language and representation.

In her sequence *How the Stone Found Its Voice* (2005) Alvi writes a poetic creation myth, answering questions such as 'How the World Split in Two' and 'How the Countries Slipped Away'. Ruth Padel suggests these poems encode a response to the September 11 attacks,[87] but their politics are balanced between the explicit and the elliptic. Where stories go untold, the urge to fill in the gaps is strong, but sometimes the art can lie in the absence itself. *The Country at My Shoulder* ends with 'Throwing Out My Father's Dictionary', a poem which reneges on its title by retrieving the dead father's much-used dictionary from the rubbish. While the poet means to continue where her father has left off, 'I daren't inscribe my name.'[88] The poem inscribes and deletes its signature simultaneously.

To Deryn Rees-Jones, the 'mulching' of cultures enacted here is a form of cultural 'composting' that carries resonances of 'birth, femininity and fecundity' as well as rejection.[89] A similar expressive dilemma is a feature of Irish poet Eavan Boland's work, where the traditional silencing of women is noted and contested, yet in a poem such as 'Achill Woman' where Boland has a chance to allow a real-live woman to speak for herself, a decision is made that she *should* not speak. Instead, the poem invites us to feel afresh the pain of absence and silencing. The danger with this is that the poet, as auditor figure or implied confidante of the ghosts of history, too readily swaps the untold tales of history for postures of anguish and commemoration that place the poet unwelcomely centre-stage.[90] Alvi's alternative approach to the drama of commemoration anticipates and neutralises this risk.

In Alvi's 'How the Sky Got a Hole In It', an unnamed force punches the hole in the sky, leaving 'the sun and the hole v[ying] for attention'.[91] There are suggestions of the Bamyan Buddhas, dynamited by the Taliban in 2001, and the eerie absence they left behind, and Wallace Stevens's distinction between the 'Nothing that is not there and the nothing that is' – the first an accidental absence, the second a deeper state of uncanniness.[92] The first can be filled in, albeit not very satisfactorily, as when Alvi asks 'What was the colour of hope? How to remember it?',[93] but the latter resists fleshing out. The final poem in Alvi's sequence, 'How the Stone Found Its Voice', leaves the question of representation unresolved, when the stone breaks its silence, with more than a little ambiguity: 'Let us be indifferent to indifference.' This pronouncement closes the poem down rather than releasing floods of pent-up eloquence, suggesting that Alvi would rather linger on the threshold of utterance than presume to fill in silences that remain the property of the voiceless.

The case of Patience Agbabi brings these debates full circle with another relationship again towards questions of Britishness and belonging. In many ways, Agbabi cuts through the modish vagueness of thresholds and marginality: she is a Black British poet, drawing on the traditions of dub and spoken-word performers (she is a skilful performer of her work) but no more or less self-conscious in her formalism or her adaptations of Geoffrey Chaucer than any other poet studied in this book. In her sestina 'Skins' Agbabi exploits a series of puns to highlight the link between bodily and literary forms. A woman can be colloquially 'fit', but in the wrong literary context may not be considered 'fit' for inclusion, prompting a 'fit /of rage'.[94] The skin is 'read', literally so with the speaker's tattoos, while a mixed-race speaker in a state of denial identifies with 'the skins' (skinheads); when romance carries the day, a condom becomes a 'second skin'. Skin and ethnicity are performative, but with real consequences in a world of racial taboos and racist politics. Among the most barbed of Agbabi's puns is 'I passed', meaning 'passed for white'. Traditionally, the Black British poet has succeeded by translating her experiences into received forms and thus 'passing', or risked non-standard forms and the marginalisation that went with it. Sarah Broom praises Agbabi's performance poetry as an antidote to the 'suspicion of the implied immediacy and authenticity of the spoken word' we find in poststructuralist theory,[95] but there is ambiguity aplenty in Agbabi's work, nor is praising its qualities as 'page' poetry to the detriment of its effectiveness in performance. Agbabi is a poet of subtlety and skill, and one who can expect to generate the critical climate best suited to her work, refashioning its categories accordingly as she does so.

Postcolonialism and Translation

'Translators want to stay at home', Vahni Capildeo writes in *Undraining Sea*.[96] Flaubert joked that rather than see the world he would like to lounge on a *chaise-longue* and have the world carried past, and while translation is ostensibly about the encounter with the foreign, many translations involve an element of asymmetry, with the stay-at-home language firmly in control. Movement between languages has been a key to much of the work considered in this chapter: the postcolonial poet will frequently be a translator, but also one who finds a quality of strangeness in the supposed native tongue. For critics too, such as Jahan Ramazani in his studies *The Hybrid Muse: Postcolonial Poetry in English* (2001) and *Transnational Poetics* (2009), movement across borders is not just a theme but a defining formal aspect of postcolonial writing. Post-war Movement poetics were hostile to translation: 'Foreign poetry? No!' Philip Larkin told Ian Hamilton in 1964,[97] but in reality Larkin was deeply influenced by foreign poetry, especially the French symbolists. *Modern Poetry in Translation* was founded by Ted Hughes and Daniel Weissbort in 1965. This was also the decade of the Penguin Modern European Poets series, giving Anglophone readers their first taste of the poetic contraband of Eastern bloc writers (Vasko Popa, Miroslav Holub and Zbigniew Herbert). The ubiquity of poetry in translation is reflected in Seamus Heaney's essays on Eastern European poetry in *The Government of the Tongue* and the Czesław Miłosz-tinged allegorical poems of his 1987 collection *The Haw Lantern*. While an early champion of foreign poetry, Donald Davie, began to inveigh against the 'translation police' (by which he meant Anglophone poets who latched onto the prestige of others' political suffering with no corresponding interest in their language), the clearest sign of the naturalisation of foreign idioms in English came in Christopher

Reid's classic *Katerina Brac* (1985), presented as a translation from the work of a Central European poet and received as such by a number of unwary first readers. In subsequent years, the book has been translated into Polish, creating the confusing to-and-fro of an Eastern European book translated from a book in English pretending to be a book from Eastern Europe. At the time that *Katerina Brac* was published, one of the great modern Czech poets, Ivan Blatný (1919–90), was still living in an institution in Clacton-on-Sea, and enduring his own private version of that fictional poet's condition. Fleeing the Communists, Blatný suffered mental collapse and wrote huge quantities of poetry in a patois of Czech, English, French and German, most of which was destroyed until his identity as a famous poet was discovered by chance. Translations of his work face complex challenges of how to mark material in English in the original, and what to do with material in languages other than Czech, but the end result is a profound sense of what a modern Babel might look like. 'Choc-ice is in Czech called Eskymo / I used to have three on a bench at Felixtow Road', writes the poet on day release, as incongruous as any Eskimo.[98] These polygot poems arise out of no postmodern affectation, but deep personal need: Blatný's work has the rare and moving ability to make us feel we are reading a foreign language – and that this language is English.

Ciaran Carson's 1993 collection *First Language* begins with a short poem in Irish, reminding us that English was not, in fact, its author's first language. The collection switches to English in 'Second Language', but the English in question is anything but organically native. Instead, it is shot through with the Babylonian dialects of the I-Ching, hieroglyphs, and tribal and sectarian shibboleths. In the Book of Judges, the Ephraimites were identified by their inability to pronounce the word 'shibboleth' and put to death, and writing in Troubles-era Belfast Carson is hyper-sensitive to the smallest tell-tale sign of accent or pronunciation. We are forced to look afresh at the tribal basis of our own dialects and the powerful complicity of language and violence. The Ephraimites who failed the 'shibboleth' test of received speech perished, and the small amount of poetry published in the UK in translation points to the abiding power of colonial and Anglocentric shibboleths. In his 1986 essay *Shibboleth* on the German-Jewish poet Paul Celan, Jacques Derrida uses the biblical metaphor to explore linguistic conflict not as a binary of native and foreign, but to express the abyss confronting all language as it seeks to articulate the unspeakable.[99] Postcolonial criticism is not a matter of bringing fresh linguistic 'colour' to British poetry, but of bringing new and sometimes disturbing perspectives to bear on the workings of language, art and society today.

W. N. Herbert, Scottishness and Nostalgia for World Culture: *Omnesia*

Osip Mandelstam defined the early twentieth-century movement of Acmeism as 'nostalgia for world culture'.[100] Many of the examples in this chapter consider the specificity of the local versus the simplifications of any would-be unitary tradition. We are surrounded by a decadent, globalised version of 'world culture' today, as satirised by W. N. Herbert in 'Petrovich's Handy Phrases for the Visiting Writer'. Herbert adopts the voice of a Slavic writer greeting a visiting bard, whose trip has perhaps been sponsored by the British Council: 'Thank you for greeting me my brother/sister. / You are a great poet. I have never / heard of you before this moment.' The visiting writer's reply is no less gracious: 'Thank you for your introduction, which / focused almost exclusively on your own work. / It is indeed a pity you are not reading tonight.'[101] The dialogue between small nations and the wider world is a multifaceted affair, and in the case of Scotland is further complicated by questions of nation and empire. Hugh MacDiarmid's modernist revival of Scottish poetry rendered Scots a vehicle of serious literary expression again, after a long period of 'kailyard' sentimentality and stagnation. It also entailed, in MacDiarmid's case, a performative Scottish identity that was by turns nationalist, Communist and Anglophobic. The situation of poets defective in conspicuous Scottishness remained problematic – W. S. Graham, who lived in Cornwall and did not write in Scots, suffered comprehensive neglect. A prime testing ground of these debates has been the fate of Scots in the decades since MacDiarmid's death in 1978.

In MacDiarmid's work there is a fateful split between the early lyrics in Scots and the later, more self-consciously internationalist work (e.g. *In Memoriam James Joyce*, 1955), which is largely in English. There is a class dimension to the use of Scots too: MacDiarmid's Scots was drawn synthetically from many sources (principally Jamieson's *Dictionary of the Scottish Language*), but when the younger Ian Hamilton Finlay published a pamphlet written in Glaswegian it was denounced by MacDiarmid as 'degenerate'[102] (we will return to the question of dialect and class in the next chapter, in the work of Tom Leonard). There is a long Scottish tradition of 'flyting', or public disputation, but among contemporary Scottish poets there is a high count of writers who have chosen simply to ignore MacDiarmid's prescriptions for a modernist nationalism on the epic scale (Douglas Dunn, Kathleen Jamie, Don Paterson, Robin Robertson, Frank Kuppner, John Burnside). It would be inaccurate, however, to suggest that the overblown ambitions of MacDiarmid's project have entirely dissipated, as shown by the example of W. N. Herbert. The condition of the Scottish poem today, Iain Galbraith has suggested, will often involve us in a bifocal act of reading, as the eye moves between Gaelic and an English translation, a Scots text and an English glossary.[103] Taken as a whole, Herbert's work renegotiates in exemplary fashion this modernist legacy of linguistic pluralism, without flinching from the awkward political questions it raises too.

'He's too clever and he makes things up', Sean O'Brien has written on Herbert, sarcastically parroting readers who might find the MacDiarmidite carapace displayed by that poet offputting.[104] Herbert (b. 1961) was born in Dundee, a city forever associated with the doggerel bard William McGonagall. Herbert celebrates his work in *Cabaret McGonagall* (1996), and throughout his career has combined not just English and Scots, but high seriousness and slapstick absurdity, local versifying and globe-trotting cosmopolitanism. The effect is one of a carefully orchestrated pandemonium, with Herbert's omnipresent humour providing the saving grace lacking in the more strait-laced epics of MacDiarmid's late phase. (Herbert was associated in the 1990s with the 'Informationist' school of poets, who explored the multiple linguistic registers of contemporary life, and the cultural politics thereof.) As a cultural icon McGonagall lacks the exoticism of a Gaelic-speaking Highland peasant, embodying instead the embarrassing aspects of a stultified provincial culture; but this is precisely the condition Herbert sets out to explore. (A similar exaltation of the secondary and the clichéd can be found in Daljit Nagra, whose *Look We Have Coming to Dover!* (2007) makes inventive use of the Asian English of *Goodness Gracious Me* stereotype.) Herbert's metaphor for this condition, and which provides him with the title of a 1990 collection, is the 'forked tongue':

■ Unlike Ireland, Scotland is not supposed to be 'different' or 'foreign' [...] The truth about Scotland, perhaps, can only be situated between the dominant and suppressed parts of language, in the region of the forked tongue.[105] □

Herbert rejects the equation of the demotic and the authentic ('boiling the idiolect down to something I'm able to say in a pub')[106] and plunges gleefully into his jerry-built epics on an ever grander scale, culminating in the stereophonic *magnum opus* that is *Omnesia* (2013). *Omnesia* rejects convention on every level, starting with its own materiality. It is published as a 'remix' text and 'alternative text', with no indication which (if either) is the original. For Heraclitus, there is no stepping twice in the same river, but where the modernists worried about the ersatz and the loss of 'aura' in the age of mechanical reproduction, it is already a given for Herbert that this position is lost. The title poem begins one volume and ends the other and addresses a goddess for the information age, in which knowledge has been displaced by information storage, and the archive or search engine has become an agent of universal forgetting: *'You'd like to think it's God that sees ya [...] / and not the eye of blind Omnesia.'*[107] Individual sections are devoted to Crete, China, Russia, Somaliland and other exotic locales, whose host cultures the poet absorbs with apparent effortlessness, exploiting and simultaneously critiquing his position as a visiting writer. A series of poems threaded through these longer sequences broods on the theme of identity and travel, pronouncing the speaker 'off-centre in the centre of my life' and 'aspir[ing] to rank non-entity', as well as dropping satirical references to the poet's institutional presence as a 'token / creative' in his home department.[108]

As a renovation of MacDiarmid, Herbert's epic makes several important advances. It trades MacDiarmid's cantankerousness for humorous self-critique, often making use of Burns's 'habbie' stanza, though his debts are as much to Henryson or Robert Fergusson as Burns. It redeems the underside of Scottish identity written off by previous generations as kitsch or beneath notice. Also, it finds a way of placing Scottish experience in an international context without resorting to sloganeering and grand gestures. Herbert's contemporary environment brings its own challenges, however. Writing on Scottish poetry's engagement with Eastern Europe, Justin Quinn draws attention to Herbert's self-consciousness about travelling to Russia as an emissary of British culture, but also his self-consciousness about his use of a host culture which, on many levels, he fails to understand. This offers opportunities as well as dilemmas: Quinn's example is Wordsworth's 'The Solitary Reaper' (1807), which was inspired by a girl singing in Gaelic, a language Wordsworth could not speak. Had he known what she was singing her words might have struck him as merely commonplace and the poem might never have been written. 'I'm happy not to understand', Herbert says in a similar vein, of the conversation of an old Russian woman.[109]

Is Herbert critiquing our globalised culture or is he a symptom of a world in which cultures are reduced to objects of cultural consumption? Quinn also points out that Herbert tends to write his poems about foreign cultures in English, saving Scots for poems about his home ground, if not without some resistance to the binary this suggests:

■ Herbert places emphasis on different Englishes within the mono-lingualism of his poetry. His asserts difference *within* English, but not *beyond* it, say, in Gaelic. Faced with the grand incomprehensibility of Russian, he introduces small amounts of incomprehensibility into his English. This is a way of saying both that 'this language does not fully belong to me, but neither does it fully belong to some notional speaker of pure English.'[110] □

Herbert's use of English, on its own terms and quite apart from his use of Scots, is already an argument with colonial notions of language and identity. These questions are not just the property or the burden of those living far from metropolitan centres, but concern all users of English and all poets within the Anglosphere. Herbert's work helps Scottish poetry take its place within this sphere in ways that happily transcend old hierarchies of dominant and subject culture, major and minor, standard and non-standard English.

Looking Beyond

Among the merits of Herbert's poetry is its reminder that postcolonialism is more than a one-way process of dissemination from the cultural centre and absorption on its fringes. The dynamic of exchanges within and beyond the United Kingdom today is more various than the opposition of centre and fringe, home and abroad, can hope to represent. With these issues in mind, Omaar Hena has suggested the label 'minor cosmopolitan poetics' as shorthand for what it means to be both 'British' and 'worldly' in the era of cultural globalisation, alive to this phenomenon without succumbing to its market-driven capitalist imperatives.[111] Where Blake Morrison worried about the performative nature of 'dialect' poetry and its rejection of traditional eloquence, the postcolonial poet starts from a presumption that identity itself is an act of performance, rather than a given (or, politically, a birthright). Postcolonialism promiscuously crosses territorial lines: it would be a subtle form of marginalisation to assume that the Northern Irish Troubles are uniquely the province of Irish poets, or the trauma of decolonisation a theme for Caribbean or African poets alone. An important counterpart to postcolonial views of Britain by Black British or Caribbean poets is poetry by British and Irish poets on the politics of elsewhere. Examples include John Ash in New York and Turkey, Douglas Oliver's book-length sequence on New York, *Penniless Politics* (1991), and Sinéad Morrissey in Japan and China. Irish poet Justin Quinn has devoted a considerable body of work to his life in the post-Communist Czech Republic, and in a poem such as 'Ukrainian Construction Workers' writes with powerful historical insight of the vagaries of empire, as the neighbours from further east who might once have entered Prague in Soviet tanks now enter the country as manual labourers, for the moment at least. Ian Duhig has written of police brutality and the murder of David Oluwale in *Pandorama* (2010); Adam Foulds addresses the atrocities of the Kenyan Mau-Mau uprising in *The Broken Word* (2008); and Douglas Oliver has tackled an entire continent in *A Salvo for Africa* (2000). Another poet who has written exuberantly about Africa, Tony Harrison, titles one of his early poems 'China is Peru', recasting a line of Samuel Johnson's. In the postcolonial viewfinder, one place mutates into another, and centre and margin interbleed. Set in Roman times, Bernardine Evaristo's verse novel *The Emperor's Babe* (2010) portrays London as a provincial outpost of ancient Rome, peopled by that empire's local ethnic minorities, or ancient Britons.

Discussing the lines of Brathwaite's quoted earlier, 'a cyan get nutten // write', Keith Tuma describes the 'frustration and powerlessness from which [Brathwaite] speaks', and contrasts this with the weight of inherited authority behind a Geoffrey Hill poem:

■ The weight of English history upon Hill leaves him only an ironic distance from the ambiguities of the word. Next to that poetry Brathwaite's rage can be understood as emanating from a troubled amazement at the very opportunity to speak.[112] □

Tuma's example of Geoffrey Hill is poorly chosen. A feature of Hill's books since *Canaan* (1996) has been the interrupting voice of the heckler, which acts as a strong dramatic counterweight to his usual seriousness, while the Biafran war is vividly present in *Speech! Speech!* (2000) in the figures of Francis Fajuyi, Chukwuma Nzeogwu, and Christopher Okigbo. The first of these died in the coup of 1966; the second, trained at Sandhurst, died in the Biafran war, as did Okigbo, who is also subject of an elegy by Hill in *Canaan*. The title *Speech! Speech!* combines the rough-and-tumble of political hustings with deeper expressive anxieties. Surveying the Nigerian battlefield, Hill juxtaposes 'semiotics' and 'semiautomatics' as he inventories the aftermath of a failed UN peacekeeping mission.[113] The international presence is 'neo-tribal' and the dead Major Nzeogwu has been blinded, but Hill's perspective does not lay claim to any saving illumination. What it does achieve, as part of Hill's larger collage, is a poetry equipped to locate the postcolonial within its English purview: if China is Peru, Bromsgrove is Biafra ('Biafra Lives').[114] Hill reacts with a troubled amazement of his own to failures of trans-local curiosity and connection and, to paraphrase Auden, teaches the free man styles of praise without borders: 'What / do I meán by praise-songs? I could weep. / Thís is a praise-song. These are songs of praise.'[115]

CHAPTER FOUR

Gender, Sexuality and Class

He Says, She Says: Confessionalism and the Male and Female Voice

A discussion of Ted Hughes's 1998 collection *Birthday Letters* in Vicki Bertram's *Gendering Poetry* (2005) begins with an unusual disclaimer: having reviewed her argument, she writes, the Hughes Estate 'refused to allow or discuss the inclusion of illustrative quotations'.[1] The literary afterlife of Plath and Hughes's relationship has lent itself to much sensationalisation, but when Hughes published *Birthday Letters* shortly before his death it was received by many critics as a confessional as much as a literary act. Hughes had finally told his side of the story, and set the record straight. The book received much hyperbolic praise on top of its Forward Prize, with Andrew Motion calling it 'the greatest book by our greatest living poet'.[2] Among the book's most audacious features is Hughes's decision to return to the scene of many Plath poems, rewriting them from his perspective and sometimes contesting the original narratives. During the 1960s Plath's name was much linked to the Confessional movement, whose style depends on a tone of intimate address easily mistaken for straight biographical truth.[3] In practice Plath's poems skilfully manipulate the expectations they set up, and only a very naive reader of 'Daddy' or 'Lady Lazarus' would assume they were born of the actual experience of a holocaust survivor, or that their merit depended on the authenticity of these comparisons. The poems are born of the post-war psychoanalytic moment in modern poetry, where dysfunctional states are explored through dramatic overstatement until a breakthrough is achieved; the stereotype of female neurosis is all part of the drama. In Hughes's hands, the male confessional poem functions rather differently. As Deryn Rees-Jones has written of the gender divide in confessionalism:

> ■ It seems fair to say that the male confessional is radical precisely because it can be seen to be exploring new territories of the male psyche; it breaks down patriarchal notions of masculinity while at the same

81

time offering an extremity of experience as a testimony of suffering that equates with prophecy and 'strength', and yet may also be disclaimed.[4] □

In 'The Rabbit Catcher' Hughes finds elegiac strength in the face of memory by painstakingly correcting Plath's account in her poem of the same name. Where Plath rampages, Hughes tidies up and reasserts normality, accusing Plath of failing to see the economic necessity behind the rabbit traps and the historical dispossession of the rural poor lost on her as a non-Briton. Plath's poem ends with a realisation of almost sado-masochistic co-dependency, but the violent force identified at the end of Hughes's poem is that of Plath's poetry alone, dictating her furious psychodrama. Throughout the book, Hughes combines a careful, observational style with astrological determinism, as in 'Flounders', which portrays the characters as puppets of the goddess of poetry. The wounded, male confessional voice masks a closely guarded helplessness, even as his redemptive role as celebrant-elegist remains unquestioned. As Bertram comments:

> ■ Hughes seems to create a Plath devoid of lust, rage, purposeful energy or agency. It is as though she has to be the innocent, frail creature in this reactionary plot; otherwise how can he be cast as her would-be rescuer?[5] □

When blame is apportioned to the voyeuristic critics in 'The Dogs Are Eating Your Mother' it is on the grounds of myth-making, yet *Birthday Letters* as a whole is nothing if not an exercise in mythopoeia. The acclaim it won from most (if not all) reviewers underlines the continuing prestige of the confessional voice, and the expectations of authentic testimony that it is able to tap, but it also highlights the strongly gendered dimension of these expectations. In the violent theatre of Plath's poems identities are swapped, whether masculine or feminine, active or passive, and reality, fiction and fantasy are dramatically blurred; the confessional voice is a vehicle rather than an end in itself. In *Birthday Letters* by contrast the female poetic impulse brings destruction and chaos, consuming Plath and requiring the belated male voice and its more reasoned account to restore sanity. Yet, as I have suggested, this takes place under the sanction of an irrational fatalism which absolves the male confessional voice of any real role in the actions he recounts. The deeper aim of *Birthday Letters* may have been not revelation but misdirection, or as Ian Sansom astutely pointed out: 'With his verse and his letters it may be that Hughes, too, has satisfied the over-curious, and kept the secret places to himself.'[6] Such are the morbid gender politics of the best-known example of contemporary confessional poetry.[7] Questions of gender, sexuality and class are easily detachable from discussions of poetry, but as the example of *Birthday Letters* suggests, bad gender politics will make for bad poetry. Jane Dowson and Alice

Entwistle have suggested that 'the future of the woman poet depends on the extent to which, and how, her work is made critically available'.[8] Questions of gender, sex and class help frame debates impossible in previous generations, but also the oldest debates of all over the good and bad, the disposable and the durable, and in doing so help make that critical availability a reality.

'Her narrative secretes its own values': Medbh McGuckian, Public and Private

The poetry of Medbh McGuckian forms one of the most mysterious bodies of work in contemporary writing. From her early collections *The Flower Master* (1982) and *Venus and the Rain* (1984) onwards, McGuckian has worked in a style that flamboyantly resists paraphrase, characterised by narrative hermeticism and sensory near-overload. Well-meaning but baffled readers might be tempted to reach for the labels 'surrealist' or *écriture féminine*, but neither is strictly adequate to McGuckian's style. Writing on McGuckian's *Selected Poems* (1997), Elizabeth Lowry expressed anxiety that the label *écriture féminine* might be shorthand for a lazy exemption from the need to make sense when the critic is reading a woman poet. Lowry singles out Seamus Heaney's reading of McGuckian and his 'gloriously magniloquent suggestion that "her language is like the inner lining of consciousness, the inner lining of English itself"', a comparison Lowry describes as 'fine as an advertisement for a wetsuit' but limited as a way of tackling the difficulties McGuckian presents to a reader.[9] Another instance of this difficulty came with Frank Ormsby's 1992 anthology of the Northern Irish Troubles, *A Rage for Order*, from which McGuckian was excluded. The anthology was highly gendered, almost entirely excluding female perspectives. Stung by this, McGuckian used a line of Picasso's as the epigraph for her subsequent collection, *Captain Lavender* (1994): 'I have not painted the war ... but I have no doubt that the war is in ... these paintings I have done.'[10] At issue is the point of intersection between the lyric poem and the larger patterns of history, and what counts as politically engaged writing. For Ormsby, McGuckian's work belonged to a private or domestic sphere that falls short of this engagement. McGuckian refuses obviousness, but at the same time refuses to cede the ground of the 'Troubles poem' to depictions of male combatants and the mythopoeia of male violence, as epitomised by Heaney's *North* (1975). In 'The Flitting', she writes of a female figure lost to a seemingly agoraphobic domestic life:

■ Her narrative secretes its own values, as mine might
If I painted the half of me that welcomes death [...][11] □

As we know from her introduction to a recording of this poem, the speaker is the widow of a murdered police officer. The poem's apparent quietism has bloody origins, and articulates in veiled form an experience of grief and trauma. The tally of lost lives, we are reminded, is higher than the four thousand or so fatalities recorded during the Troubles, as whole generations are forced to live with the poisoned legacy of conflict. In the circumstances it is unsurprising that the woman should want her narrative to 'secret[e] its own values'. This gendered perspective on political violence is one that Clair Wills has addressed in her study *Improprieties* (1993). Contrasting McGuckian with Paul Muldoon and Tom Paulin, poets who offer more of a public register in their work, Wills is at pains to rescue private or domestic spaces from connotations of the secondary or the apolitical. She stresses the ways in which McGuckian translates the public discourses of sex and gender into ostensibly private narratives, with an implied critique of the former coded into our experience of the latter as resistantly obscure. The stable, private self as a counterbalance to the public realm is decentred and estranged. Full though they are of stock symbols of the feminine – tides, the moon, flowers, scents – McGuckian's narratives call out for symbolic 'translation' back into an experiential referent only to reveal the chimeric nature of these referents the more we accept the poems' power to set their own interpretive terms. On this reading, the frequent images of childbirth in McGuckian become correlatives of the poems' self-production and fecund relationship with the array of male figures that populate them. Yet here Wills enters a caveat:

■ [B]y setting herself up as the object for investigation, the mystery to be solved, is the woman not colluding in her own fetishization before the male gaze? The representation of woman 'in all her complexity' for a male readership surely necessitates a re-presentation or alteration of the traditional images and symbols which normally surround her.[12] □

Even allowing for the poet's desire to subvert 'feminine' modes (if this is truly McGuckian's intention), should we be worried that the poet's language remains so beholden to the templates of gender convention? (In an introduction to one of her early pamphlets, Paul Muldoon applied the archaic term 'poetess' to McGuckian, apparently without irony.[13]) Is McGuckian's project an extended exercise in parody? Wills deflects this possibility by steering her readings repeatedly back from the private to the political, as in her comparison of childbirth to the experience of the 1981 IRA Hunger Strikers in 'Dovecote', from *Captain Lavender*. As the mother nurtures her child and receives confirmation of her self-image from it, so the Catholic nationalist community uses the Republican prisoners to bolster its sense of shared political purpose.

But as Wills is the first to admit, 'there is nothing within the poem itself which would determine such a reading',[14] and the comparison is dangerously inexact and dependent on a subjectivised view of history. Our reading of the poem is marooned between public and private and the inability of either to provide completion for McGuckian's fractured and elliptical narratives. The critique is thus turned back on the opposition itself, and our ability to compartmentalise these poles of experience quite so tidily. This is a very different conclusion from a reading of McGuckian which would synthesise these two poles, proclaiming her debt to the 'recognizably local' over the reassuring ground-bass of the 'universal themes of birth, love, death'.[15] It is the elements of dissonance, of failed unity, that form the most interesting entry-points into this work. Wills's view of the critique of the body that emerges from these poems is best summed up in her observation that 'Rather than a celebration of maternal nature, the reader is continually confronted with the prior colonization of this space, as the discovery of an origin is perpetually delayed.'[16] The true battleground is language itself.

Intertextuality, Gender and the Canon

Mention of the extra-textual source of a recorded introduction to 'The Flitting' raises another level of difficulty again where McGuckian's work is concerned. Readings such as Wills's helped stabilise McGuckian's reputation against accusations of obscurantism and did so through extensive use of feminist and post-structuralist theory (Irigaray, Kristeva), but did not prepare her readers for subsequent discoveries made by her most devoted critic, Shane Alcobia-Murphy, which have decisively reoriented approaches to her work. As he describes it in his study *Sympathetic Ink* (2006), examination of McGuckian's drafts and composition habits led to a realisation of how much her poems depend on intertextual borrowing and rewritings of existing works. The ratio of borrowings was sufficiently high for many McGuckian poems to be effectively centos or collages of her sources, which have included the work of Russian poets and biographies of the great modern painters. It now seemed that the hothouse feminine imagery of her early collections concealed a very different project, and one to which critics arguing only about gender and domesticity had been blindly inattentive. Alcobia-Murphy describes a correspondence with McGuckian in which the poet vents her anger at her composition methods being rumbled, only for the anger to give way to a more symbiotic relationship with the critic (she went on to dedicate a poem to him).[17] More so than Wills, Alcobia-Murphy sees a critical force in McGuckian's use of intertextuality, but makes the small concession to more conventionally-minded readers of defending her palimpsests as 'original' gestures. Marjorie Perloff titled her study of the vogue for 'appropriative' writing in recent poetry, especially in the United States, *Unoriginal Genius* (2012), but McGuckian's deep involvement in the lyric tradition, especially the Northern Irish lyric tradition, suggests the time is not yet ripe for such an outright break with Eliotian 'individual talent'.

Yet, in the words of Eliot's 'Gerontion' (1920), 'after such knowledge, what forgiveness?' Intertextual readings such as these raise fundamental questions as to how our knowledge of a poem's sources should (or should not) inform our readings. The most encyclopaedically-minded of critics, Christopher Ricks, has devoted a whole volume to the question of allusion (*Allusion to the Poets* (2002)), differentiating it from the more modish concept of 'intertextuality'. When Ricks edits a poet, as in his edition of T. S. Eliot's juvenilia, *Inventions of the March Hare* (1996), he lovingly annotates layer upon layer of canonical allusions. Coincidentally or not, these allusions tend to be to other poets favoured by Ricks, such as Milton, Keats and Tennyson, rather than those less favoured, such as Yeats. Is the allusion really there, or wilfully projected like the 'figure in the carpet', in Henry James's novella of that name? Need poet A have read poet B to be influenced by, or allude to, him or her? Despite the extravagance of the allusions he records, Ricks works from a model of strong canonical filiation and authority, even when discussing poems from which the author appears to have vanished altogether such as *The Waste Land* (1922). 'Allusion' stops well short, in other words, of the postmodernist high jinks licensed by theories of the death of the author. (By way of an example of the latter, in Jorge Luis Borges's 'Kafka and his Precursors' Kafka's achievement retrospectively turns writers into his precursors, promoting them to a status they would not enjoy without Kafka's belated intervention; literary history goes into reverse, as the present acts on and changes the past.) Intertextuality of the kind we find in McGuckian pushes the concept of allusion to breaking point and beyond, but also raises difficult questions for feminist readings concerned to 'gender' a text as male or female. If a text originates from a male author and is appropriated by a woman whose 'own' contribution is small, to what extent is the poem a 'feminine' text? Wherein lies the difference?

Yet another complicating factor is the status of McGuckian's own interpretive remarks on her work. Reference has been made to her explanatory comments on 'The Flitting', but in interview McGuckian will frequently make pronouncements that seem gender-essentialist in ways that flout her intertextual practice, as when she ascribes the complexity of her work to its source in 'the feminine subconscious or semi-conscious, which many men will or do not recognise and many women will or cannot admit'.[18] Another student of her intertextual borrowings, Leontia Flynn, has commented that 'It is difficult to know in what spirit to take these remarks.'[19] The critical anxiety behind this observation touches on the sensitive issue of how critics should solicit interpretive assistance from the poets they study. Philip Larkin was a master of the entertaining but misleading interview, offering his public a version of the blimpish poet at war with modernist pretension, but leaving critics to rescue him from the ensuing simplifications. This style of deliberate indirection is risky, but hardly less so than the fondness of more contemporary poets for releasing insider information to favoured critics. The poet is thereby able to shape or control interpretations; an example of this can be found in Clair Wills's study of Muldoon, in which the highly opaque rhyme scheme used in his long poem 'Yarrow' is passed on to the reader courtesy of the poet himself.[20] Flynn's impatience signals a desire for the critic to retain her freedom to manoeuvre, whatever the author may say in interview or wherever the intertextual trail may lead us as readers. McGuckian has attracted ingenious and sophisticated critical readings, yet it remains possible to read and enjoy her work in utter ignorance of its local debts to Mandelstam, Van Gogh or other sources of her palimpsests: her intertexts enhance but do not restrictively define her work. The transformative, liberationist urge remains supreme. As she writes in 'The Albert Chain', in lines that appear to come to rest in the 'prison' of the self before the reversal of the penultimate line-break: 'I could escape / from any other prison but my own / unjust pursuit of justice / that turns one sort of poetry into another.'[21]

'And I hesitated': Identity, Dislocation and Carol Ann Duffy

Few readers, on a first reading of Carol Ann Duffy's poetry, will find themselves turning to theories of intertextuality to help them with its interpretive difficulties. Unlike McGuckian's, this is not poetry that places conspicuous obstacles in its reader's path. Duffy's ambitions for poetic language seem utilitarian rather than formalist: 'I'm not interested, as a poet,' she has claimed, 'in words like "plash" – Seamus Heaney words, interesting words.'[22] Antithetical to Larkin in so many ways with her liberal-left politics (though unlike Larkin, Duffy chose to accept the post of poet laureate, in 2009), Duffy represents a significant strain of the Larkinesque inheritance. Hers is a poetry of persona and statement, on bantering terms with the national mood but reserving the right to explore states of disaffection and solitude too in the poetic monologues that represent her best work. Angelica Michelis and Antony Rowland suggest Duffy's essential joco-seriousness when they classify her as a 'naughty poet', their evidence being her rhyming the words 'hillock' and 'pillock'.[23] As humorous effects go, this connects Duffy to a strain of poetry as light entertainment in the tradition of Betjeman and Pam Ayres, but also raises questions of tone and seriousness. Comedy, poetry and mass appeal need not be mutually exclusive, but Michelis and Rowland show the difficulty of tracing the overlaps, where Duffy is concerned:

> ■ On the subject of cheeky rhyme, Sheenagh Pugh argues that 'Mrs Icarus' 'isn't even vaguely funny'; hillock/pillock is so extraneous to the poem that it's obvious it's been introduced purely for the rhyme' [...] Other detractors from Duffy's poetry may argue that the jokiness of the verse offers teachers an opportunity to interest pupils in a genre that might otherwise appear opaque, or that she writes children's poetry for adults.[24] □

The reference to teachers connects to another theme strongly associated with Duffy: comprehensibility. 'Duffy's style aimed at accessibility from the start', John Redmond writes, describing how Duffy's monologues 'try to close the distance from their audience by imagining the reader to be immediately present'.[25] Where social exclusion enters the mix, this acquires a therapeutic dimension. Duffy is sensitive to the exclusionary basis of identity categories in times past, as we find in 'Originally'. The poem describes a childhood uprooting experienced by the speaker as mildly unsettling rather than traumatic, but with the vagueness of origins presented as a welcome relief from the violence of categorisation:

> ■ Now, *Where do you come from?*
> strangers ask. *Originally?* And I hesitate.[26] □

This is an elective if slightly embarrassed silence, but Duffy is aware of the blocking agents behind other failures of eloquence. Redmond has suggested that Duffy's satires on Anglocentric attitudes (the racist undertones of the news in 'Translating the English') identify gaps in the cultural map but do not fill them in, or not with the same bravado and audacity as Christopher Reid's *Katerina Brac*.[27] For all its faults, the Anglocentric world becomes an object of nostalgia. Sarah Broom notes the importance of nostalgia to Duffy, but questions readings which would view this as a sign of sentimentality: Duffy's revisitings of the past, she argues, 'point us towards important questions, contentious and unresolved in contemporary theory, about the relationship between the body and consciousness'.[28] 'Language embarrassed them', Duffy writes of the remembered housewives of her childhood,[29] making them belatedly welcome, in her repetition of the brand names that formed their daily vocabulary. Her punishment for repeating a playground swear word – to have her mouth washed out with soap – inculcates the lesson of self-censorship, punishing the girl for an utterance whose force belongs far above her properly meek and inoffensive station. In 'The Captain of the 1964 *Top of the Form* Team' the warm currents of nostalgia (again) associated with childhood brand names and pop culture trivia are tempered by a sudden chill of dislocation. Just as Duffy's collection of quiz answers atomises knowledge into a series of discrete facts requiring no real understanding, the speaker's synecdochic trophies of childhood do not constitute an overcoming of her deeper alienation: 'My country. // I want it back.' But there is no recovering it.[30] In a different context, this last phrase might sound like an expression of aggrieved racism. While Duffy has tackled violent subject matter (in 'Psychopath') the dominant note of these poems is a wistfully captured distance between ideology and experience. Reading Duffy's work for evidence of a broader social critique, David Kennedy suggests that the 'debased language' in which she delights highlights the ways in which 'culture and society [...] function as debased texts' today.[31] This is undeniably true, but also a starting point for further debate about appropriate artistic responses: other poets, from Tom Leonard to J. H. Prynne, have had different ideas of what to do with and about this debasement. Nevertheless, Duffy's best work manages to fuse Larkin's inheritance with, on the one hand, the class politics of Douglas Dunn and the Liverpool poets and, on the other, the gender psychodramas of Sylvia Plath.

More recent Duffy books have taken concerted steps to hold gender ideology in particular to account. The genre of feminist fairy tale popularised by Angela Carter in prose has been taken up enthusiastically by Duffy in *The World's Wife* (1999) and *The Feminine Gospels* (2002). Ideally, corrective justice and poetic freedom go hand in hand, since in Dowson and Entwistle's formulation '"kicks" at tradition, if occasionally antagonistic, are often skilful manoeuvres with language and form in the context of a shared, albeit unlevel, playing field'.[32] While these books have won her a large audience, augmented by Duffy's appointment to the post of poet laureate in 2009, it would be problematic to bracket this poetry with the more radical styles of women's poetry we will consider in Chapter 5. John Redmond has written of Duffy's younger contemporary, Simon Armitage, that his conversational tones give him the voice of a 'professional *involver*', a description no less applicable to Duffy.[33] In response to criticism of 'You Jane', a monologue spoken by a brutish man, Duffy has conceded that 'I doubt I would now write a poem in the male voice',[34] implying that gender roles are consciously fixed in her work, rather than being theoretical constructs that emerge in performance. Duffy's dramatisation of feminist concerns involves a degree of bathos, as figures from history and myth are transplanted to a contemporary world of body-anxiety and celebrity culture. Her back-cover blurbs hail Duffy as the 'representative poet of her day', but in her absorption with the *Zeitgeist* there is an element of commerce with its degraded discourse lacking in the work of Denise Riley or Helen Macdonald. A critical engagement with the lives of women today must be a critique of language too, but Duffy's less interesting work becomes a largely theme-driven poetry nourished by mild ironies and identity politics. At other times, however, the experience of Duffy's women is the difficulty of representation or adequate language. Sean O'Brien corrects a reading of Duffy by Ian Gregson that interprets the poem 'Warming Her Pearls' as an act of empathy between its maid and her inaccessible mistress. It is also a poem of violent desire, O'Brien insists, for all its apparent poise, and the mistress remains 'physically unknowable to the maid'.[35] The temptation is to impose a narrative of recuperation on the maid's experiences, bringing her in from the cold: while the poem ends on a striking image of separation and frustration, O'Brien equates Duffy's 'meetings with otherness' with a 'sense of the positive' that they make possible.[36]

At its most colloquial, Duffy's language avoids both the richness of classical myth and the satirical daring that might transform the follies of our times. Of the heroine of 'Beautiful' we read: 'Guy fell / in love, dames copies her [...] / She married him. / The US whooped.'[37] When Glyn Maxwell titles a poem 'We Billion Cheered', he is capturing the blankness at the heart of the pseudo-narratives of fame and sporting achievement, deliberately bleaching his poem free of affect or aura. In Duffy's poem, by contrast, there is little inducement to take the fairy tale as anything other than sincere. The transparency of Duffy's language, her reluctance to place any obstacles in the way of immediate understanding, militate against the dramatic shifts and reversals on which sophisticated satire depends. As Stephen Burt has written of *The Feminine Gospels*:

> ■ too much of Duffy's recent verse is what might be called predigested or proto-poetry, the sort of verse that telegraphs us about where it intends to go long before it gets there, and which shows us mostly what we already know. It is the sort of verse every age admires and the next will find unreadable, having replaced our certainties with its own.[38] □

As poet laureate, Duffy must grapple with the public role of poetry in Britain, as Andrew Motion and Ted Hughes did before her, also with mixed results. The paradox of her earlier versus more recent work, for all the former's focus on marginalised and silenced figures, is that it communicates a more dramatic sense of the public sphere too, giving us figure and backdrop, contemporary drama and allusive tradition, the rawness of social injustice and the unexpected patterns of achieved art too. It is here, perhaps, rather than in the 'fixed and stable femininity' that Deryn Rees-Jones has found in the later Duffy,[39] that her most effective challenge to poetic orthodoxies can be found.

'Even the Grammar of Branches / can't be pinned down': Sex and the Lyric

'Do women poets write differently to men?' asked Pascale Petit in a 2012 essay for *Poetry Review*.[40] Her examples quickly come up against the problem that styles of writing proposed as distinctively feminine are rarely theorised within an equally-weighted dichotomy of male and female. The male position will often be the default, containing and outweighing its female counterpart. The problem thus becomes terminological. To F. R. Leavis, 'sinewy' or 'muscular' were terms of approbation, adding an athletic lustre to the vocabulary of criticism while hinting at a competitive, male ethos. Picking over objections to the term 'man-sized' by a reviewer to describe Les Murray's poetry and insisting that, masculine though he is, Murray is also an empathetic poet ('assuming that empathy as a trait is more feminine than masculine!'), Petit reveals how deeply embedded the gendering of critical vocabulary goes. In its place she proposes a good-humoured progressivism, with a reference to the 'confidence' of recent writing by women taking the edge off what might, in a previous generation, have been a spikier, separatist aesthetic:

■ There are women who write like men, who engage with the tradition on its own terms, and there are those who are re-inventing that tradition. Alice Oswald is an example of a poet who engages fully with the tradition, but also re-invents it. Recent single-sex anthologies such as *Modern Women Poets* [2005] and *Women's Work* [2008] display the confidence and sheer range of women's writing [...][41] □

A problem with talk of 'confidence' and 'sheer range' is how unexceptionable these terms are, except as a direct riposte to critics concerned to brand women's poetry as mousy and unambitious. A more stimulating answer to Petit's question is poetry which confounds the question of sex and gender altogether, or throws up contradictory responses, as has happened with the work of Vona Groarke. Discussing Groarke's work in his study *Poetry and Privacy* (2013), John Redmond explores a debate that took place at a 2006 symposium on the question of feminism and its implications for the reading of poetry. The terms of the debate are not new, and have been reproduced with a varying focus down the decades. To begin, a critic might lodge a feminist objection to how male-centred criticism has traditionally proceeded, as in this case Moynagh Sullivan does when she accuses commentators of deploying 'a lexicon of aesthetic defence that is steeped in a fascination with, and deep fear of, woman'.[42] In response, one might quote Seamus Heaney's claim that while feminist concerns are all 'perfectly in order as a form of intellectual exercise and political protest [...] it is not what the thing in itself is',[43] meaning that even as the male imagination recognises the validity of feminist critique something remains unaccounted for: poetry, the thing itself, whose real life is somewhere apart from these debates. The stand-off is not easily defused, but one challenge it raises is how to transcend the opposition of ideologically-based feminism on the one hand and formalist appreciation of poetry on the other, operating in a rarefied atmosphere above our fractious gender politics. Another contributor to the symposium, Selina Guinness, addresses this crux by trying to locate her feminism in a close reading of a poem by Groarke, 'The Annotated House'. After two stanzas describing a domestic interior and dropping playful erotic hints, Groarke ends the poem with the following lines:

> ■ A sequence of breath cuts a dash in the hall.
> In the kitchen, the evening bucks its rhythm
> and lull. Even the grammar of branches
> can't be pinned down. As the smoke flirts
> with meaning and falls back into disarray
> above the clean, straight-talking roofs,
> so my pen, scratching through loose leaves,
> comes to a dead stop at the very moment when
> the boiler downstairs, like breaking news,
> shunts the here and now into one full clause.[44] □

Describing the reaction of the symposium participants (including the present writer) to a group reading of this poem, Guinness comments 'It took an embarrassingly long time for a room full of close readers (myself included) to register the scene of female masturbation that climaxes at the end of the third stanza, and once pointed out (by Moynagh Sullivan), discussion closed down as if the text had been "solved".'[45] If Groarke's poem does have a sexual theme, it has chosen to approach it in an oblique way, making heavy use of tropes of concealment and secrecy, displacing it onto the domestic surroundings ('the boiler downstairs'), the noises off of 'breaking news', and the action of language itself (the closing 'one full clause'). One signal form of frankness has been allowed, however: the assumption that the poem's speaker is a woman. As John Osborne has shown in his work on Larkin, many of the readings which most egregiously pronounced Larkin a misogynist after his death did so on the basis of unwarranted assumptions as to the gender of the speaker in any given poem.[46] There is a reference to 'stockinged feet' in the first stanza of Groarke's poem, but a man in socks is 'stockinged', not to mention other transvestite possibilities. We do not know for a fact that 'The Annotated House' is spoken by a woman.

Redmond traces the ways in which Guinness's reading (whose ingeniousness should be acknowledged) construes 'The Annotated House' as an allegory of female negotiation with the male realm, and with a world of objects variously friendly and hostile. This accounts too for the poem's intertextual play, in its allusion to what Guinness calls 'the masturbatory confessions of Seamus Heaney's "digging"'.[47] The final 'boiler downstairs' achieves an 'immolation of all such lineages' in its 'one full clause', which Guinness interprets as the articulation of female *jouissance*. Rejecting the power dynamic of the male tradition, the female is free to speak *in propria persona* at last. If a reader objected to the essentialist fallacy of the assumed female speaker at this point, Guinness might point to a line in the second stanza ('I will take myself off to lie in a bed / silken with usage') as a demand to trade 'acquired subjectivity' (the 'acquired' voice of a woman poet within a male tradition) for the true experience of female pleasure, as authenticated by 'usage'. But even here complications pursue us, in the word 'lie' (reminiscent of the rich gender politics of a Larkin poem, 'Talking in Bed', with its play on 'lying together'), and the polysemous potential of the 'cover' beneath which the speaker shelters. When we reject a 'literary tradition where partriarchal prejudice has been seen to shelter'[48] do we move beyond artifice and distortion altogether, or merely trade one form of artifice for another?

Redmond's response to the impasse of gender essentialism and feminist subversion is resourceful: he displaces the auto-eroticism at work in the poem from the speaker onto the house itself. There are practical clues in support of his reading, such as the fact that the speaker may not have entered the bedroom at all, but where Redmond's reading takes on a polemical edge is in his refusal to read the poem's challenge to 'critical and poetic decorum', in Guinness's phrase, as coded by Groarke in male–female terms. The branches outside the window, for instance, are gendered as male and hostile only by the critic, and not the poet. The liberating force of female sexuality is represented by the heavily phallic image of a pen, though one whose power stops short, 'com[ing] to a dead stop' at the point where the image of female pleasure begins. Guinness's reading depends on the opposition between inside and outside, which becomes a version of the private and the public, but Redmond proposes that we go beyond this opposition to a more detached perspective:

> ■ [T]he poem depends on the same motif of interrupted consciousness which animated the most important poems of Derek Mahon. The house is *almost* silent, which makes any noise a candidate for interrupting the author's stream of thought. When the boiler comes on it specifically interrupts the act of writing but it also more generally disrupts the narrator's solipsism. Far from representing the rarefied possibilities of an *écriture féminine* the boiler is a reminder of those blank workaday tasks which interfere with the time to write. In quest of some form of imaginative sovereignty, the poem figures the various noises off as 'rivals' to that potential state. Indeed the poem is more explicit about its underlying concerns than equivalent poems by Mahon – one thinks of 'A Disused Shed' and 'Leaves'.[49] □

The real difference between Redmond and Guinness is over how poems frame bodies, and how they understand the transition from the physical body to its literary representation. For Guinness, the male tradition embodied by Harold Bloom's 'anxiety of influence' is about coded initiation rites: 'male poets show they have passed their apprenticeship exams in poetic tradition via knowing inter-textual allusion'.[50] Feminist readings by contrast go beyond this into a more purely physical realm of the real bodies of real women ('the female body in all its physicality is invoked by several Irish female poets as a riposte, yes, to the too easy symbolic appropriation of that body as nation or nature or nurture'). Yet as that 'invokes' reminds us, the body is no more physically present here than it is in a Derek Mahon or Seamus Heaney poem, and the vocabulary of 'The Annotated House' has been almost obsessive in its evasiveness and failures of presence: a page 'hangs limp', the speaker is 'killing time between lines', he or she asks 'something pointed but oblique', will 'lie' beneath a 'cover', experiences profound stasis, and seems at a loss for direct utterance. If the poem does build up to the expression of *jouissance*, it chooses that very moment to come to a halt. As a full-bodied presence, answering back to male tradition by being simply *there*, the poem would be a failure. As a feminist poem, regardless of who is speaking, the poem succeeds through a tissue of teasing and testing allusions, engagements and reversals. What it does not do, however, is enter a realm where female physicality is no longer subject to these allusions, for good or ill. From Guinness's point of view this may be a disappointing surrender to literariness, rather than a door opened onto other forms of feminist action. But the symbolic field on which these interpretations are contested allows for both 'feminist concerns' and 'what the thing in itself is', even if we are denied any guaranteed outcome. There is no reason, one might add, why we need choose between the two.

'Will Eh hae tae *explain* it tae ye?': Maleness and Postmodernism

In interview with Andy Brown, David Kennedy makes a striking observation on the gendered voice of male poets, or *some* male poets rather than others:

> ■ Why do Simon Armitage and Glyn Maxwell attract eager critical and popular attention and yet the work of Charles Boyle is hardly discussed at all? [...] The answer, I would suggest, is that Boyle doesn't write obviously like a male poet, or should I say a bloke poet. He lacks the hard-boiled voice they both share but, more interestingly, where Armitage and Maxwell ironise male behaviour, Boyle seems to ironise even the possibility of being able to say what male roles are any more.[51] □

(An irony to note in passing is that Charles Boyle, after a long hiatus from his poetry, re-emerged as a fiction writer under the female *nom de plume* of Jennie Walker.) The 1990s were the decade of lad lit, of Tony Parsons and Nick Hornby's sentimental reconnection with rock music and football as tokens of middle-class maleness, but more so than Armitage or Maxwell it is Don Paterson among poets of the New Generation who has most interestingly explored the state of contemporary masculinity. 'Postmodern', from Paterson's second collection, *God's Gift to Women* (2005), addresses questions of sex and gender in a comically grotesque way. Its title should make us wary, given Paterson's much-advertised scepticism of postmodernism, and in this prose poem we witness a disturbing uncoupling of sexuality from reality. A man acquires a pornographic film in the pub and uses a camcorder to make a copy of it. The film is then passed round among his friends from the pub, whose humorous reactions suggest a private joke from which the protagonist is excluded. Watching the film again, he becomes aware of his image on screen, masturbating. When he ceases masturbating in real life, his on-screen image continues:

> ■ That's cuz it's no his fuckin reflection. He's only jist taped himself haein a wank, huzzee. Dye no' get it? Will Eh hae tae *explain* it tae ye?[52] □

There are many layers within layers of illusion here. Pornography is a heavily distorted version of sex, onto which the male viewer projects and overwrites his own fantasy needs. Paterson's narrator does this not figuratively but literally. If he is slow to realise this, it is because of the element of projection we bring to any artistic representation we consume, finding in it what we want. While the other men laugh at the narrator for his *naïveté*, they too have consumed the image of his obscene enjoyment, suggesting an unspoken homoerotic complicity, not unlike the scene in Bram Stoker's *Dracula* (1897) where the male protagonists offer Lucy a blood transfusion, transforming the female body into a conduit or pretext for male sexual bonding. Pornography can be seen as a substitute for or even improvement on real sexual activity (the narrator watches the film while his wife is out), but the narrator's mishap suggests that, whether the sex is real or not, our enjoyment remains profoundly self-involved and even solipsistic. On a cruder level, the poem might also simply be saying that our postmodern age is, in so many words, a pile of wank.

Vicki Bertram has noted the performative laddishness of Paterson's early work, and the ways in which the 'new territories of the male psyche' noted earlier (its exploration of working-class Scottish experience) offset what might otherwise seem unpalatable sentiments. (A comparable example from the 1980s would be Blake Morrison's *Ballad of the Yorkshire Ripper* (1987), designed to provoke but also critique the 'civilised outrage' of those who live at an insulated distance from the attitudes it describes.) The violent and even murderous fantasies of *God's Gift to Women* overlap with a despairing highbrow allusiveness. '*From* Advice to Husbands' parodies Heraclitus: 'No one slips into the same woman twice.'[53] Bertram concedes that 'It is possible for a woman reader to find this entertaining', but judges the collection's sexual baggage 'disconcerting'.[54] The anxiety of these poems alternates between guilt-laden sex and a fear of paternity. Paterson's subsequent collections have reined in the sexual *grand guignol*, and used their near-custodial view of literary tradition (as in Paterson's elegising of his friend Michael Donaghy) to assuage this fear of lineage and tradition. Paterson's poems display the most classicist surface of any New Generation poet, and the most turbulent undercurrents. The sexual politics of his early work will date, if they have not already done so, but their effect on his formal evolution remains very much a work in progress.

Thom Gunn: Bad Taste and the Gay Lyric

The concept of heteronormativity entered literary discourse with a 1980 essay of Adrienne Rich's, 'Compulsory Heterosexuality and Lesbian Existence', and applied to contemporary poetry it flushes out a myriad of concealed assumptions. Seamus Heaney's *North* for instance, already a battle ground of warring interpretations, has attracted critical ire for its treatment of gender roles: while one male tribe wars with another over who gets to occupy and master the feminised land, the essential rightness of these gender roles (male as active and penetrating, female as passive and receptive) is never seriously questioned, critics have claimed.[55] As a gay poet born in 1929 Thom Gunn was more than familiar with heteronormativity, going to the extreme of composing an early poem with the unlikely title 'First Meeting with a Possible Mother-in-Law'. When Gunn achieved popular success with *The Man with Night Sweats* (1992), an account of the ravages of the AIDS pandemic on the gay scene of his adoptive San Francisco, it reintroduced to British readers a writer who had fallen slightly out of favour, after decades of living outside the UK and a fallow period in the 1980s. As feminist poetics had developed in the intervening period, so had awareness of the dividends to be won from an interrogation of heterosexual identity too. This was not without strains, however, as when Eavan Boland upbraids her contemporary Derek Mahon for failing to audit his heterosexual assumptions:

■ I learned a lot from him, but I notably failed to persuade him that a radical self cannot function authoritatively in the political poem if the sexual self, which is part of it, remains conservative, exclusive and unquestioning of inherited authority.[56] □

Boland has in mind a certain kind of lyric form, with a firmly anchored narrative voice, secure in its sexual privilege. As a gay poet Gunn knows all about the intersection of sexual and political authority, yet throughout his work he shows a strong commitment to traditional form, which he turns against heterosexual gender assumptions in a playful and sometimes even perverse way. I have mentioned the masculine cast of Leavisite critical language, in its heyday when Gunn made his debut, and there is something unapologetically muscle-clad about Gunn's language too. He will often toy with gay stereotypes and homophobia: in 'Troubadour', from *Boss Cupid* (2000), he devotes a sequence of poems to the gay serial killer and cannibal Jeffrey Dahmer. When these caused a walkout at one of his poetry readings, Gunn heckled the protestors, suggesting a poem on Julius Caesar or Napoleon, who killed far more people, would not cause anything like the same outrage (and at least, he added, Dahmer had fun with the bodies afterwards).[57] What is most disturbing about the poems, though, is the surface innocuousness of their language. When we read 'Oh do not leave me now. / All that I ever wanted is compressed / In your sole body',[58] we are (almost) in the territory of boyband song lyrics. In so far as Jeffrey Dahmer formulates his thoughts romantically, they exhibit an uneasy overlap with ours, while for our part we are forced to recognise the implicit threat that underwrites the corny language of love: 'Oh do not leave me now' – or else. The jaded pop song contemplates the beloved with the mind of a rapist or killer. Love speaks the language of violence, and no less in high than in low cultural forms. Gunn's poem relishes the bad taste of this discovery, just as it relishes the cognitive dissonance of its toying with the abusive identification of gay men with paedophiles. A merely worthy poem on a gay theme would stress the virtuousness of its subjects; a truly democratic gay poem, Gunn reminds us, gives the imagination as free a rein as any heterosexual poem to explore the darker side of human sexual identity, whatever its forms.

The freedom won in a Gunn poem is closely allied to formal restraint. Writing on Gunn's Movement beginnings, Stephen Burt finds the poems' hyper-control at risk of becoming 'a grim end in itself'.[59] 'Much that is natural to the will must yield', Gunn writes in his early anthology piece 'On the Move',[60] subordinating spontaneity to deliberation, and exploring fetishistic pleasures while flinching from postures of emotional exposure. At every stage in his career Gunn's gender politics are tied to the pulses and currents of his lines: Britain and America, freedom and inhibition, metre and free verse all collide in knots of lyric energy, which it takes several books for their author to begin to unpick. Burt identifies *Touch* (1967) as the book in which Gunn's defensiveness gives way to empathy. Touch is the most mutual of the senses, and tactilely exploring the world, Gunn begins to register its pressure pushing back against him: 'His tactile talents let him get all these supposed opposites into the bodies his poems imagine, the people they create.'[61] Freedom from his previous defensiveness also opens the door to the vulnerability of the male confessional voice once more, most famously in *The Man With Night Sweats*. Here there is no controlling narrative fatalism to compare with Hughes's *Birthday Letters*, and when the poet meets two drug-users in a bath-house ('In Time of Plague') who suggest sharing a needle with him, there is a terrible poignancy in the persistence of reckless pleasure in the face of death ('I love their daring, their look, their jargon, / and what they have in mind').[62] Gunn's elegies are uniquely suited to synthesising sex and death, but this surplus enjoyment, as in the poems on Jeffrey Dahmer and in the face of all good taste, is what lifts them into the realm of true artistic freedom, 'carrying in their faces and throughout their bodies / the news of life and death'.[63]

'I talk as I write': Class and the Lyric Voice

'So did you always talk like you do now?' an unnamed speaker asks in Roy Fisher's 'Mother-tongue, Father-tongue'. 'I talk as I write', comes the answer.[64] Rarely is the answer so straightforward in contemporary poetry; nor, indeed, is it so straightforward in Fisher's poem. Different voices imprint themselves differently in the words on the page, and different readers will hear the words differently too. One point of origin for class in post-war poetry is the Butler Education Act of 1944, which raised the school leaving age and introduced the principle of free education for all: from this act flowed the careers of Tony Harrison, Seamus Heaney, and Douglas Dunn. Richard Hoggart's *The Uses of Literacy*, a classic study of working-class culture and its access to the written word, was published in 1957. For the contemporary poet, the era of the Angry Young Men and the Third Programme may seem hopelessly remote from present concerns. There is a danger, as we read work that revisits this period, such as Harrison's sonnet sequence 'The School of Eloquence', that we assume its hierarchical class politics have withered away, never to return. Harrison, Dunn and O'Brien, however, tend to apply a strongly comparative framework to their depiction of class politics. Sean O'Brien, writes David Kennedy:

■ uses the fictionalising impulses of the imagination to dramatise the 'master narratives' of English culture and to explore how the deferentiality and mastery implicit in those narratives determines the individual's everyday and historical experience.[65] □

These master narratives reach back into O'Brien's dour allegories of the 1940s and 1950s and forward into post-Thatcherite times. The closer we come to the present day, the greater the risk of 'master narratives' seeming out of joint with the times, since, as Sarah Broom writes (in 2006), '"Class" in recent years has started to sound like a rather old-fashioned term, as politicians avoid it and Marxist class-based analyses have fallen out of favour in academia.'[66] The overcoming of class politics is frequently preached, but the assault on free education and the public sector by New Labour and the Conservative–Lib Dem coalition should give pause to any such whiggish or 'end of history' theories of progress. A more accurate reading of this generational shift would be that the relaxed view of education we find in Simon Armitage, where anxieties tend to be about sex and girls rather than class and accent, capitalises on the victories Harrison has won on his behalf.

The teacher who interrupts the young Harrison's reading of Keats in 'Them and [Uz]' is ignorant of Keats's lower-class origins, blinded by the equation between high culture and social privilege. In his compensatory zeal to 'occupy your lousy leasehold poetry'[67] Harrison has always been drawn to formalism, and the position of fruitful antagonism with tradition and authority in which it places him. The successful Harrison poem requires a careful rhetorical balance to spark into life, and when a poem on the death of Ted Hughes attacks the laureateship, Harrison undercuts his position by hubristically rejecting a job he has not been offered. Just as damagingly, the dialectic of high and low on which he depends cannot function when his formal verse becomes clunking and doggerel-like, as in *Laureate's Block* (2000) and *Under the Clock* (2005). As Robert Potts observed of the former: 'There is much to dislike in the volume, but the worst thing about it is that the verse is bad.'[68] There is a strong suspicion in these books that Harrison is picking the wrong fights, in the wrong style, with the wrong people. Class politics becomes a problem of address: for whom does the poet speak and in whose language? If the poem chooses solidarity above all else it risks failing to connect with its target, but if it overshoots it risks propelling the poet into the shadow-boxing of Harrison's later work, where the conflict loses all dramatic tension. More so than other themes, class places the poet on the spot historically, and what may be possible in one generation may not be possible in another. Although the target remains the same, the poet must constantly recalibrate his or her style to keep it properly in focus.

'Seepage from "Background"': Douglas Dunn

The appropriate mode of representation has long been a concern of Harrison's younger Scottish contemporary Douglas Dunn. 'They suffer, and I catch only the surface', he writes in his early poem 'The Cameraman'.[69] On the surface Dunn's debut collection, *Terry Street* (1969), is a classic of post-war British social realism, but Sean O'Brien has counselled that it is 'hard to view' the collection as 'simply "realistic"', while David Kennedy too diagnoses something deeper at work, coloured by the collection's deep 'ambivalence'.[70] At the time, Dunn was living in Hull, where he was a colleague of Philip Larkin's, and in *Terry Street* he describes with empathy and wit life in a row of working-class terraced houses. Larkin's characterisation of the people among whom he lived was keenly aware of social class (the 'cut-price crowd' of 'Here'), and concerns over community and belonging animate many of Dunn's short lyrics too. Dunn has spoken of the effects on his career of the 1944 Education Act,[71] but in the Hull of *Terry Street* education seems a remote possibility. With his Scottish Presbyterian ethos of self-advancement, Dunn believes in education, unlike the unregenerate locals. Terry Street men 'come in at night, leave in the early morning' to perform low-paid but exhausting jobs, their 'masculine invisibility mak[ing] gods of them'.[72] Stuck in his house studying, Dunn lacks this masculine authority and is a subject of mockery for the local girls, whose taste in pop music he derides as vulgar. The window pane between the girls and the studious poet emphasises the barriers blocking their path to self-improvement, though not without a queasy touch of self-conscious superiority on the poet's part. Enforced proximity brings a knowledge of distance in 'Incident in the Shop', a description of a domestic abuse victim. In this short poem reference is made to the woman's bedraggled appearance ('the slow expanse of unheld breasts'),[73] allowing the speaker to offload feelings of sympathy, helplessness and voyeurism all at once. The poem remains an 'incident', however, refusing any follow-up or further engagement. *Terry Street* was written just before the Cod War and the collapse of the North Sea fishing industry, but the city it depicts is already implicitly doomed. When Dunn rises to anger it is the anger of vituperation and fatalism: drinkers staggering home are 'agents of rot', 'street tarts', and Hull is 'a city of disuse, a sink, a place, / Without people it would be like the sea bottom.'[74] Ian Gregson has coined the phrase 'ruined lyricism' for this side of Dunn's style, prompting David Kennedy to comment: 'What seems clear is that Dunn's lyricism is "ruined" because it carries within it the expectation of location within both a particular place and a particular community.'[75] A decade before the arrival of Thatcherism, this expectation is already cruelly dashed.

The dead-end quality of the lives Dunn describes is mirrored by the undeveloped style of his short lyrics, their Lowryesque qualities suggesting timeless poverty and neglect. By the time of the Thatcherite revolution, more radical responses were called for. Dunn's role as a link between poetic generations can be traced, first in his influence on the younger Hull poets Peter Didsbury and Sean O'Brien, and second, in the reinvention of his style announced with his 1979 collection, *Barbarians*. Detachment and anecdote become commitment and tirade; the unselfconscious short lyric becomes an angry meditation on the basis of literature and civilised values. As in Harrison's 'School of Eloquence', the writer experiences his situation as a rhetorical impasse. He is educated into fluency in a bourgeois medium, literature, which he turns against itself in defence of a working-class audience who may never read his poems. This is the condition explored in 'The Come-On':

■ To have watched the soul of my people
  Fingered by the callous
  Enlivens the bitter ooze from my grudge.[76] □

As the poem continues, Dunn angrily lists the ways in which the ruling culture recuperates through stereotypes the lives of the underprivileged. As David Kennedy has pointed out, the political backdrop to *Barbarians* was the Black Papers on education and their conservative attack on comprehensive schools and student radicalism.[77] The unnamed 'vile' in 'The Come-On' with their '"coal in the bath" stories' (mocking speakers of non-standard English) aggressively proclaim their ownership of high culture. Rhetorically speaking, the poem has a number of options open to it by way of response. It could defuse this tension by assimilating to 'high culture' and bourgeois values; it could propose art as a site of reconciliation in which high and low meet harmoniously; it could use the formalities of art in the service of a confrontational politics; or it could reject the notion of eloquence and formality as an extension of bourgeois ideology and pursue a more formally anarchic line of out-and-out attack. It is not as simple, however, as equating the formality of art with a conservative political stance, or the injection of radical material with achieved radical art; the quotation marks Dunn places round 'background' elsewhere in the poem suggest a reluctance to harness his experiences in such a mechanical fashion. 'The Come-On' ends with a vision of cultural democracy, from whose perspective 'Our grudges will look quaint and terrible',[78] but gaps remain, between our current predicament and victory, between bourgeois entitlement and the shame-filled poet, and between an art of lyric contemplation and one of activist anger. Is it the fate of Dunn's poems to occupy a vanishing point somewhere between these poles? Sensing the failure of traditional (Arnoldian) solutions, whereby culture provides the harmonising element amid this discord, David Kennedy attempts to answer the question:

■ What all these statements engage with is a sense of the English language losing its natural authority and evocative power and of the corresponding need of poets to work harder in the language, to remake it as an active instrument. The English language has become a place of diminished energy because it has dissipated itself in 'arts of bland recoveries' and, more importantly, because it is now the language of an historical 'afterwards', a period which may be described as a code or postscript to either the end of Empire, the collapse of the post-war consensus or the project of Enlightenment depending on one's perspective.[79] □

Dunn's books since *Barbarians* perform something of a retreat from its high-water mark of indignation. Without abandoning politics altogether, he availed himself of his return to Scotland to perform a repatriation of his muse in the Horatian odes of *Northlight* (1988), but in *Dante's Drum Kit* (1993) Dunn is hostile to Scottish nationalism as any kind of panacea. He thus falls somewhere athwart the dilemma Kennedy describes: becoming the Scottish poet he wants to be is presented not as a political victory but as the exercise of a private citizen. In Ireland, even a private lyric by Seamus Heaney can still be seen as possessing a public dimension, but because of the weakened public sphere sketched by Kennedy, the same conditions do not obtain in Britain – a factor to which, consciously or not, Dunn may be responding in his lyric retrenchment. In 'The Come-On' Dunn feels an 'ooze' from his grudge, just as the poet in Shakespeare's *Timon of Athens* says of his art, 'Our poesy is a gum, which oozes / From whence 'tis nourished.' It is the ooze of indignation that endures, of poetry as a witnessing to impasse, whether political or rhetorical.

The impasse of class politics in Dunn is not so total that he has not been deeply influential on the work of Sean O'Brien (b. 1952) and, once again, Don Paterson (b. 1963). Pursuing his analysis of 'voice and ownership' in British poetry from Dunn to O'Brien, Kennedy notes the attraction for O'Brien of the 1940s and 1950s, decades in which the post-war consensus (broken under Thatcher) was forged, and that help to shape a 'central, defining tension in O'Brien's poetry between transformation and immobility'.[80] Just as Dunn had his imaginative poles of lyric stillness (if not 'immobility') and political transformation, O'Brien's work swings between a style of philosophical whimsy influenced by Didsbury and Wallace Stevens and political confrontation. The last of these is much to the fore in his 1987 collection *The Frighteners*, where political poems rise to political occasions only to be swallowed up by them ('We change our cars and eat our meat. / There are no negroes on our street').[81] This is not the style, needless to say, in which O'Brien's political imagination has been best served.

'The Need-to-Know Basis of Beauty and Truth': Sean O'Brien and Don Paterson

For the poet keen to describe working-class life, the problem remains one of moving beyond naturalism without indignation becoming an end in itself, or mere repetition of the postures of a previous generation. O'Brien's answer to this has been a turn to a highly personal strain of political allegory. Reviewing his *Selected Poems* (2002), Adam Newey followed the clichéd route of hailing 'a poet of unabashed political engagement' and celebrant of a 'quintessential England', or its Northern subset at least, before voicing a misgiving: an O'Brien poem of direct political commitment is 'very atypical', and much of his work proceeds instead by 'witty or sardonic observation'.[82] Another critic, Peter Davidson, contests Newey's verdict of 'quintessential Englishness' by making O'Brien a case study in *The Idea of North* (2005), alongside other authors such as Auden in Iceland and Nabokov in the Arctic – writers from varied geographical 'norths', but responding to a mood or atmosphere, as much as any political territory (O'Brien is 'steadily directed towards far imaginations of north – Arctic voyages, icebreakers, the wintry Europe of war films').[83] In O'Brien's portraits of working-class life, politics are omnipresent yet the irruption of the political into the naturalistic is a practised rhetorical move, usually involving recourse to a more abstract register and – a favourite technique – appeals to history with a capital H. The impoverished Northerner lacks agency: power resides elsewhere, and his or her life becomes an allegory for a distant ruling class's callous neglect. Railways are omnipresent in O'Brien, the closure by Dr Beeching of unprofitable branch lines in the 1960s furnishing the poet with a perfect metaphor for the dismantling of the welfare state. Thus, a typical O'Brien poem might situate us among ghosts waiting for a train that will never come, 'On the wrong side of England, forever / (...) And if we should wonder what for, we must hope / That as usual it does not concern us.'[84]

There is a desperate irony at work in the narrator's identification with the forces which marginalise these people. James Joyce spoke of 'the big words which make us so unhappy', and there is a similar desperate irony in O'Brien's use of 'The Ideology' as a poem title, summoning the language of old-style Marxist dogma but also our sense of its out-modedness and the ghosts of radicalism past. O'Brien's response is once again to mimic artistically the victimisation inflicted on his working-class subjects, who are happy 'on the need-to-know basis of beauty and truth'.[85] The Romantic consolations of art are a lie. Poor people live in squalor and die far from our sympathy or concern. Another poet who has written about working-class life in similarly fatalist terms, Tom Paulin, has been accused by Edna Longley of 'misappropriat[ing]' his subjects' culture and language 'in order to despise them'.[86] Must the poet always speak *for*, in the absence of the underprivileged subject's ability to speak for him- or herself? This would be to succumb to the airlessness Maria Johnston has found in O'Brien, leaving 'no space' for 'the vivifying forces of ambiguity, multiplicity'.[87] Discussions of poetry and politics can reach over-speedily for Auden's nostrum that poetry 'makes nothing happen', but O'Brien's admission of political impotence can direct us in its despair only to a 'different poem', one in which these blighted lives find fruition. The failure of the oppressed to challenge their conditions is ascribed in classic Marxist theory to false consciousness, and 'The Ideology' cannot imagine its poor people's happiness except as similarly false. Yet all they, and the poem too, can do is maintain the lie in the absence of any alternative but death.

The downgrading of the celebrated Keats line (from 'Ode on a Grecian Urn') to the 'need-to-know basis of beauty and truth' is an admission of defeat but also a refusal fully to let go of the Romantic legacy. As in Dunn's *Barbarians*, the poetry of class is at its most intense in its moments of angry self-interrogation, doubt and defeat. The closed circle of rhetorical self-arraignment never quite opens onto the political action that would overcome this sense of failure. No wonder then that a guilty state of poetic in-betweenness – between mute origins and guilty social advancement, inarticulacy and eloquence – remains the emblematic state of the contemporary poem about class. Self-directed feelings of inadequacy aside, there is one other easy outlet for these frustrations, as chosen by Don Paterson at the conclusion of his poem 'An Elliptical Stylus'. The poem, from Paterson's debut collection, describes his father's attempts to purchase a replacement needle for his record-player, only to meet with jocose dismissal from the shop assistant. The 'elliptical stylus' of the title is adept at 'bring[ing] out a' the wee details', and like a stuck record the incident repeats endlessly in the adult poet's head. He could extract a poetic fable from the experience but chooses not to, since the point of the story is obvious to us and was not lost on his father at the time. Instead, he spells out what is at stake by imagining a violent reaction to any 'cunt' who would attempt to put his father in his place, a threat from which the reader is not exempt ('which probably includes yourself. To be blunt').[88]

The pleasure of execration is achieved only through an admission of defeat: the reader too is a bourgeois enemy. Peter Howarth locates a similar moment in Paterson's 'Nil Nil', where the account of a Scottish football team's declining fortunes suddenly gives way to an angry second-person address: 'You've been taken for a ride, in other words, and the mixture of gangster menace ("this is where you get off") and brisk self-dismissal is characteristic.'[89] If readerly sympathy is called for, the narrator is too embarrassed to receive it and prefers to keep a mask of aggression in place. A dialogue *is* taking place, but one that boomerangs back on the speaker, leaving him angrier and more beleaguered than ever. That clunking full rhyme of 'An Elliptical Stylus' places Keatsian beauty and truth very much on a 'need-to-know basis', but the real brunt of the attack here is taken by the speaking voice himself, as the poem shuts down in an issueless defeat. These attitudes die hard, and when poets are still routinely described as writing 'proudly about working-class roots', we witness again the unthinking condescension of class politics (do middle-class poets write 'proudly' of their roots?).[90] O'Brien's work has snagged itself obsessively on this rhetorical crux, with an ever more elaborate appeal to the ghosts of history, but for Paterson – as we have seen – the pugnacious stance of *Nil Nil* (1993) and *God's Gift to Women* has softened in recent times.

'Phonetic Urban Dialect': Tom Leonard and Peter Reading

In March 2014, a government adviser on child poverty suggested that children from working-class backgrounds would experience difficulty 'fitting in' in later life unless exposed to middle-class experiences such as visiting theatres and restaurants. The condescending assumption that culture (and restaurants) are a middle-class purview, onto which the working class trespass at their peril, typifies the snobbish class politics against which Tom Leonard has taken a stand throughout his career.[91] Glasgow poet Tom Leonard offers a counter-example to Paterson of a writer whose career refuses to move in the direction of reconciliation or the overcoming of class tension, either in theme or style. His poems in Glaswegian cultivate illegibility: when a football fan asks another 'ma right insane yirra pape', 'Pape' meaning Catholic or Celtic sup-porter, the rendering of 'right in saying' as 'right insane' is its own eloquent comment on the introspection of a tribalised culture.[92] As for any writer who uses Scots, Leonard is highly self-conscious about which of his two languages he writes in, with English representing the pole of would-be detachment or successful class mobility. In 'Fathers and Sons' (written in English), Leonard remembers his shame at how his father would whisper the words aloud as he read the newspaper, which he then juxtaposes with an audience member challenging the poet on the 'constrictive' effects of using 'phonetic urban dialect' in his work. Rather than answering, Leonard writes: 'The poetry reading is over. / I will go home to my children.'[93] What for the poet is his life and identity is for his audience member a literary device or affectation, and since he too has been moving his lips as he reads, perhaps his children can now feel embarrassed by their father, or equally embarrassed by his failure to deliver an indignant reply to his inquisitor. Sarah Broom cites another example of his politics hitting home for Leonard, when his work was placed on the GCSE syllabus despite his having polemicised against the educational system and its 'essentially acquisitive attitude to culture'. Broom finds a positive aspect to Leonard's dilemma:

> ■ The role of the literary critic, says Leonard, is 'to categorise, that the bourgeoisie might safely possess'; an exam demands that a student show his or her mastery or possession of the literary text rather than allowing any meaningful and challenging entanglement with it. [...] Such views are bound to induce a perhaps salutary sense of awkwardness for literary crit-ics attempting to write about Leonard's own work, but they also suggest ways in which the education system can change for the better.[94] □

There are many affinities between Leonard and Tony Harrison, but in 'Fathers and Sons', with its economy of effect and refusal of poetic editori-alising, Leonard has compressed any number of sonnets' worth of wisdom into under fifty words. 'Fathers and Sons' is the final poem in his *Selected Work* (1995), closing the book on a note of unfinished business. Contem-porary satirists divide into those who believe that exposing injustice helps to drive it out and those with a more pessimistic view of the poet's powers.

If Leonard tends towards the latter, the most distinctive anti-progressive satirist in modern English poetry is Peter Reading. Reading explores poverty and destitution in poems of savage indignation, and has been hailed by Tom Paulin as the 'laureate of grot',[95] but Paulin's radical politics sit uneasily with Reading's snarling misanthropy, unless we class him with radical Tory satirists such as Swift, flaying the fallibility and sinfulness of the human condition. Reading's work from the 1980s captures perfectly the Thatcherite moment of social polarisation, the crass consumerism of the *nouveau riche* class, and the seething rage of the excluded, but it may be a step too far to dress up the squalor of sequences such as *Perduta Gente* (1989) and *Stet* (1986) as seriously considered political statements. Sean O'Brien experiences a stumbling block in his attempts to read Reading as a political poet: his work 'leaves a huge hole where causality ought to be'.[96] Who is speaking in the average Reading poem, and might thus be in a position to assign causality, is not always immediately apparent. Trained as an artist, Reading is irresistibly drawn to the screaming headlines of tabloid newspapers, whose graphic awfulness, in style and substance, he likes to incorporate into his work. There is an element of childish glee in his tabloid-filtered reports of violence, with an occasionally unpleasant racial dimension too. Likewise, representations of the artistic temperament or the intellectual in Reading's work (such as the unfortunate philosophy professor in *5x5x5x5* (1983), luridly assaulted by skinheads) will often veer sarcastically towards tabloid distrust of the namby-pampy, effete egghead. One critic at least wrongfooted by Reading's tone is Isabel Martin, who (as O'Brien notes) can seem to take this at face value ('His no-nonsense outlook never leaves the realm of common sense, thus also appealing to those readers who tend to favour the normally less ethereal world of prose fiction').[97] To believe Reading believes in poetry as an 'ethereal' medium beside the common-sensical novel is to succumb to a peculiarly Readingesque prank. Nevertheless, and despite Martin's misprisions, the anti-lyric demands of poetic anathema will not be denied. In 'Shropshire Lads', from *Ob.* (1999), for instance, Reading begins with a sound bite of Tony Blair's ('Clear Beggars from Streets, says Blair'), before describing a row of Shropshire lads queuing to buy their cheap cider from the local supermarket. Readers expecting a thoughtful allusion to A. E. Housman will be disappointed: 'Oh yes, even in Salop, they are there, / anathemas of Tony fucking Blair.'[98]

Outside and Inside: History and the Canon

The intersections of class, gender and contemporary poetry play themselves out in narratives of exclusion and inclusion, of progressive democratisation, conservative distrust, and radical impatience with the slowness of this process. Prizes and anthologies for writing by women and Black British authors persist in the face of journalistic sniping that the equivalent for men or Caucasian British only would be unthinkable or illegal. It is a common feature of conservative backlashes to borrow the language of victimhood, but genuine questions can be posed about the usefulness of these categories, and when they become a self-inhibiting purdah. Some women writers, notably Elizabeth Bishop, have taken a stand against women-only anthologies (though Bishop has featured in such volumes), and in her essay 'Inside and Outside History' (1992; 1998) Anne Stevenson engages with the point at which reclamation of lost histories and suppressed voices becomes an enemy of creative promise. Her target is the Irish poet Eavan Boland, whose work frequently turns on emblematic autobiography, with Boland's story of poetic formation made to do duty for the generations of women before her, denied a hearing in their day. Boland sets up a duality of myth versus history, in which myth is man-made and distorting, denying access to the more redemptive arena of history in which we at least have a chance to work out our destinies, on our own terms. Stevenson contests the blanket condemnation of myth, while expressing scepticism too at the warmth of the welcome that history can afford us instead:

■ What worries me chiefly is a feeling, or half a feeling, of being present at the creation, not of a new approach to history but of a new myth. Look at what actually happens when, from a comfortable niche in middle-class modern Ireland, a woman poet looks back at the horrors of the past and *decides* to choose history over myth. Not being able really to enter history, she instead creates a highly imaginative scene – 'roads clotted as / firmaments with the dead' – in which she and other poets participate as a chorus of mourners.

Now, does not such a poetic tragedy as Boland creates partake more of myth than of history? It seems to me that there is no way a poet can choose history and reject myth without giving up poetry altogether and taking instead to medicine or social work, or martyrdom. The very making of a poem – especially one in which the poet acts the leading role – ensures that the past is reshaped and fictionalized.[99] □

Stevenson's modest proposal encountered resistance from Nuala Ní Dhomhnaill, who saw, in her polemic, evidence of a divorce from the world of 'chthonian aboriginal earth energies'.[100] For Ní Dhomhnaill, Stevenson preaches an uninspiring poetic *embourgeoisment*, whose claims on our attention must remain secondary as long as the great forces of nationalism and myth retain their current hold on women's lives. Answering back, Stevenson remained unconvinced: female archetypes such as the Virgin Mary imposed on suffering women are 'no longer so relevant'. In their place, she suggests the poet 'distrust all cultural generalizers and, as a woman or man, allow oneself to make poetry out of the particular'.[101] The debate turns on the extent to which women feel convinced of their status 'Inside History', and how this might affect the imaginative debt they feel to those who remain on the far side of such a categorisation. Evidently, there are risks on both sides. On the one hand, Stevenson's universalism may seem premature or insufficiently responsive to the different conditions under which women poets write today. Is it wise of Stevenson to suggest that writers should transcend forms of victimisation she may not have experienced, or fully understood? On the other hand, when Irish poet Mary O'Malley announces by way of pricking our political consciences that she addresses us across 'the staked thighs / Of the unsaved women of El Salvador'[102], we are dealing with a form of moral narcissism, commodifying and debasing the suffering of the women for whom it purports to speak. Expressions of solidarity and poetic merit are not the same thing, least of all when they neutralise the distance between writer and subject, victim and survivor, as in O'Malley's ill-judged example. Poetry which fails to be 'interesting primarily as a verbal artefact' threatens, in Kit Fryatt's formulation, to make 'of social conscience mere worthiness, and of protest mere protestation of virtue'.[103] The distinction is not between poems that engage, versus poems that transcend questions of gender and class; nor is there a single right way for poems to engage with these questions. Stephen Burt has warned us of the dangers of 'predigested poetry [...] that shows us mostly what we already know'.[104] Reading Thom Gunn, Medbh McGuckian, Tom Leonard or Vona Groarke, we encounter work that thinks seriously about gender and class in the uncertain space between artistic conflict and resolution, preserving amidst so much that is treacherous and hostile to poetry 'a place for the genuine'.[105]

CHAPTER FIVE

Experiment and Language

■ as the filling seeps out of a self
   – Veronica Forrest-Thomson, 'Tooth'[1] □

Just as the filling seeped out of Veronica Forrest-Thomson's self at her dentist's, the post-war period appeared to witness the filling seep out of the modernist revolution of the 1920s and 1930s. Modernist writing did not go away, but discontinuity remains a strong feature of attempts to chart the history of modernist writing through the contemporary period. Where non-modernist poetry forms a continuous tradition, modernist poetry tends to be seen as a series of revivals, sometimes across intervals of decades, with radio static or silence in between. Contemporary poets can experience an anxiety of belatedness beside their modernist forebears, uncertain what to do with such titanic energies. Keats's late poem 'Hyperion' (1818–19) was inspired by the burden of his great Romantic precursors and the poet's struggle to make his own way. In an Irish joke, a tourist asks directions only to be told 'I wouldn't start from here.' Seeking to reconnect with modernist radicalism from the grid-location of the Movement, a mid-century poet would have had frequent occasion to think the same. If there seems no connecting route from the one to the other, the question arises as to the reliability of the map. Terminology is important, but can be variably or contradictorily applied. As modernism ages, how does it maintain an oppositional stance? Does it enter the mainstream culture and lose self-definition or mutate into postmodernism? Searching for a label for Cambridge poet J. H. Prynne, Ian Gregson settles on 'retro-modernist'; to Neil Corcoran, the poets Christopher Middleton, Roy Fisher and Prynne are 'neo-modernists'; and Roy Fisher has described himself as a 'sub-modernist', harking back to 1920s Russian formalism.[2] The label 'postmodernist' by contrast has proved itself capacious to the point of meaninglessness. To some, it is Prynne and Tom Raworth who are the true postmodernists, but to Sean O'Brien it is the dandyish Oxford formalist John Fuller. For Ian Gregson, the metaphor-rich Martians of the late 1970s and 1980s and the dialogic style of Carol Ann Duffy prove that mainstream poetry has now 'accommodated postmodernism', even if only 'up to a certain point'.[3] In her 1978 study *Poetic Artifice*, Forrest-Thomson discussed modernism as a resistance to 'naturalisation', or the binding of art to a realist outlook, a resistance she links to structuralist and post-structuralist literary theory. Resistance to 'naturalisation' can be compared to the estrangement-effect or *ostranenie* of the Russian formalists, later adapted theatrically as Bertolt Brecht's *Verfremdungseffekt*, which depends on our cultivating a critical relationship with language and thereby seeing the world anew.

Describing the readerly need for an 'overview', to make sense of the disorientations of modernist poetry, Peter Howarth suggests that 'the experience of actually reading a lot of modernist poetry is more like an immersion, where there is no longer a clear distance between what you are seeing and the position you are invited to see it from'.[4] Blurring is a feature of another interpretive paradigm discussed by Forrest-Thomson, the duck-rabbit optical illusion used by Wittgenstein in his *Philosophical Investigations* (1953). Looking at this figure we alternatively see a rabbit with long ears or a duck with its bill open. Which is correct? In our hesitation, we show resistance to a linguistic system which would have us choose one or the other. Ian Gregson comments:

■ There is a sense, then, in which a good poem for Forrest-Thomson is a kind of 'duck-rabbit', a chimera that combines the familiar and the unfamiliar, the world and an interpretation of the world, meaning and form.[5] □

Unlike ducks and rabbits, the duck-rabbit is not so easily tracked down in its natural environment, and the critic who would study it is forced to assume the role of field researcher. More so than with other kinds of poetry, the experimental critic cannot presume a consensus view of the field, and must remap and redefine it on a constant basis. Who the major figures are and how we most usefully discuss them – all is up for discussion and in a state of constant evolution.

'Rubbish is / pertinent': Experiment and the Question of Value

In 1999 J. H. Prynne broke the habit of a lifetime, or almost, when he chose to publish a *de facto Collected Poems* with a commercial press, Bloodaxe Books. The doyen of Cambridge poetry, he had for many decades circulated his work semi-privately, and made an unlikely match for the style of populist engagement that is Bloodaxe's stock in trade. While Bloodaxe's editor Neil Astley has long polemicised against poetry that holds fast to coterie privilege, Prynne refuses to read in public (in Britain at least) or to allow his work to appear in anthologies, and does not allow his books to carry an author photograph. How to account for this publishing mismatch? The modest blurb offered few clues, limiting itself to a description of Prynne as 'Britain's leading late Modernist poet'. Here was the 'modernist' poet as retro specimen, quasi-incomprehensible perhaps but free of the spin and self-promotion that drive postmodernism and its offshoots. Prynne's fellow Cambridge poet John Wilkinson begins an essay on the sequence *Not-You* by acknowledging the forbidding aura surrounding the older writer's work. Trying to orient himself, he wonders whether the poem's specialist vocabulary might be a description of the 'use of lithium salts in psycho-pharmacology as a mood-stabiliser' – not, it must be confessed, most people's idea of promising poetic subject matter.[6] Answering this objection, he reminds us of the intense engagement with lexis we can expect as readers of Prynne, and the 'dictionary neurosis' in which this is likely to result. If we put in this effort but still find something is missing, we must cultivate 'counterfactual' expectations of what we can expect by way of meaning. Traditionally, Wilkinson argues, 'poetic authority' exempts the artwork from 'mak[ing] appeal to the reader by enjoining pity or sympathy, or explaining itself';[7] he then cites the case of American poet Laura (Riding) Jackson, whose disillusionment with the slippery nature of poetic language led her to abandon poetry altogether and take refuge in dogmatically self-explaining prose. But this is not how Wilkinson sees Prynne's poetry as working. I have used the word 'forbidding', and Wilkinson comments sarcastically on the use of the word 'rebarbative' as a label for Prynne, but his aim is to overturn these conceptions and teach us to take this difficult poetry on trust. Prynne will not be taking to prose commentaries to explain himself, but his work remains radically readable and available none the less:

■ In a universe where trust is endlessly solicited by objects, persons and every stray phrase, Prynne has been drawn towards a counterfactual practice with its attendant formalism, but his scrupulousness, and his powerful moral conscience are not still, and enjoin a trust in his writing which is earned as by no other contemporary poetry.[8] □

Accepting the good faith of Wilkinson's position does not unlock the mysteries of Prynne's work, but helps to bring its special difficulties more clearly into focus. The question of 'scrupulousness' asserts a continuity between Prynne's attitude towards publication and his lyric practice. If poetry likes to believe it transcends the market economy, this is work that presents a zero degree of commodification, full of bizarre and minatory pronouncements on capitalism and modern culture and making no claims for its own innocence, but lacking any pointers for the bewildered. Like an archaeological find from a lost civilisation, it resembles a mysterious fetish object, designed for unknown rites and addressing us in an unknown language. These are the qualities that attract Sean O'Brien's attention, writing on experimental poetry, when he draws a distinction between work that 'offers a challenge to the reader's imagination' and 'the kind of obscurity which has less to do with substance than with signalling a superior exclusivity'.[9] For O'Brien, the *avant-garde* combines incomprehensibility with grandiose ambition in a spirit of what Lenin termed 'revolutionary defeatism'. Michael Donaghy too is scoffing, when he wonders how an experimental poem 'composed from punctuation marks will help bring down the arms trade'.[10] This is a joke, but Donaghy's parody of the experimental poet drunk on self-delusion depends on simplistic ideas of how poems *are* expected to interact with the arms trade: do the poems of Michael Donaghy or Sean O'Brien 'help bring down the arms trade', but in a sensible and mainstream way? If not, are they too as redundant as Prynne's? As it happens, the quality of redundancy is one to which Prynne's poems pay close attention, as in 'L'Extase de M. Poher', which concludes its meditation on culture and time with an intimation of its own 'refuse-nik' status as a piece of cultural detritus:

■ any other rubbish is mere political rhapsody, the
gallant lyricism of the select, breast & elbows,
                    what
else is allowed by the verbal smash-up piled
under foot. Crush   tread   trample   distinguish
put your choice in the hands of the town
clerk, the army stuffing its drum. Rubbish is
            pertinent; essential; the
            most intricate presence in
            our entire culture; the
ultimate sexual point of the whole place turned
            into a model question.[11] □

To the reader untrained in Cambridge poetry, certain features will stand out here. After the scientific interlude that precedes these lines, the poem reinforces its critical distance from lyric verse with an arch dismissal (as 'rhapsody') of the 'gallant lyricism' it confines to the rubbish dump. The unexplained transition to 'breast & elbows' may be triggered by this reminder of lyric intimacy, which may in turn trigger the guilty crackdown that follows in which the poem mimics the violent effect on the lyric of contact with the social process. Unexpected transitions are everywhere: Prynne is the supreme poet of parataxis, or juxtaposition without explanatory connections (e.g. Julius Caesar's

'*Veni, vidi, vici*', 'I came, I saw, I conquered'). Yet in the lines quoted above a peculiar, if semi-strangled, lyric voice is clearly in evidence, and a compelling linkage made between redundancy and eros that places Prynne in a long line of melancholy Romantics. Comparing Prynne to Geoffrey Hill, Natalie Pollard has discussed how both poets 'achieve an ethics of address in "establish[ing] relations not personally", and in speaking at odd angles, "to one side" and "aside from" violent urges for comprehension and lyric genius'.[12] The strangeness of its address does not mean the Prynne poem is not still speaking to us, or seeking to cultivate an intimate register purged of cliché and cant. O'Brien's 'superior exclusivity' is a relative term, but this is a poem whose effects depend on the fate of culture and the individual in an era of mass consumption, the persistence of the lyric impulse amidst the white noise of the information age, and most importantly the poet's ability to wring dramatic pathos from this situation. So where is the problem?

To one interested in the link between culture and waste, the poet or critic can be a kind of rag and bone man, searching for value where others see nothing of worth. Where experimental poetry is concerned, questions of worth are closely linked to those of publication, dissemination and reception. Can one be a major British poet yet almost entirely unknown to the public at large (though we are told Prynne commands a large popular audience in China[13])? Here we revisit the terrain of Larkin's polemic against modernism, which he accused of breaking the contract between artist and audience. A roundabout answer to this question would start by looking more closely at the terms of access between poet and public today. Even for those published by Cape or Picador the economics of the poetry market are harsh and unforgiving, but for those writers published by Shearsman or Reality Street, review coverage or festival invitations are scarce to non-existent, while critical visibility too can be severely compromised; in his 1973 study *Poetry Today, 1960–1973*, written at the height of the British Poetry Revival of the 1960s and 1970s, Anthony Thwaite dedicates a mere three pages to experimental work, allowing at his most generous that it deserves 'something other than contempt'.[14] Then and now, experimental poets unwilling to wait for a Copernican revolution in mass taste have found alternative cultural spaces in small-press publishing, underground magazines, collaborations with visual artists and a migration to online writing.

A founding moment for the contemporary *avant-garde* is the aforementioned British Poetry Revival. During a controversial tenure at *Poetry Review* (1971–77), Eric Mottram steered what had been a sedately amateur journal towards work influenced by the Beats and the Black Mountain poets, using the Poetry Society's Earls Court headquarters to host experimental performances by Bob Cobbing, cris cheek and others. Nor was the *avant-garde* wing without a popular following: in 1965 an 'International Poetry Incarnation' featuring British and American Beat poets had filled the Royal Albert Hall. The Arts Council reacted with alarm, and attempted to win back control of the journal while withholding funding from small presses allied with the Poetry Society. Amid much acrimony and pandemonium (described in Peter Barry's study *Poetry Wars* (2006)), Mottram resigned in 1977, providing the *avant-garde* with a fall narrative which it has rehearsed rancorously ever since. The elements of this dispute have an uncanny knack of reproducing themselves, historically: in 1949, after a bitter struggle with the board of the Poetry Society, the young Muriel Spark resigned from editing *Poetry Review*. Narrative and counter-narrative wage war across the generations, with Spark's departure from the magazine mirrored six decades later by that of Fiona Sampson. The tension between the public/educational remit of the journal and the desire editors have felt, in their different ways, for increased autonomy has never been definitively resolved. While their grievance over Mottram's treatment has fuelled many a conspiracy theory among experimentalists, others might question the usefulness of a strategy of 'entryism', or attempted co-opting of the organs of mainstream culture. Prynne's phrase 'the verbal smash-up piled / under foot' describes all too well the intensity of the *Kulturkampf* driving these fractious debates. The image of the 'smash-up' returns us to the rubbish tip through which we pick for something of value. Like a Rembrandt found in the attic or a Shakespeare folio in a charity shop, value in a Prynne poem is offset by its unexpected surroundings. Readers tempted to preen themselves on cracking the code and unlocking the poem's secret wisdom are never entirely able to shake off the suspicion that the whole process may have been a joke, and at their expense too. As Peter Howarth comments:

> ■ You knew you were reading something very few others would, but at the same time the poem's complexity outlined how much its meaning would never be yours to own [...] Prynne's limpid, remorseless relativisation of the self's interiorities and intentions through language meant his readers could never really tell whether their own interpretations were precious finds or complete rubbish.[15] □

'What does it matter who is speaking?': Experiment and Voice

'"What does it matter who is speaking," someone said', writes Foucault, quoting Samuel Beckett, in his essay 'What is an Author?' (1969).[16] Experimental poetry is most often seen as floating free of identity politics, though its rootedness in certain institutional affiliations (such as Cambridge University) has had clear effects on its demographic make-up. Much contemporary poetry thinks of itself as giving a voice to previously unrepresented groups, but from another point of view this is merely a perpetuation of identity politics by other means. As Keith Tuma has written of the dissenting working-class voice in a Tony Harrison poem, '"he" is meant to be no less representative [than the neutral "I" of the classical lyric]. It is *what* or *who* he represents that differs, but the poetry is no less vessel [*sic*] for the expression of a recognisable and coherent identity, albeit one set dialogically among other voices.'[17] Nevertheless, the work of Prynne, Tom Raworth or Andrea Brady does not emerge from a vacuum, and some readers have chosen to read it through the prism of *its* recognisable identities, with controversial results. Writing on 'Prynne and the Movement' for a *Jacket* magazine symposium, Steve Clark draws attention to Prynne's striking from the record of his debut collection, *Force of Circumstance* (1962), a volume closer to mainstream poetics than anything he has published since. Wishing to 'contest the aspiration of autochthony implied by this erasure', Clark links Prynne to socio-cultural currents of the time, as numerous critics have done with his Movement contemporaries. In an unfortunate echo of Larkin's posthumous critical fate, Clark's reading finds a violent and even far-right political dimension to early Prynne. He is 'almost parodically susceptible to post-imperial recuperation', and the most innocent-seeming imagery delivers unsuspected political subtexts, as when a boat-trip ('We shrug too quickly / At sailing from islands') becomes a metaphor for post-war decolonisation.[18] For all the intertextual echoes Clark finds between Prynne's work and that of Larkin and Donald Davie, his argument leaves itself open to a simple counter-thesis taking its cue from Foucault's 'What is an Author?': Prynne's work, even within single poems, should not be seen as the product of a unified speaking subject, and to frisk it for evidence of unsavoury political attitudes is a basic category error. Even so, it is worth pausing on the problem of experimental versus identitarian styles of reading. Few people are tempted to bring to a Keston Sutherland or Drew Milne poem the same biographical assumptions they bring to readings of Heaney or Carol Ann Duffy, or if they do they find this poetry stony ground for their interpretive projections. In her poem 'When I say I believe women ...' Cambridge poet Emily Critchley consciously foregrounds herself as a female subject. In doing so she addresses the easily overlooked submersion of gender in discussions of innovative poetry (none of the contributors to the aforementioned *Jacket* Prynne is female), and also the question of where the trace effects of gender are expected to go in a poetics that believes itself beyond identitarian concerns. Men and women 'read differently', she writes, before asking whether this is biologically 'essential' or

> ■ because women have a subordinated relationship
> to power in this guts I don't know. Is this clear
> enough for you to follow. I don't know.[19] □

Critchley repeats her opening claim, as though putting sceptical responses ('women & men what?') down to mishearing. The connection of deep power structures to the trivial example of a piece of burnt toast adds a comic veneer to her critique, while the notion of a Cambridge poetry reader trained in reading Prynne but unable to follow something as 'clear' as gender injustice (because of its very clarity?) is also not without sour hilarity. As Linda Kinahan has asked, 'Is female subjectivity expressible in the arena of an anti-lyrical aesthetic dominant in this reading community?'[20] Exploring the double-bind for women experimentalists that their tradition declares gender a 'non-issue'[21] while continuing to uphold a heavily male lineage (Ezra Pound, William Carlos Williams, Louis Zukofsky, George Oppen, Charles Olson, Basil Bunting, David Jones), Kinahan directs our attention to the many female modernists whose influence has been felt in British and Irish writing (Lorine Niedecker, Marianne Moore, Gertrude Stein, Mina Loy, H. D.). Here again the conduits represented by small presses are crucial: though little known even in the US at the time, the Objectivist Lorine Niedecker was published by Ian Hamilton Finlay's Wild Hawthorn Press and Stuart Montgomery's Fulcrum Press in the 1960s, to high praise from Basil Bunting and Roy Fisher. Acts of retrieval such as Patrick McGuinness's rescuing of forgotten Welsh modernist Lynette Roberts have also adjusted our sense of the post-war scene (her long poem *Gods with stainless ears* (1951) had been out of print for more than half a century before its reissue in 2006). Anthologies have redressed the balance (Maggie O'Sullivan's *out of everywhere* (1996), which mixes UK and North American poets, and Carrie Etter's *Infinite Difference* (2010), which confines itself to the UK),[22] but to adapt Critchley's thesis, men and women continue to be read 'pretty differently', as we see from the reception of one of the best-known contemporary experimental poets, Denise Riley.

'You principle of song': Voice and Desire in Denise Riley

'Expectant contexts that seem designed to invite or provoke failure are particularly pertinent to the poetry of Denise Riley', as David and Christine Kennedy have written.[23] Denise Riley's 'Shantung' is a short poem about love and desire combining baby-talk ('Ouf, ouf'), remembered pop lyrics ('Come on everybody') and a darkened mood that pitches the whole affair suddenly into failure ('Each day I think of something about dying').[24] On the face of it, it is a throwaway poem, like snatches of overheard conversations. Is the tone serious or comic? Is it an example or critique of the language of contemporary desire? As we have seen, Prynne takes a keen interest in junk culture, but something in Riley's work struck Prynne's fellow Cambridge poet, John Wilkinson, as lacking in high-mindedness. Reviewing *Mop Mop Georgette* (1993), the collection from which 'Shantung' comes, he accuses Riley of 'working with the narcissistic grain which cannot divert or obstruct its pathological logic'.[25] As a theorist of identity, Riley takes a keen interest in narcissism and identity formation, and has devoted a poem, 'Affections of the Ear', to the Narcissus myth. While the narcissist converts identity into a closed circuit, refusing to move beyond the mirror stage, the healthy adult acknowledges the self as shaped by forces beyond our control. Under Althusser's theory of interpellation, ideology functions not unlike a shout in the street: hearing a random cry of 'Hey, you!', we turn around and recognise ourselves in its call, just as we recognise ourselves in the demands of bourgeois subjecthood. Riley's 'Laibach Lyrik: Slovenia, 1991' is full of examples of ideology dictating people's identities in this way, with the brutal force of the civil war in Yugoslavia. A speaker becomes aware of ethnic hatred based on 'where / I came from, which I never used to know', while another responds to violence by realising that she has now assumed an identity she could never have foreseen ('But that blood lost means I must take that name').[26] David and Christine Kennedy note the shift of locale to London and the narrative rendering of exile and displacement for a young and old woman:

■ [The young girl's] comments seem to blur linear and cyclical time in an attempt to present meaningful time in terms of the life cycle and reproduction. Or perhaps it is more correct to say that her complaint is partly that something has violated cyclical time and made it linear.[27] □

The speaker is forced to take on 'new designations' whose complexity may be lost on a British observer, or exoticised as the traces of a difficult or failed assimilation. The poem closes with an allusion to *Twelfth Night*, set in the Central European territory of Illyria (present-day Croatia). As Wilkinson comments, the Illyrians spoke an 'extinct and unrecorded language', and in identifying with them the poem chooses 'to speak something unknown, to stutter and halt *and* bring to light, to speak in tongues "like 'the unconscious'"'.[28]

Her problems with identity lead some readers to take a pessimistic view of Riley's belief in emotion and interpersonal relations ('Much of Riley's writing concerns the impossibility of human contact or communication'),[29] but difficulty and impossibility need not be the same thing. Leaving the narcissistic stage does not mean a farewell to 'pathology' when our new identities are shaped on our behalf by the collective madness of civil war.

Riley's use of childish and adolescent material thus acquires a critical dimension, lingering on the stage where gender and identity remain molten and unformed. There is a constant tension in Riley's work between exemplarity and the individual: the individual may wish to speak out for others against injustice, but it is also a condition of freedom that she not feel the need to be representative of anyone or anything, should the mood so take her. Sometimes, in other words, a silly pop song is just that and nothing besides. As she writes in 'A Note on Sex and "Reclaiming the Language"': 'The work is / e.g. to write "she" and for that to be a statement / of fact only', but it is in the nature of poetic language to be perennially overdetermined. The 'she' of Riley's narrations experiences this as a series of negative feedbacks: when the female 'Savage' goes on holidays 'she is asked to buy wood carvings, which represent herself'; women are asked to consume the commodified simulacra of themselves they become under patriarchy.[30] A further aspect of Riley's immersion in childhood is its Forrest-Thomsonian resistance to 'naturalisation', or the verification of a poem's truth by reference back to its presumed real-life origin. The suspicion of realism was a strong feature of poststructuralist theory, and leads Forrest-Thomson to value parody and pastiche as forms in revolt against the conventions they inherit – lessons clearly learned by Riley's poems too.

A test case for a poem unable to test its verity against its object is elegy, and when Riley published her first poem since 2000, 'A Part Song' in 2011, it was an exercise in maternal bereavement (though Riley herself prefers to avoid the term 'elegy').[31] A part song is a form of choral music, though as the pun in Riley's title suggests, one crucial voice is necessarily absent. This adds extra sensitivity to the question of 'speaking for'. Riley inverts the dilemma by imagining her dead son's voice speaking for her, and surrenders authorial control so far as to imagine herself being 'dictated to' by the absent voice:

> ■ Who'd laugh at the thought
> Of me being sung in by you
> And being kindly dictated to.[32] □

This is a savage twist on the usual elegiac convention of the poet reconstituting the voice of the departed. 'A Part Song' takes us far from poetic narcissism, of any stripe, and discovers the freedom of major poetry in the midst of grief and powerlessness.

Infamous and Invisible: Institutions and Anthologies

We have seen in Chapter 1 the central role played by anthologies in shaping contemporary poetry, but experimental poetry is a special case again.

From the experimental perspective the anthology form as much as its contents is problematic, telescoping all the vested interests whose public face the anthology often presents to the world. Much of the contemporary poetry classed as experimental is bypassed altogether by commercial anthologies, or the possibility of the experimental is appeased through notional crossover figures (Roy Fisher, Denise Riley). This should not be mistaken for peaceful coexistence. As previously noted, Don Paterson devoted much of his introduction to the US-published anthology *The New British Poetry* (2004) to a denunciation of postmodernist poetry despite not naming even one of the writers in his sights. The most plausible explanation for this is a perception that experimental poetry is a purely academic phenomenon, as embodied in the US by the Language poets, and that Americans tempted to study British poetry might apply the same academic-led approach, with disastrous results. This belief can be traced back to the critical writings of Michael Donaghy, a major influence on Paterson's generation. An American-born poet who made his career in the UK, Donaghy felt strongly about the takeover of poetry in the United States by an institutionalised *avant-garde* that divorced the art from the common reader and its oral traditions (Olson's Projective Verse was a particular bugbear). In the States, those who shared Donaghy's views banded together as New Formalists, but while Donaghy's formalism was less dogmatic than this and possessed of a knowing and self-deflating wit, there is plenty of oppositional energy on show in his prose manifesto, 'Wallflowers'.[33] Where some might regret the decline of the genuine *avant-garde* into a tenured élite, Donaghy finds little to distinguish between its later etiolations and its modernist beginnings, stressing the element (as he saw it) of bourgeois self-punishment and distrust of the artistic pleasure principle. As he told Andy Brown in interview:

■ The audience for avant garde art is a middle class audience that pays to be shocked, to be horsewhipped. Whether it's a urinal on a pedestal in 1910 or a poem composed entirely of semi-colons in 1997 ('everything changes but the avant garde', said Auden), the audience expects to retreat from a direct and complex experience of the craftsmanship, to ideas about art.[34] □

Contra Donaghy, it is an over-simplification to see British experimental poetry as a purely academic phenomenon or as emanating only from established academic beachheads. In his sequence *Pearl* (1995), Barry MacSweeney addresses 'paranoid Marxist Cambridge prefects'[35] with the jocular awkwardness of one whose experiments took place in working-class Newcastle, while Michael Haslam, though taught by Prynne, spent his working life as a labourer in Yorkshire. More recently, in interview, Paterson has retreated from his hard line and confessed to finding a 'healthy and perhaps necessary dialectic' between the mainstream and the *avant-garde*, but only 'when people are prepared to caricature their positions a little'.[36]

Given the strength of preconceptions, the language of *avant-garde* polemic will sometimes veer towards the apocalyptic, as we find in the combative approach Iain Sinclair brings to his 1996 anthology, *Conductors of Chaos*. Best known today as a novelist and non-fiction writer, Sinclair was briefly the poetry editor at Paladin, where he suffered the indignity of having his poetry list pulped when the press was acquired by Harper Collins. Unlike the elusive Prynne, Sinclair is a practised controversialist, forever jousting against the philistinism and narrowness of British culture: when Randall Stevenson praised Prynne in a volume of *The Oxford English Literary History* in 2004, the fact was seized on by reviewers, and Sinclair duly appeared on the BBC's *Today* programme, to answer the question 'Who is J. H. Prynne?'[37] The gladiatorial edge to these stand-offs – Prynne versus Larkin, the underground versus Harper Collins – is a feature of *Conductors of Chaos* too. The anthology is published by Picador but one of its first texts, by Caroline Bergvall, consists largely of punctuation marks. In his introduction Sinclair veers between a flaunted disregard for the mainstream and a desire to reappropriate it from the cuckoo-in-the-nest of the Movement generation and their poetic descendants. Swinging between these poles induces something akin to editorial sea-sickness in Sinclair, which he works off in attacks on the anthology form: the anthology, he insists, is a power-grab, dependent on a slash-and-burn erasure of previous generations and the reduction of complexities to packageable sound bites:

> ■ At their worst, anthologies are lies: the absolute betrayal of the programme they presume to promote. Ireland, a swamp of corrupt decisions, is reduced to a package for export. Bog and bomb and blarney a heap of glittering similes burnished for westward transit. The whole sorry 'problem', the anthologist suggests, can be made fit for the syllabus by the industrial conversion of charm (myth/metaphor/weather) into strict metre.[38] □

This is Sinclair's response to the commercial and critical success of the Belfast poets, well into their second generation by 1996, and shows the difficulty for the *avant-garde* of connecting with a sense of national tradition, especially when more than one nation is involved. To Sinclair, the existence of an Irish *avant-garde* remains unthinkable. Even allowing for heavy sarcasm here, Sinclair's reduction of all Irish poetry to 'bog and bomb and blarney' is crassly over-simplifying. The 1930s produced a promising but abortive generation of experimentalists in Ireland. Circumstances conspired against their work entering the mainstream but by the late 1960s interest in their work had been revived by the poets associated with the New Writers' Press and its journal, *The Lace Curtain* (1969–78). These poets include Trevor Joyce, Maurice Scully, Catherine Walsh and Michael Smith, and have long defined themselves against the unexamined realist and identitarian assumptions of much other Irish poetry. Why then are they invisible to Sinclair? Trevor Joyce has written of the tendency of the 'international' *avant-garde* to flatten out in practice to Anglo-America, and despite his commitment to overlooked traditions Sinclair shows himself culpably incurious.[39]

There are other ways too in which Sinclair's canon exhibits historical flattening-out. *Conductors of Chaos* reaches back to the heroic period of high modernism, but a disparity between the careers of early-century modernists and Sinclair's contemporaries becomes awkwardly apparent. The selection from Anglo-Welsh poet David Jones in *Conductors of Chaos* is prefaced by an essay devoted to salvaging Jones from the 'toxic qualities' of his 'modernist Catholicism'. For Jones, as for Pound and Eliot, modernist poetics came with a strongly implied endorsement of reactionary politics, often with a crypto- or not so crypto-fascist tinge. Drew Milne's response to this is to locate Jones's redemptive radicalism in the gap between the hierarchical vision and the fragmentary actuality of the texts: 'it is the extremity of his work's estrangement [...] which deserves attention. Jones's integrity is reflected in his inability to tidy up his fragments of crystallized writing.'[40] By the time we come to *A Various Art*, a 1990 precursor of *Conductors of Chaos*, the problem has inverted itself: minus any whiff of sulphur or the promotional cunning of the New Generation ('pod people', in Sinclair's view), that volume's editors had only a languorous dilettantism to fall back on: '"Various Artists". It sounded too much like a tea-chest of unattributable dross in a poorly attended Fenland auction.'[41]

The *modus operandi* of Sinclair's assembly is performative contradiction: the work he values most 'seems most remote, alienated, fractured', to the point of not really wanting to be there: his poets are a 'quarrelsome bunch; dealing with them is like dipping an arm into a sack of vipers'.[42] Where so much canon-making has shaded into PR and marketing, it may seem like the decent thing to dispense with the canon altogether. A comparison of *Conductors of Chaos* with *A Various Art* and Richard Caddel and Peter Quartermain's *Other: British and Irish Poetry since 1970* (1998) reveals a mere four writers in common, from a field of 36 writers (*Conductors of Chaos*), 55 (*Other*), and 17 (*A Various Art*). They are: Andrew Crozier, John James, Douglas Oliver and Peter Riley. While Oliver wrote one of the great, angry political poems of the contemporary era (*Penniless Politics*, 1991), none of the other three shares Sinclair's confrontational stance and one, Peter Riley, has been prominently sceptical of the *avant-garde*'s own cherished myths. Other models are possible, and in their introduction to *Other*, Caddel and Quartermain (while still repeating the post-Mottram narrative of British poetry) place their analysis in the context of a larger sociology of art. What they oppose, broadly, is the empirical and rationalist worldview, and its compulsion to interpret disagreement as deviation:

> ■ Power structures rest upon claims to transcendent identity and unity, and in laying claim to the universality of moral, ethical, and aesthetic values they deny their own historical contingency. They install centrist monologic utterance as the norm.[43] □

While this critique of what Adorno and Horkheimer might call 'instrumental reason' is cogent and appealing, and Caddel and Quartermain make considerable efforts to look beyond a narrow white Anglo-Saxon demographic, their invocation of William Langland's fourteenth century as 'already an intensely plural society' shows an unexpected conjunction of organicism and multi-cultural *pietas*, not to mention the ability of experimentalists to talk in blurb-speak too. One of the final poems in *Other* is Catherine Walsh's 'Nearly Nowhere', and between Langland's mediaeval 'fair field full of folk' and the fugue state in which many of the poets in *Other* function, signs of unresolved conflict persist. The challenge for a critic who would make sense of this conflict is to provide a narrative of the *avant-garde* driven by neither visions of Eden-like beginnings nor the charge sheet of betrayal and recrimination that drives *Conductors of Chaos*.

Andrew Duncan and 'The Failure of Conservatism'

In his 1930 essay on Baudelaire, T. S. Eliot mounts a defence of that French poet's outspokenly blasphemous side. Though a Christian himself, Eliot defends Baudelaire against a world in which blasphemy is no longer possible, as indifference and ignorance gain the upper hand over belief and disbelief. Among modern critics, Andrew Duncan makes a model blasphemer (one of his essay collections is titled *The Council of Heresy* (2009)). Matching Sinclair for anger at his Movement bogeyman, Duncan has written a series of provocative books to harness the scattered energies of the British *avant-garde* into a coherent history of the recent past. Among these is *The Failure of Conservatism in Modern British Poetry* (2003), one of the most unusual and maverick studies of contemporary poetry. Flouting the widespread assumption that only academic critics are interested in innovative poetry, Duncan's writing owes more to the world of punk fanzines than to the monograph. It begins with the claim that 'No modern British poet has an international reputation',[44] which if true attests to an isolation of British poetry on the world stage drastically at odds with perceptions closer to home. The example of Keith Tuma's *Anthology of Twentieth-Century British and Irish Poetry* showed how revealing (and, for some, enraging) foreign perspectives on British poetry can be, but when Duncan further insists that 'It is half a century since any British poet acquired a world-wide reputation', we are dealing not with the time-lag of overseas reception but a principled and absolute rejection of the boosterism on which his hated mainstream depends.

This lends an inflammatory edge to Duncan's prose. Taking the pulse of the contemporary mainstream he examines Armitage and Crawford's *Penguin Book of Poetry from Britain and Ireland since 1945*, whose introduction charts a progressivist narrative of the 'democratic voice'. Duncan begs to differ:

> ■ [Crawford's] definition of the democratic voice, then, is mystificatory; what he is not saying is 'dumbing down'. As a description of the cultural field, it is a screen behind which the issues of market preferences, the division of the market, the clash of classes represented by different educational levels, and the process of making taste, are hidden. Crawford has no interest in educating public taste; some critics or editors want to help the reader to deal with complex, dense, and innovative poetry, but not this one. If Crawford does not engage with a thirty-year lag between public taste and the practice of poets, it may be because he personally is 30 years behind. This is not a crime, but he fares badly from a comparison with Iain Sinclair or Ken Edwards, as anthologists. Much modern poetry is critical of conventional poetics and of the dominant social order. Crawford finds this shocking and unpleasant – and therefore unaesthetic and not part of real poetry. The chronology within the volume reveals that age brings legitimacy and authority: he is able to stomach senior rebels but not ones under 70. Someone who enforced order is not going to be happy about critique or dissidence.[45] □

Duncan is impatient with critics who use the unseating of Eric Mottram as an alibi for the failure of more recent *avant-gardes*, as though some eras can sustain radical art and others not, but when he accuses Crawford of a thirty-year knowledge gap he too is arguing from an implied dissociation of sensibility (in Eliot's phrase): at some point in its recent history British poetry was offered the chance to broaden its horizons, but has chosen instead to retrench, masking its insularity with an unconvincing vocabulary of democratisation. Duncan's critique shares the blame for this between privileged institutions such as the Anglican Church and their unresponsiveness to cultural change (T. S. Eliot and Geoffrey Hill do not loom overly large on Duncan's neo-modernist map), to which he opposes countercultural movements such as protest and pop poetry. His *Council of Heresy* is subtitled *A Primer of Poetry in a Balkanised*

Terrain, and with its proliferation of *groupuscules* Duncan's map can resemble that of the far left, another cultural arena where messianic pretensions and small bands of true believers do battle over ultimate truths.

Forty years after Alvarez on the Movement, the opposition of middle ground and the treacherous cultural fringes remains self-fulfillingly irresistible. The charge of Crawford's recoiling from poets whose language represents a real challenge to the 'dominant social order' only to anoint rebels safely over the age of 70 is an interesting one, especially in the context of Scottish poetry. As Duncan writes elsewhere in *The Failure of Conservatism*, MacDiarmid's role as keeper of the Scottish *avant-garde* flame did not prevent him responding to younger Scottish experimentalists with incomprehension and fury, notably Ian Hamilton Finlay, whose use of demotic Glaswegian he angrily denounced. One *avant-garde* will not necessarily overlap with, understand, or support another. Cambridge poetry is not Language poetry is not Informationism is not Conceptualism. The real imperative is to match the rhetoric of inclusivity with a care for the legions of lost and forgotten radicals, from the New Apocalypse poets of the 1940s to the present day.

Another way in which Duncan flouts (innovative) convention is the unpredictability of the choices for his alternative canon. While Prynne, Raworth and Barry MacSweeney all feature extensively, Anthony Thwaite is also unexpectedly singled out for praise. No less than Leavis or Yvor Winters in their day, Duncan is savagely judgemental in his personal canon, a canon he is happy to spell out in lists of touchstone volumes. His choices for the 1990s range from the obvious (John James, Denise Riley, Roy Fisher), to neglected older poets (F. T. Prince, Christopher Middleton, Charles Madge), to apparently mainstream figures (Alison Brackenbury, Alan Ross), and other poets not normally the subject of any kind of critical interest.[46] While his more extreme pronouncements may seem perverse or attention-seeking, Duncan meets the test of a radical criticism as few other writers have done: identifying, explaining and championing work which he believes can transform how we read.

'Between Cup and Lip': Translation, Experiment and Peter Manson

Translation is an under-examined aspect of British poetry today, both in its own right and as a synecdoche for thinking about poetic language in general. It has been of central importance to modern experimental writing, both as medium and metaphor. Some of the strongest voices in contemporary British poetry are both non-contemporary and non-Anglophone. Homer, Ovid, Mallarmé, and Tsvetaeva, are living presences in the translations of Christopher Logue, Ted Hughes, Peter Manson, Elaine Feinstein and others. From the outset, translation was centrally important to modernism, effecting a dramatic realignment of the concept of voice and originality. Pound's 'Homage to Sextus Propertius' (1919) was attacked for its failures of literal fidelity, but provided Pound with a vehicle for his disillusionment with England and critique of imperial values. The versions of Chinese poetry he published as *Cathay* (1915) were decisive in reorienting the movement of Pound's verse music away from the pentameter and towards the open forms that make up *The Cantos*. The opening passage of the epic poem is a translation within a translation, from Andreas Divus's Latin rendering of Homer's Greek. A side-effect of modernist translation is its reminder that our current Anglocentric culture is the exception, historically, rather than the rule, and that the circulation of texts between languages and across contexts is a part of any healthy tradition. As Pound tries to condense world culture into a single poem, we are offered foreign poems in untranslated, translated and re-translated form, all mixed in together in an impossible collage. The effect is strongly inimical to Forrest-Thomson's 'naturalisation': never is the reader allowed to settle into the luxury of equating the poem with the voice of a single, definable narrator. This is our experience of reading Eliot's *The Waste Land* too, whether or not (as is often the case) this passage in question makes use of adaptation or translation. A logical conclusion of the modernist style is that we begin to experience 'original' text in English as though it were a translation too. This is the effect exploited by Christopher Reid in *Katerina Brac*, but also in Geoffrey Hill's 'The Songbook of Sebastian Arrurruz', a purported translation from the work of a non-existent Spanish poet. To Robert Frost, poetry is what gets lost in translation; to the writer working with fictive translations, the poem becomes a powerful metaphor for cultural restoration and wholeness, the 'dreams / Through which the excess of memory / Pursues its own abstinence.'[47]

Translations do not have to be fictive to explore the estrangement effects we find in Reid and Hill. Given the global dominance of English, a translator will approach a text in any other language from a position of power. Hence the popularity in contemporary poetry of the 'version', in which a poet without expert knowledge of the target language produces poems 'after' Dante or Mandelstam, sometimes with updated cultural references, and which the Anglophone poet can publish under his or her name. In the marketing of these books, it is often the translator or versioner's name that carries the product: his third book, *The Eyes* (1999), features Don Paterson's name on the spine, with a smaller acknowledgement, 'after Machado', author of the Spanish originals, under Paterson's name on the front cover. Where styles of translation are concerned, a belief in the availability of the foreign in English means that many poets will attempt to carry over the formal aspects of original texts, despite the different conditions under which rhyme is used between one language and another.

Describing his translations from French symbolist poet Stéphane Mallarmé, Peter Manson takes a stand for the contrary impulse, rejecting the false equivalences and expectations of rhymed translations:

■ These translations were done in the conviction that a translation of Mallarmé should at least be allowed to sound like interesting modern poetry, and that the strict (or even the very lax) use of rhyme and regular metre is one of the surest ways of forbidding that from happening.[48] □

Metrically, translators tend to assume equivalences between French forms such as the alexandrine and the English iambic pentameter, despite English prosody being accentual-syllabic and French not; these, too, Manson rejects. Mallarmé's is a poetry haunted by silence, nothingness and death, and if there is any truly shared ground between the verso and recto pages in a translation of this poet it is most likely to be found in the white space between the blocks of text, a temptation encouraged by Mallarmé's envisioning of the book as a *tombeau*, or tomb for the writer's soul. While Manson has produced a (comparatively) 'straight' translation of Mallarmé's *Salut* (1893) as part of *The Poems in Verse*, a version in his 2008 collection *Between Cup and Lip* demonstrates a novel approach to linguistic incompatibility (as well as exemplifying the condition of textual pluralism within Manson's own *oeuvre*). There is proverbially many a slip between cup and lip, and Manson introduces some original slippage in his own voice in between the translated French text, which he places in capital letters. The capitalised text can be read separately or across the interpolated text, giving two different narratives:

■ what hope REFERS TO NOTHING BUT THE CUPidity
SO SLOWLY knocked, with the candle, UPSIDE DOWN: this one A TROOP
OF SIRENS ON THE CEILING could not awaken DROWNS in blood liquor.[49] □

Manson's patternings can be characterised as exercises in the 'deviant translation' that Dónal Moriarty has diagnosed in the case of another devotee of Mallarmé, Irish poet Brian Coffey.[50] Moriarty compares Coffey's translations to those of Derek Mahon, whose renderings of French poets such as Nerval and Rimbaud are elegant, witty and rich in rhyme. Mahon's translations aim, above all else, for readability, whereas Coffey's take a perverse delight in their awkwardness. Coffey pays close attention to etymologies, and will deliberately flaunt *faux amis* lookalikes between English and French such as 'flames' for *flammes* in a Rimbaud translation, *flammes* meaning 'banners'. Moriarty comments:

■ Such is the nature of Coffey's method of translation that the reader is continually made aware that English is constructed out of foreign materials. A stimulated awareness of the diachronic dimension of language enriches the meaning of the line but, more significantly, it is another way of inscribing foreignness into the translation.[51] □

The most celebrated instance of this approach in modern poetry is perhaps Nabokov's 1964 translation of Pushkin's *Eugene Onegin*. Abjuring the liberties and readability of the 'version', it preached fidelity above all else, and was widely attacked as an eccentric curiosity. The readable versus the awkward, the surface versus the model, produce an opposition of smooth versus rough. Pound's early translations shocked readers with their slangy register, but also had frequent recourse to archaisms, as in his translations from the Anglo-Saxon and Cavalcanti (a poet that Manson has translated 'after Ezra Pound and Louis Zukofsky'). Whether erring on the side of the slangy or the archaic, what the translation refuses is the transparency of a naturalised text, readable as though an English original. This is the contribution of translations such as Manson's to the innovative tradition, returning our focus to the source and accepting the burden of difficulty rather than skimp on the full complexity of the original text. In his translations of Mallarmé's *'tombeau'* sonnets, the words pine for the materiality of a funeral monument, but turn from the loss of the dead poet (in this case Edgar Allan Poe) to dazzling visions of futurity:

■ calm block fallen down here from an unseen disaster,
let this granite at least set for all time a limit
to the black flights of Blasphemy scattered in the future.[52] □

'Melody exchanged for atonality': Keston Sutherland and Late Modernism

The work of Keston Sutherland resists easy paraphrase, but numbers among its chief concerns the fate of late capitalism and the cult of commodity fetishism, the chimera that is bourgeois subjectivity in the age of the administered society, and the possibility of meaningful artistic activity almost half a century after Adorno's *Aesthetic Theory* (1970). It is also much preoccupied with police brutality, UK foreign policy, bad sex, information theory and the inspired randomness that leads him to name a recent work, *The Odes to TL61P* (2013), in honour of a discontinued brand of Hotpoint tumble dryer. Taught by Prynne at Cambridge,

Sutherland combines the most forbidding aspects of Cambridge poetry with an unstinting political aesthetic heavily indebted to Marxist critical theory. Despite its hieratic patina, Sutherland's work comes across strongly in performance, allaying any suspicions that this is poetry for the page (or Cambridge cloister) alone. To open his long poem *Odes to TL61P* is akin to opening a door on a typhoon, admitting a headlong and unrelenting textual onslaught. Sutherland delivers the cacophonous, competing voices of twenty-first-century politics with a deliberate suppression of framing devices or anything that might reduce them to a manageable narrative. A Sutherland poem will require some acclimatisation from a first-time reader, but the text's shock-value is an important part of the experience too.

Sutherland makes for an implausible formalist, but the form of poetic utterance and the horizon of formal possibility are central to his project. With his apocalyptic side, Sutherland is not without a romantic dimension too, as noticed by John Wilkinson. Of the conclusion of a previous political sequence, *Neocosis* (2005), he writes:

■ These lines, which so intricately cross-cut neoconservative idealism, Old Testament sacrifice, and eschatology with a descent into the gut of empire, figure a particular constraint on the reach of lyric poetry. The problem is that the lyric surge operates at a level which can overwhelm or obliterate any counterflows at the semantic level.[53] □

In the Jim Carrey film *Man on the Moon* (1999), comedian Andy Kaufman is showing a pilot for his TV show to a room of network executives when the picture-frames begin to skip, prompting one executive to stand up and slap the top of the television. Kaufman explains that the picture is meant to behave like that, to an incredulous reaction. Sutherland wants to snap the frames that hold the conventional lyric poem in place, but also the readerly assumptions that tend to greet lines like the following with incomprehension:

■ Each time you unscrew the head the truths burn out
and fly away above the stack of basements inundated
in aboriginal mucus, elevating the impeccable[54] □

The opening section of the poem from which these lines are taken begins *in mediis rebus*, giving the impression that its narration has already been in motion for some time. 'Make sense who may', says a character in the Beckett play *What Where [Quoi où]* (1983), and one is aware in reading Sutherland of the violence of interpretation involved – the extreme efforts required to parse this most quicksilver of writers, but also the power structures and workings of language in general

which Sutherland aspires to lay bare. Nevertheless, this is not to say that
Sutherland defers or dodges the question of meaning in a deconstruc-
tionist or self-absolving style. A plausible source for the above passage
(coupled with a later reference to the 'oblong top of the freezer') might
be a user's manual for a domestic appliance, which has deviated into
a playfully sexual register ('hereafter congenitally depilated Janine')
before exploding into questions as to the text's linguistic status, again
in the manner of late Beckett, as it wonders 'who the fuck / I am now
speaking to or at or for or not at this moment'.

Worrying about Sutherland's more operatic moments of high drama,
Wilkinson writes: 'The danger [...] lies in too little mediated a relationship between poetic discourse and social-economic structures of
authority, which in turns suggests the poet's exceptionalism as well as
his instrumentality.'[55] If this interface is problematic for Sutherland, his
poems are informed by a painful consciousness of this fact. It is in the
nature of modernist art to be self-referential, and this condition risks
tipping the poem into excessive pleasure at its status as a self-consuming
artefact (to paraphrase the title of a 1972 Stanley Fish book); Sutherland's work, though, is aggressively resistant to tropes of achieved
resolution, or what we might once have called the 'well-made poem'. It
helps that he can declare that 'this is a comic poem', though he also says
of the general public, 'what a cunt'.[56] When Joyce attracted criticism for
Work in Progress (later *Finnegans Wake*) he incorporated the voices of his
detractors into his text, and Sutherland does the same thing with swipes
at the *Times Literary Supplement* columnist 'J. C.', with whom he had
had a hostile exchange over matters *avant-garde*. The reader must judge
whether the explanatory statements that pepper this passage are in ear-
nest or constitute leg-pulls for the reader who sees the modernist poem
as sealed-in, hierophantic utterance and nothing else. Sutherland has
just dissented from Philip Larkin's statement in *All What Jazz* about the
unnaturalness of modernist art, and continues:

> ■ The administration of modernism is to be
> difficult on purpose, to love the confusion of others as much
> as your own. Melody is exchanged for atonality,
> proving their trail by fungibility; however much these
> words dispirit me I love the experience of making
> them.[57] □

An unsympathetic reader of this passage might pause on 'difficult
on purpose', 'love the confusion', and 'atonality', but another phrase
that leaps out is the closing insistence that the author 'love[s]' the experience' of making these words. The final chapter of Sutherland's prose
study *Stupefaction* (2011) is titled 'Happiness in Writing' and returns to

Sutherland's *maître-à-penser* Adorno and the gloomy post-war meditations of *Minima Moralia*. Adorno demands the 'utterly impossible' from thinkers as a precondition for philosophy, but as Sutherland adds, 'Happiness in writing is found in the trial of enduring, intense and ineliminable doubt or not at all.'[58] That this insight arises from a reading of Wordsworth's *Prelude* (1799; 1805; 1850) is another reminder that Sutherland is connecting with a larger tradition than that of 'paranoid Marxist Cambridge prefects'. As Jeremy Noel-Tod has written of Sutherland, his is an *oeuvre* that 'pursues a revolutionary – and increasingly psychoanalytic – concern with "the significance of love"'.[59] Without quite amounting to Sutherland's Larkinesque 'What will survive of us is love' moment, the lines quoted from *The Odes to TL61P* are a reminder that experimental writing has its intense emotional core too, without which it is nothing.

'The dust of our wasted fields': Experiment, Tradition and Uncreative Writing

Narratives of rupture and discontinuity will always be to the fore in discussions of modernism, but it is also worth insisting on deeper continuities. To Jeremy Noel-Tod, surveying the links between the experimental and Romantic traditions, Prynne's project is 'essentially Wordsworthian', confirming affinities across centuries which only the vagaries of contemporary anti-modernism serve to obscure.[60] Reading an early Prynne essay, 'Resistance and Difficulty' (1961), Noel-Tod uses the first of those terms to suggest an alternative to the more usual accusation levelled at Prynne's poetics, unintelligibility. The Romantic landscape offers resistance to our too-easy progress, and requires careful thought and engagement before it can be negotiated. Landscape is encountered rather than mastered, in the sense that familiarity does not exhaust a Wordsworth landscape, whereas a field in the path of a motorway is recognised and assessed as an obstacle and swept aside. As Prynne's style develops in the 1960s, the ground covered by his poems becomes ever more diverse, encompassing the scientific and technical vocabularies we see in 'L'Extase de M. Poher'. The collections in which this growth-spurt are most noticeable are *Kitchen Poems* (1968) and *Brass* (1971), volumes whose relationship to their period Ben Watson has compared to the role of Captain Beefheart's jarringly atonal *Trout Mask Replica* (1969) in 1960s rock history[61] – artworks whose mythic status is won at the expense of a reputation for indigestibility. Sifting through these poems' frequent images of waste and refuse, Noel-Tod refuses to allow the case for Prynne to become one of sealed-in 'refuse-nik'-dom, stressing instead the persistence of the Wordsworthian ideal but also the 'murderous' act of will required to clear a path through the rubbish mounds of contemporary discourse in search of green thoughts in contemporary green shades ('We walk / in beauty down the street, we tread / the dust of our wasted fields').[62] We will see further examples of the meshing of the experimental and ecopoetic traditions in the next chapter, in the work of R. F. Langley, Peter Riley and Helen Macdonald, but no special pleading is needed to see the deep connections with the Romantic tradition not just in Prynne, but in other writers such as Michael Haslam, Peter Larkin and Zoë Skoulding.

It is when we look forward rather than back that the canon of experimental writing seems uncertain. One paradox of the institutional rise of creative writing is that it has coincided, first, with the age of literary theory and its critique of subjectivity and the romantic concept of individual inspiration and genius but, more recently, with the rise in the United States of 'uncreative writing'. Students taking a seminar on the Victorian novel or literary theory become inured to the death of the author, or the 'author function' in the conceptualist longhand, only for it to spring unexpectedly back to life in a class on their own poetry. 'Uncreative writing' can be seen as a response to this discursive impasse, and in her *Unoriginal Genius* (subtitled *Poetry By Other Means in the New Century*), Marjorie Perloff draws attention to the number of writers or practitioners whose work involves framing, citing and recycling existing texts rather than generating any of their own. Among the best known of these is Kenneth Goldsmith, whose books include *Day* (2003), a transposition of the entire text of a copy of *The New York Times*. Pondering the meaning of works in this vein, Perloff repeats a question of the Language poet Ron Silliman's: 'What does it mean for a work of art to be eminently likeable and almost completely unreadable?'[63] Behind Silliman's question and Goldsmith's frank confessions of the tediousness of his texts lies an assumption that they are to be engaged with as concepts, as ambushes and gimmicks even, rather than as words on the page. The affinities with conceptual art are salient: an artist in the early twenty-first century can achieve public recognition through controversial subject matter (Tracey Emin's unmade bed) and the media debate this generates, entirely bypassing old-fashioned questions of style and technique. Debates about conceptual art can resemble the white noise of an untuned radio, as artists and critics fail to agree on the criteria by which to evaluate this work. Similarly in poetry, Silliman applies the pejorative label 'school of quietude' for writing that remains committed to the individual subject, authentically rendered by a unified voice, but the element of schoolboy taunting in his use of the term suggests that a two traditions model, locked antagonistically together, retains a strong psychological appeal.

With his hucksterish air, Goldsmith's post-avant projects might appear a passing folly of American academe, and it would be a mistake to see the emergent trends of 'uncreative writing' as necessarily overlapping with British experimental writing, any more than Language poetry shares its aims and strategies with Cambridge poetry; but there is a larger (non-American) dimension to these developments. Perloff draws attention to the role of the internet in reshaping the locations of today's *avant-garde*: if up to very recently geographical location came first and a group of like-minded individuals second, the exploitation by 'uncreative writing' of material found online facilitates, in theory at least, a globalised community. Given the prominence attached by Perloff to Adorno's theory of 'resistance' ('the resistance of the individual poem to the larger cultural field of capitalist commodification'),[64] it is peculiar that she sees only positives in the use of social networking sites as agents of connection and as inspiration in their own right. Why is the ubiquitous Facebook not merely another tool of commodification and control? Why is globalised capitalism a bad thing but a globalised *avant-garde* of instant connections, bypassing previous barriers of language difference and the nation state, intrinsically good? Under this model, previous models of modernism which combined linguistic experiment and nationalism, such as that of Hugh MacDiarmid's in the 1920s and the Scottish Renaissance that followed, cease to be readable, their nationalist dimension merely an embarrassing anachronism (England, Ireland and Wales offer their own variants, *mutatis mutandis*).

Hugh MacDiarmid also features in a forecast by Robert Crawford of poetry's future, in his study *The Modern Poet* (2001). Crawford quotes a singularly clunking line of MacDiarmid's ('Shirkogoroff's *Psychomental Complex of the Tungus*'), and then its author's parenthetical addendum: '(If that line is not great poetry in itself / Then I don't know what great poetry is!)'.[65] The passage interests Crawford for its very ugliness, and MacDiarmid's self-consciousness about expecting the reader to follow him into the unaccommodating terrain of his pseudo-omniscient later epics. Here we see the expectations of what a poem can be stretched to breaking point, and which for Crawford prefigure the great breakthrough of our age – cybernetics. Though quick to qualify his praise for MacDiarmid's late style ('It may indeed have provoked more hostile reaction than sympathetic reading'), Crawford shares the common belief that the new knowledge environment of the internet has changed our relationship with the world as deeply as any technological advance has ever done. What, in the age of Google, still constitutes a 'natural' environment? W. N. Herbert's *Omnesia*, as studied in Chapter 3, is proof enough of how soon the alien territory glimpsed by MacDiarmid can become natural (if not 'naturalised' in the Forrest-Thomson sense) by the contemporary poet.

A Marxist critique might compare the newfound prestige of Goldsmith's found texts to the surplus value analysed in Marx's *Capital*

(1867), with the internet-surfing, textual recycler acting as the exploiter of someone else's labour. The most interesting British and Irish writers who have exploited (or foreshadowed) these techniques have tended to incorporate a dimension of self-critique into their projects. Having succeeded in hoaxing some readers with the poems of a non-existent Central European poet in *Katerina Brac*, Christopher Reid ended his next collection, *In the Echoey Tunnel* (1991), with the sequence 'Memres of Alfred Stoker', the memoirs of a semi-literate centenarian whose experiences stretch back to Victorian times. As a Martian poet, Reid might seem far removed from the canon of the British *avant-garde*, but the 'Memres of Alfred Stoker' are both found and faked, artful and artless, at once, and one of the most important interrogations of voice in contemporary poetry. Other glimpses into poetic futurity such as Nathan Hamilton's anthology *Dear World and Everyone In It* (2012, discussed in Chapter 7) show current trends exploring forms and media undreamt of by Prynne and his contemporaries in the 1960s, and converging on the territory explored by the 'uncreative' Americans. Cambridge and Sussex universities continue to foster young experimental writers, but art schools and the spoken-word scene are important conduits too. When a Faber poet, Sam Riviere, uses a social networking website to explore for satiric purposes the instantaneous nature of communication today, he is reaching a very different accommodation with the poetic medium and its audience from the traditional small-press poet whose print-runs might barely break into three figures. New media create new horizons of possibility, and to reject them out of hand would be to condemn oneself to Ian Gregson's 'retro-modernist' status. In 1994, Ian Hamilton had applied an almost blanket exclusion of the experimental tradition from his *Oxford Companion to Twentieth-Century Poetry*, but when a second edition appeared in 2013 under the title *The Oxford Companion to Modern Poetry*, dozens of experimenters took their place alongside the stalwarts of Hamilton's Londoncentric canon, even in some cases displacing them. This is welcome progress, but in an amusing sign of the larger literate audience adjusting its sense of the poetry world, the book was parodied by the satirical journal *Private Eye*. Among the fictional poets it described was 'A. D. Penumbra', credited with 'writing in every known register, simultaneously vatic and encrypted', and a sample of whose work it helpfully provided: 'hark to the wing-nut's stark periphrasis, gold the beat of the stoat's multitudinous heart'.[66] If *Katerina Brac* had been a fictional Cambridge experimenter rather than East European, her work might have sounded very much like this. Yet, in another example of Prynne's 'verbal smash-up', it might also be urged that A. D. Penumbra sounds uncannily like the late Prynne of the comically named *Her Weasels Wild Returning* (1994) or *Red D Gypsum* (1998). No less than Prynne and Ian Hamilton, Prynne and *Private Eye* make unlikely bedfellows. Yet the juxtaposition is no less improbable or alarming than those creative tensions that drive Keston Sutherland's *The Odes to TL61P*. In the version of experimental poetry passed through the intestinal tract of the *Private Eye* parodist we see again its 'atonality' and 'difficult on purpose' side, but also a successful communication of the pleasure in language, the fine excess and gusto in which the parodist confirms Sutherland's claim: 'however much these / words dispirit me I love the experience of making / them.'

CHAPTER SIX

New Environments

The Human and the Non-human: Principles and Pragmatism

In his *Poetry and Privacy* (discussed in Chapter 4) John Redmond examines the ways in which poems are interpreted by readers intent on giving them a public dimension. The junction of public and private in poetry is often a matter for debate, but what Redmond seeks to identify are over-interpretations, 'the *determination* to read poetry in publicly oriented ways, the *determination* to make it fit with one kind of public program or another.'[1] Redmond follows the American pragmatist tradition, which downplays ideology and stresses finding practical solutions to the problems that texts present. In a chapter on Robert Minhinnick and ecopoetry he addresses the way in which attitudes towards the natural world have shaped poetry, from Ted Hughes to Minhinnick and John Burnside, and diagnoses large amounts of Romantic ideology. If 'nature' as understood today is a largely Romantic creation, so is the role of artist as saviour first seen in Shelley's *Defence of Poetry* (1821; published 1840), in which poets feature as the 'unacknowledged legislators of the world'. Since Auden, who quipped that this role more properly belonged to secret policemen, readers have learned to be sceptical of artists' messianic delusions, but as contemporary poetry seeks a public role for itself, ecopoetics is a prime arena for its reconnection with the Romantic legacy. A crude version of this would be poems filled with lectures on recycling and reducing our carbon footprint, but Minhinnick has explained in interview why a genuine artist will tend to resist this impulse:

■ I don't think the poet has a moral role though a moral message might be perceived by the reader. Of course I have a moral standpoint on many aspects of life, but I wouldn't wish it to intrude too obviously in my poems, because I simply don't see myself as some kind of moral arbiter.[2] □

One might imagine a separation between a writer's poems, in which the natural world found pure expression, and the same writer's prose, in which he or she carried out the unlyrical work of activism and agit-prop. While poets have featured prominently in the resurgence of nature writing in prose (e.g. Kathleen Jamie, in her essay collections *Findings* (2005) and *Sightlines* (2012)),[3] this would be a false and unsustainable opposition for a number of reasons. First, it would beg the question as to what constitutes nature in its pure state. Only the bravest or most foolhardy writer would claim to have access to this realm. Draining a wetland to build houses on it is an act of appropriation, but nature writing has designs on the wilderness and mines it for its own 'use-value' – less obviously than the property developer, but in ways that amount to appropriation too. Post-Romantic concepts of wilderness risk collapsing into a guilty inversion of suburban life, blind to their pre-packaged form. Writing on Robert Macfarlane's prose study *The Wild Places* (2007), Kathleen Jamie recoils from the egocentricity she finds at work:

■ The danger of this writing style is that there will be an awful lot of 'I'. If there is a lot of 'I' [...] then it won't be the wild places we behold, but the author. We see him swimming, climbing, looking, feeling, hearing, responding, being sensitive, and because almost no one else speaks, this begins to feel like an appropriation, as if the land has been taken from us and offered back, in a different language and tone and attitude. Because it's land we're talking about, this leads to an unfortunate sense that we're in the company, however engaging, of another 'owner', or if not an owner, certainly a single mediator. [...] What's being reduced is not the health and variety of the landscape, but the variety of our engagement, our ways of seeing, our languages. There are lots of people, many of them women, who live in, or spend long seasons in places like Cape Wrath, St Kilda, Mingulay, thinking about the wild, studying its ways. Interesting people, with new ideas. It's a pity we meet none of them.[4] □

Related to the question of purity is that of knowledge. How do we know nature on its own terms, and not just as a human projection? Redmond quotes John Burnside on the need to 'step away from the narrowly human realm' and, given the practical impossibility of such a quest, questions the underlying motives:

■ As pragmatists never tire of saying, we are already in the world and the only values and preferences which we can satisfy are our own. The idea of the 'more-than-human' itself aims to satisfy purely human, and mainly sentimental, ends.[5] □

For Redmond, the pleasure we get from contemplating a landscape is a human, not a natural pleasure, and the sorrow we feel at natural disasters is 'because they interfere with our own dreams and purposes, not because they are breaking an imaginary law of nature'; the song of the earth is a song of ourselves.[6] Even when poets such as Robinson Jeffers or Hugh MacDiarmid take an apparent delight in contemplating landscapes purged of humanity, or Sylvia Plath in her poem 'Pheasant' says 'I trespass stupidly. Let be, let be',[7] they do so from an anthropocentric perspective.

This conclusion lends itself to contrasting applications. If nature is immutably alien to us we might decide that no great difference exists between Keats's nightingale and a cartoon kitten on the internet since both are designed to meet human needs, leading us to give up on the non-human altogether. As a piece of pragmatism this would seem petty and unimaginative, though when Clov in Beckett's *Endgame* (1957) announces 'There's no more nature' he does so to shock us into a realisation of the benighted state of a world – a post-apocalyptic future world, but by implication the one we already inhabit – in which all connections with nature have been severed.[8] One possible response to this is to see the gap between the human and non-human as a zone of artistic possibility, in which concern for nature expresses itself through meditations on its fragility and essential alienness.[9] It is the latter option that drives the work of Kathleen Jamie, Alice Oswald, Michael Haslam, Helen Macdonald, Peter Riley and others who have engaged intelligently with their environments. A further refinement of this would be to argue that ecopoetics overcomes the false division of art and activism and offers a transformative medium for how we relate to the world around us. The term 'ecocriticism' has a longer pedigree, but J. Scott Bryson's *Ecopoetry: A Critical Introduction* (2002) and the journal *Ecopoetics* have helped to popularise the specifically poetic aspect of environmentally sensitive writing, and the anthology *Earth Shattering* (2007; see below) is subtitled *Ecopoems*. One sign of the infancy of ecopoetics as a discipline is how little it featured in the early reception of a poet as steeped in the natural world as Seamus Heaney, where it is often seen as secondary in importance to the sectarian or postcolonial themes, or an all-purpose foil to them; the 'naturalness' of the land, as the ground bass under Heaney's work, casts it for many critics in the role of redemptive but voiceless goal of the warring tribes staking their claim to it.[10] For the ecologically-minded critic the cause of nature must be pressed for its own sake, and not just as an adjunct to our human concerns. Not all the writers I will consider use the term 'ecopoetics', and I use it here to designate the full spectrum of contemporary engagement with the natural world in poetry, criticism and prose. A good starting point for this – the starting point Jamie finds missing in Robert Macfarlane – is the moment of encounter with the unknown.

Encounter/Non-Encounter: Kathleen Jamie

Kathleen Jamie began her career with a series of travel poems that took her to Pakistan, Tibet and China, and it is only comparatively recently that the natural world and the landscapes of Scotland have come to the fore in her work, notably in the collections *Jizzen* (1999), *The Tree House* (2004) and *The Overhaul* (2012). Combined with this is Jamie's increasing use of literary Scots from *The Queen of Sheba* (1994) onwards, of which collection Sarah Broom has written: 'the use of Scots words and phrases situates the [title] poem itself (and implicitly the author) within the community it critiques'.[11] The unity of speaking subject and community is never without subtle qualifications in Jamie's work, however. While her poem 'The Stags' does not use Scots, it shows how neutral-seeming words acquire different resonances in different settings. Jamie frames an encounter with a herd of deer within the context of a human relationship. The 'you' addressed in the poem wants to display the stags to the speaker, who compares the animals to 'signatories of a covenant'. Covenanters were radical religious dissent-ers in seventeenth-century Scotland, often forced to go on the run to escape persecution, just as the 'covenant' that humans strike with wild creatures grants them freedom within certain conditions, while reserv-ing the right to manage and cull their numbers too. When the sighting finally takes place, it is lacking in various ways: the stags' faces look 'toward us, toward, / but not to us', and the poet is mainly conscious of her companion's desire to impress her with this display, to lead her on to the site of encounter, coupled with a fear of startling the animals. Consequently:

> ■ you're already moving
> quietly away, sure I'll go with you,
> as I would now, almost anywhere.[12] □

Jamie satirises the custodial equation of nature with an object of consumption: the stags are not returning the humans' rapt attention, but are inconvenienced and impatient to be alone again. Yet when the poet's companion senses this and moves away, the speaker chooses just this moment to declare her loyalty ('sure I'll go with you'). The (non-)encounter with the deer is the catalyst for a breakthrough in the human relationship which, once made, renders the animals redundant. The poem appropriates the deer only to reject this appropriation and return the animals to a state of innocence beyond whatever the poem has made of them. Responding to the trope of partial or frustrated reve-lation so often encountered in Jamie, Peter Mackay has questioned the amenability of her work to Romantic *Song of the Earth*-style green readings:

■ We are once more in a process of infinite regress, in which knowledge is always at one step removed. This is not poetry as the song of the earth, or of a revelation of dwelling, but as a stymieing and troubling of communication. Contemporary poetry is often an art of non-communication, a resistance, a making strange: what we have in *The Tree House* is a consummate communication of this non-communion, a tilting of the world in all its unchanciness.[13] □

The close of 'The Stags' is closer, rather, to the 'devotional attentiveness to the natural world and the poem as organism' that Maria Johnston has found in Jamie's work, but an attentiveness willing to coexist with the 'non-communication' and 'making strange' diagnosed by Mackay.[14] The ambivalence of 'The Stags' recalls Peter Riley in his sequence 'Western States': 'We turn our backs and the deer / come to drink in the dark.'[15] Once again the elusive deer are there, but in the dark and only when the observers turn their backs; but here too there is a framing 'we', on whose approach and withdrawal the poem's epiphanic payoff heavily depends. Jamie's poem dramatises its fraught interaction of the human and non-human in a way that undercuts the structural centrality of the human perspective.

'Ach, perhaps I should have left the moth alone', Jamie writes of a field trip in her essay collection *Sightlines*.[16] According to Heisenberg's uncertainty principle we interfere with the objects of our study in the act of studying them, and Jamie displays a scrupulous resistance to winning her epiphanies at the expense of the creatures she describes. Frequently in her essays she will be accompanied on her trips to far-flung places (St Kilda, North Rona) by a research scientist, with Jamie supplying the raw curiosity and the scientist the more hard-headed answers. Nor, it emerges, are these places quite as empty as we might imagine. Depopulated in 1930, St Kilda is now an important scientific and military base; the empty North Atlantic fringe is fertile territory for research into sustainability and renewable energy. In her essay 'Pathologies' (2008, collected in *Sightlines*, pp. 21–41) Jamie attends a conference on our relationship with other species and listens uneasily to talks that include a 'thrilling [...] encounter with sea-lions' and a 'transforming experience with polar bears', concerned by the narrowness of these definitions of 'nature' and our tendency to dramatise and misunderstand such interactions. Vaccinations, she reminds herself, are a way of formalising our distance from nature, and when it comes to lunch time 'what did we just eat, vegetarians aside? Deer meat, and very nice, too.' Jamie acknowledges the contradiction here between the animals

we exalt (the polar bear) and those we exploit (the deer), and is faced
with a choice between the reformist and the radical worldview. For the
reformist, animals and the environment are resources to be farmed and
consumed, and our human energies are best deployed in working out
the most sustainable methods of doing so. The simplistic appropriation
of polar bears and sea-lions for action adventure narratives is not in
contradiction with the venison on the menu, but coextensive with it:
both are symptoms of exploitation, conscious or otherwise. For the radical, by contrast, the animals are not ours to consume and should be left
entirely in peace.

Within ecopoetics, this difference manifests itself in a tension
between poems that respond to the environment as a theme, and those
that seek to incorporate their response into the form of the poem itself.
Contra Robert Minhinnick's advice, many serious writers have engaged
with the environment on the level of theme alone, with mixed artistic results. One example is Derek Mahon, whose early work exulted
in images of alienation, from oil-covered seabirds to abandoned mine
shafts: the opening line of his great poem 'A Disused Shed in Co.
Wexford' ('Even now there are places where a thought might grow')[17]
is almost a mantra for art-works resolved to create their own unique
environments far from the madding crowd. In recent years, he has
drifted increasingly towards Gaia-inspired poetry of reconciliation with
the earth. The critical question is whether justice to the earth and justice to poetry can be held together in sympathetic balance, or whether a
state of aesthetic dissonance is truer to the contradictions and conflicts
of our contemporary *malaise*. When Mahon spurns modernity in 'World
Trade Talks' (from his 2010 collection, *An Autumn Wind*) to reconnect
with classical pastoral ('Next spring, when a new crop begins to grow, /
let it not be genetically modified / but such as the ancients sowed / in
the old days'),[18] the reader is entitled to some scepticism as to who these
ancients might be and how confidently we might identify with them.
The pose of sage is too seductive, too readily taken up. Mahon turns an
amused gaze on Kinsale 'yoghurt-weaver' hippies in 'Homage to Gaia',
but between this, condemnations of over-consumption, and a paean to
an agreeable-sounding restaurant, we seek in vain for an over-arching
critique that might justify his title, *Life on Earth* (2008).[19] Formally too,
there is a lack of tension in the poem, suggesting the journey from
eco-complaint to holistic solution has taken place too quickly, and without sufficient engagement with poetry as the form of Mahon's homage.
A different line of attack can be found in Christopher Reid's 'Men
Against Trees', which opens with *sangfroid*, 'I note that the deforestation
of Brazil / is going ahead at a cracking pace', before saluting the work of
a chainsaw-wielding council worker ('You had to admire the insouciant
slob!').[20] Sometimes it is necessary for art to incorporate the chainsaw-like

disturbance of contrary positions, the illuminating dissonance without which art becomes a self-directed call and response, eliciting only what it already knows.

Jonathan Bate: Poetry and Prophecy

The best-known example of ecopoetics as a marriage of art and activism is Jonathan Bate's *The Song of the Earth*. Bate grafts contemporary ecopoetics onto the Romantic tradition with a strong belief in poetry's utopian force. At the heart of Romanticism is a paradox: nature is rediscovered and invented at the same time, as the modern dialectic of nature versus culture takes hold, supplanting the earlier definition whereby culture simply meant a cultivated field or piece of land.[21] Even as nature is championed, it is simultaneously consumed and exploited. In old age Wordsworth decried the extension of Victorian railway lines to the Lake District, but in his younger days had written a *Guide to the Lakes* (1810): then as now, no wilderness is so wild that it cannot become an object for imaginative colonisation. The cult of the Romantic artist involves separation from roots and the land, requiring an 'egotistical sublime' to articulate the values of country folk stripped of their power of self-determination and self-expression by industrial modernity. These generalisations might lead to a gloomy vision of alienation, but while he meditates on ecopoetics as 'a way of reflecting upon what it might mean to dwell with the earth' (rather than a series of practical prescriptions for change),[22] Bate is supremely confident of the power of poetry to bring about (or be) the change it envisions.

There is a long tradition in modern criticism of casting poetry in the role of last line of defence against barbaric modernity, the usual riposte to which is Raymond Williams's *bon mot* on the 'organic community': the one thing certain about the organic community is that it has always just vanished. The pattern reproduces itself continuously in modern nature poetry. As we have seen, Philip Larkin's 'Going, Going' goes in search of a lost England but finds only its heritage *ersatz*. Ted Hughes depicts the scarring of the Yorkshire moors by the industrial revolution in *Remains of Elmet* (1979) and campaigned against river-pollution, while remaining committed to the hunting and fishing of the countryside's traditional squirearchy-exploiter class, as explored in his account of life as a farmer-poet in *Moortown Diary* (1979) (never was there a less vegetarian poet). These are tense contradictions, not susceptible to easy resolution. Leavisite criticism prized 'organicism' as a bulwark of liberal values in a decadent world, though Leavis's hero D. H. Lawrence despaired of liberalism and toyed with more authoritarian political systems (the violence of nature in Hughes's work is a clear effect of Lawrence's influence). Bate has his version of this crux too, when he comes to the work of one of the greatest modern thinkers on nature, Martin Heidegger, who uncomfortably combined his environmentalism with a commitment to National Socialism and its search for racial purity. Resolving this contradiction is beyond Bate, whose argument comes to rest on an ontological ambivalence: poetry is a language that restores us to our home, or leads us to the realisation that language *is* our home. Politics yield to ontology.

Bate supplies a political reading of Keats's 'To Autumn' (1820), with its vision of dispossessed gleaners (rural poor dependent on scraps from the harvest and, like John Clare, recent victims of the Enclosure Acts), though without the more fevered speculations of Tom Paulin, who has seen the poem as a coded response to the Peterloo Massacre of 1819.[23] If anything, Bate is keen to remind us of the failures in store once we convert poetry into environmental agit-prop. He takes issue with the anthropocentrism of the word 'environment', 'because it presupposes the image of man at the centre, *surrounded* by things; ecosystem is the better word exactly because an ecosystem does not have a centre, it is a network of relations'.[24] It is when these relations are threatened, and the ecopoet is placed on the defensive, that unity of artistic vision comes under pressure. Among his examples is the Beat poet Gary Snyder, whose work preaches peaceful coexistence with nature but is sometimes forced to adopt a more hectoring tone ('The living actual people of the jungle sold and tortured – / And a robot in a suit who peddles the delusion called "Brazil"'). 'Worthy as the sentiments may be,' Bate notes, 'they do not in any sense grow from the poetry.'[25]

Desiring a social purchase for his words beyond the realm of art, the poet takes up the role of seer. A British equivalent would be Heathcote Williams, who has written best-selling but low-quality poetry books on the plight of the dolphin, the whale and the elephant, those poster-boy animals for environmental awareness. The greater the sense of unheeded urgency, the greater the appeal for the poet of the Cassandra role of spurned prophet, diluting her art with dire warnings of the catastrophe to come. Rejecting Snyder's example, Bate holds up for our approval instead poems by Elizabeth Bishop and Seamus Heaney. Lacking Hughes's out-and-out 'feral' quality, Bishop's 'The Moose' and Heaney's 'Crossings' use the human in the landscape as a focus for a more humanistic uncertainty and estrangement. A bus in Nova Scotia is stopped by a moose in the road; seeing a fox at dawn from his car, Heaney enjoys a moment of connection with nature but knows he is a visitor there. Bate's answer to the problem of back-to-nature absolutism (the problem being that it is not attainable) is to linger on the knowledge of separation, while accenting the epiphanic pleasure of the moments when nature does make itself available to us. Thus Bishop's is 'a poem not about getting back to nature, but about how nature comes back to us'; nature displays 'ineffability' and 'natural holiness', and our moments of contact with it are 'indescribably (save in poetry) precious'.[26] When the Heaney sequence moves on to deal with armed soldiers at a border checkpoint, Bate observes that 'Poets may sing the song that names earth and all living things upon it, but sometimes they have to stop and ask who lays claim to sovereignty over their land.'[27] Yet no sooner does he raise this question than he drops it, conferring a certain 'ineffability' on the political questions which Snyder, in his cruder way, had tried to import into his own poem. The stance of self-conscious nature poet, the role of intermediary between mute nature and alien- ated urbanites, and the show of concern at the encroachment of politics (regardless of what the political quarrel might be) – all add up to a powerful restatement of traditional Romanticism. Here again then, politics finds itself trumped by ontology, and Heaney's poem emerges from Bate's reading considerably watered down.

The picture of environmental despoliation painted by Bate pushes him towards an activist stance on the great issues of the day such as global warming, but how poetry is expected to tackle these issues in practice is never spelt out. Instead, his conclusion is unabashedly messi- anic. Nature is threatened not merely by property developers 'but more insidiously by the ubiquitous susurrus of cyberspace' (Bate's synecdoche for all that is inauthentic in how we live now), and only art can save us: 'if poetry is the original admission of dwelling, then poetry is the place where we save the earth'.[28] 'Think globally, act locally', the green slogan enjoins us. To speak of poetry saving the earth in this way marks the point at which criticism and wish-fulfilment meet, and the deep-green ecology of Heidegger and nature as the sphere of unified being promise to cancel our fall into modernity and its disastrous aftermath. Not all contemporary poets are so convinced of the ease of this manoeuvre, however. Traffic between the local and the global is a feature of much ecopoetry, but the cultural politics skated over by Bate have a way of reasserting themselves, and demanding admission into the fabric of poetic – and critical – discourse.

A Wind-Encircled Burial Mound: Michael Longley

Even when he is looking at otters or wader birds on a lake in the West of Ireland, there are few contemporary poets more deeply enmeshed in the politics of environment and poetic form than Michael Longley. Longley is a Northern Irish poet of English background, intimately influenced by the First World War poets and in particular Edward Thomas; his best critic, Fran Brearton, notes the 'particular ecological conscience' he shares with Thomas and John Clare.[29] When Longley writes of the West of Ireland – a frequent backdrop to his work – he is conscious of doing so at an oblique angle to local traditions, but conscious also of emulating another Northern Irish Protestant poet, Louis MacNeice, whose father's roots were in County Galway. Thomas is unusual among serious poets of the First World War in addressing himself not to the trenches and horrors around him, but exclusively to the remembered landscapes of home. He thus leaves himself open to the charge of pastoral escapism, but to paraphrase a line of Picasso's quoted in an earlier chapter, if he did not write of the war there is no doubt that the war is in his poems. So it is with Longley, whose Mayo landscapes might strike as escapist a reader who visualised the poetry of the Northern Irish Troubles as a form of on-the-spot reporting from the theatre of war. This is not how Longley's poetry works: often it is from the West of Ireland that he writes most probingly of the Troubles, and most probingly of the natural world to which he turns for elusive consolation. As an urbanite, Longley is more likely to be found looking at birds through binoculars than standing in the fields contemplating his ancestral connection to the land. Longley's wife, the critic Edna Longley, notes the presence in the West of Ireland of the great English-born cartographer Tim Robinson, and contrasts his and Michael Longley's work with the 'Heaney–Wordsworth georgic'. The work she has in mind 'doubly problematizes its own construction: wariness about intruding on other people's landscapes meshes with wariness about human intrusion on nature'.[30] Longley's second collection, *An Exploded View* (1973), features a series of verse letters to his contemporaries that place the city and the country in delicate juxtaposition. In the letter to Derek Mahon, written in Marvellian octosyllabics, Longley writes of 'the burnt-out houses of / The Catholics we'd scarcely loved', underlining the mismatch between his elegant stanzas and Belfast's sectarian violence. He takes refuge in memories of the Aran island of Inisheer, yet the images of the West are insistently muted by inhibition and failure. The visiting poets' footsteps are 'Hung with the failures of our trade', they are 'tongue-tied', 'strangers in that parish', keeping company with a local God 'we couldn't count among our friends'.[31] This may be Longley signalling the elaborate courtesies shown to visitors by country people, but it is also a way of undercutting the privilege on which pastoral traditionally rests. In the larger literary-political scheme of things, it is also an act of reconciliation between different and often non-communicating traditions. As Brearton writes:

■ The pull to-and-fro between Inisheer and Belfast [...], the complex identification with neither and both simultaneously, offers an alternative to the 'stereophonic nightmare' of one-dimensional communal loyalties: it suggests at least the possibility of both/and not either/or, a redefinition of what is or is not 'our own'.[32] □

In the next letter, to Seamus Heaney, the conservational tug of the rhyming couplets encompasses professional chit-chat and weak puns ('the sick counties we call home') before once again shifting scene to the West of Ireland. Though the poet 'slams his door' on the commotion of politics, they reappear in nightmare imagery. Longley performs an exorcism encompassing Orange marches, No Man's Land, coffin ships, all jumbled into one before turning to the elemental purity of the natural world at last, prolonging his 'sad recital':

> ■ By leaving careful footprints round
> A wind-encircled burial mound.[33] □

Ventriloquistically, the cry of the disturbed lapwing lodges in the poet's throat, even as the image of the startled bird in the mud evokes one of Longley's First World War scenes. Longley is drawn to elegy, and the closing 'wind-encircled burial mound' becomes a vanishing point in the verse letter for the opposition of urban ironies and rural escape. The footprints round the burial mound carry the elegiac impulse into the natural world, inscribing it wordlessly. As Brearton notes, there is a tension between the 'seductiveness of purity' and 'the necessary engagement with impurity', and 'a door half open between the two'.[34]

To write a poem about a bird or a landscape is to engage in anthropomorphism, filtering the non-human through language and reconfiguring it in our image. Some writers engage with this problem through verbal extravagance, catching the natural world up in the sublime raptures of the Romantic style. When Shelley writes of the skylark, 'Hail to thee, blithe spirit! / Bird thou never wert' he sublimates the bird almost out of existence (a more banal explanation is the height at which the skylark flies, making it invisible even as its song remains audible). When George Oppen writes in his poem 'Psalm' of some deer in the undergrowth, 'That they are there!' it is as if, by contrast, the poem is pulling away from describing the animals, imitating the speaker's reluctance to disturb them:[35] that they are there is enough in itself. Longley's verse letters are undoubtedly extravagant, while feeling the pull of a more windswept and anti-anthropocentric impulse. In an influential reading of the Northern Irish poets, Christopher Ricks coined the phrase 'self-inwoven simile' for poetic conceits of the 'x of itself' type (Seamus Heaney's Grauballe man weeping 'the black river of himself').[36] For Ricks, the turn inwards was a response to the violent pressures of civil unrest, but also a mark of defiant linguistic exuberance. In Longley's later work, after a creative hiatus in the 1980s, elegy remains central but acquires a new starkness as he abandons the rhyme of his earlier collections. A child being deported from a ghetto in Poland is described with the line 'Your last belonging a list of your belongings';[37] the self-inwoven simile has become the mark of despairing interiority, shorn of all external aid. Returning to his County Mayo landscapes, however, Longley keeps faith with this starkness while finding bold new ways of imprinting the landscape on his poems. In 'Form' he echoes a short lyric of W. B. Yeats which plays on the fact that a hare's nest is known as a form. 'Trying to tell it all', writes Longley, is like waking a hare from its form: 'In that make-shift shelter your hand, then my hand / Mislays the hare and the warmth it leaves behind.'[38] As in Yeats's poem, the hare and even its warm aftermath give the poem the slip. What remains is pure 'form', a form that is all the fuller for encompassing the absence it describes. Poetry may not be able to check or reverse the tide of loss and politics, but like no other art it retains their imprint in the living stream of lyric form.

Radical Earth and Edgelands: Mapping the Terrain

The tension between reformist and radical strains in environmental activism finds expression in the canons of ecopoetics too. One way of framing the difference is between the holistic and a more post-lapsarian worldview. Does there exist an originary wholeness to which we gain access through nature? The anthology *Earth Shattering: Eco Poems* (Bloodaxe Books, 2007) is divided into nine sections, of which the first is titled 'Rooted in Nature'. Wang Wei, Li Po, Wordsworth, Rilke and Don Paterson are yoked together in a vision of shared natural patrimony. The second and third sections, 'Changing the Landscape' and 'Killing the Wildlife', contract their focus from the global to the Anglosphere, following an arc from Goldsmith's 'The Deserted Village' (1770) to Tony Harrison's 'Art & Extinction' and suggesting that the destruction of nature is very much a by-product of Western capitalism. This is then complemented by a recovery narrative that draws on the wisdom of non-Western cultures to restore our lost wholeness, such as we find in the work of American poets Gary Snyder, Joy Harjo and Mary Oliver. Among British poets, Ted Hughes occupies a central position and appears solidly anti-Enlightenment in his ecological stance, seeing pollution as part of our belief in the right to exploit nature unhindered for our own ends. Yet Hughes's conservative vision also extends to a passion for blood sports and, as *Earth Shattering* points out, a mystical belief in monarchy as the 'essential centre'[39] on which society is grounded, as reflected in his laureate poems. How can concern for ecology coexist with the vast estates held by the aristocracy and their use as game reserves? The contradiction is deeply threaded through Hughes's work, emerging in the flailing and undirected violence into which his poems often descend, most famously *Crow* (1970).

Answers to these questions go beyond the scope of *Earth Shattering*. A different approach can be found in Harriet Tarlo's 2011 anthology *The Ground Aslant*, a volume that reports from more marginal zones, as hinted in its subtitle, *An Anthology of Radical Landscape Poetry*. In her introduction, Tarlo admits to trouble with terminology: landscape poetry is not pastoral is not ecopoetry. While the exact dividing lines are a matter for debate, readers more used to the Kenneth Baker map of the territory-as-national-possession will recognise how far from the usual nature trail we have strayed when confronted by the work of Colin Simms, Tony Baker, Wendy Mulford or Helen Macdonald, poets who publish with Shearsman and Reality Street rather than the bigger commercial presses, and the authors of collections with titles such as *Terrain Seed Scarcity* (2001) and *Lessways Least Scarce Among* (2012).

Through its very existence alone, *The Ground Aslant* helps to correct a number of widespread but groundless assumptions. The first is that British experimental writing operates in a realm either of rarefied abstraction or of metropolitan indifference to anything beyond the city limits. A second misconception is that landscape poetry belongs to an organic tradition (that of Frost and Edward Thomas), onto which experimental writers trespass at their peril: if Pound or Olson or their British followers write about nature it goes against type, runs the argument, whereas Frost, Thomas and their contemporary heirs simply belong by river and tarn, in the natural order of things. A third assumption is that experimental writing proceeds from theory to practice, bypassing any individual sensibility and producing clone poetry much as urban planners now produce clone towns, when in reality Peter Riley is as different from Frances Presley or Nicholas Johnson as Gary Snyder is from Robert Hass or Mary Oliver. As Tarlo writes:

■ Whereas Pastoral often sentimentalizes the rural life, radical landscape poetry is more realistic in its view of contemporary landscape, rural people and past and present agricultural and social issues. Here [...] we find ample examples of work which resists narrative and realist *conventions* in poetry in favour of evolving techniques and structures which aim to create a truer reflection of reality itself.[40] □

The equation of the experimental with the urban has also thrown up a peculiar obverse of Tarlo's revisionism in the form of psychogeography and its contemporary variants. Originating in French situationism and the work of Guy Debord, psychogeography is best known in Britain through the work of Iain Sinclair and Peter Ackroyd. For the psycho-geographer, the sites of unregarded urban experience become occasions of mythopoeia, often with a gothically hysterical dimension, as in the picaresque adventures of *Lights Out for the Territory* (1997). Sinclair's editorship of *Conductors of Chaos* and hostility towards the mainstream has further cemented the link between urbanism and experiment. Yet in *London Orbital* (2002), which charts a walk around the M25, Sinclair confronts the unenchanted suburban landscapes in which the metropolis peters out, and in *Edge of the Orison: In the Traces of John Clare's 'Journey Out Of Essex'* (2005) he re-creates a journey of one of the greatest of all ecopoets, John Clare. Just as Sinclair was getting out of the city, Paul Farley and Michael Symmons Roberts staged an attempt to occupy Sinclair's patch in *Edgelands* (2011), which addresses itself not so much to cities as to the overlooked spaces round their edges: the ring roads, conference centres and business parks in which so much of contemporary life takes place, and the industrial canals and disused mills where voles, falcons and foxes often enjoy less persecution than they do in the coun-tryside. Where Sinclair is twitchy and angst-ridden, Farley and Symmons Roberts are warmly nostalgic. Marginal, unoccupied or ruined build-ings possess a potent cultural charge: the unresolved tension between works such as *London Orbital* and *Edgelands* lays bare the struggle between estrangement and naturalisation as ways of building them into the fabric of poetic environments.

R. F. Langley: Landscape, Enclosure, Text

One of the great shifts in the relationship of Britons to the land came with the Enclosure Acts of the nineteenth century, under which large tracts of the countryside were taken out of public ownership, causing much suf-fering to the rural poor. They also caused much distress to John Clare, the poet singled out by Harriet Tarlo as the lodestar of radical landscape writing. Where his contemporary Shelley is ethereal and abstract, Clare is incura-bly descriptive, displaying a loving attention to the 'creaturely' dimension of the natural world in his native Northamptonshire, and winning him many contemporary admirers. Clare's work engages with the nature of public space, seeing the natural world as part of a 'commons' at risk of pri-vatisation. He spent the final decades of his life in an insane asylum, and in a bizarre twist his work has been the subject of a textual 'enclosure', with his twentieth-century editor claiming exclusive control of his copyrights. Clare has thus become a focal point not just for ecopoetics but textual scholarship too. A striking engagement with Clare's legacy can be found in the work of R. F. Langley, whose poem 'Matthew Glover' explores what rootedness in, or attachment to, the landscape might mean today. Langley (1938–2011) was a Cambridge contemporary of J. H. Prynne, but produced an *oeuvre* whose modest dimensions (his *Collected Poems* of 2001 contained a mere seventeen poems) bespeak an aversion to maximalist shows of ambition. In ornithology, the term 'subsong' is used of the sounds produced by a young bird before it has learned to associate song with territorial display – tuning-up noises, almost – and beside a more orthodox Romantic style Langley's too might be described as 'subsong'. The poem begins with a description of a village before the Enclosure Act, and while it has a certain Edenic quality, Langley shies away from parading his fair field full of folk in conventional pastoral style, preferring an elliptic presentation. As Jeremy Noel-Tod has observed, 'His poems shrink interestingly from the single, arrogating point of view, the self-possessed lyric "I". You, I, he, she, we, and it are liable to take each other's place without warning.'[41] Amidst this uncertainty, the landscape acquires its reality in terms of textual imprints or traces:

> ■ this tract waited
> for a mark, for a –
> they would call it
> navel[42] □

Where Clare's poetic world suffered from the prosy impositions of the enclosures, Langley's poem subtly alters perspectives as it advances, shifting to a more formal style to describe the effects of the change on village life. Neither for nor against the enclosures, the eponymous Matthew Glover is too bewildered to express his feelings. Langley succeeds in giving voice to Glover's place (or lack of place) in the new dispensation, by aligning him with a nature henceforth seen as decorative but impotent, as the poem slips almost furtively away, a willow-wren's colours disappearing into 'no hint // or half a hint // not enough to decide'.

In Philip Larkin's 'Afternoons', something pushes the women 'to the side of their own lives', and what Langley gives us here is the sense of the shift itself, like a slowly moving tectonic plate. The Italian thinker Gianni Vattimo has coined the phrase 'weak thought' (*pensiero debole*) for modes of thought which seek the emancipatory dimension of pessimism, and beside other poets' responses to social change and injustice (such as Tony Harrison) Langley is a prime exemplar of a self-consciously weak, undemonstrative style.[43] Like the willow-wren's song, 'Matthew Glover' aspires to be almost 'too slight' for its own good, making of its textual condition a site of resistance. As it wanders between registers, a poem such as 'Matthew Glover' brushes the lyric voice up against the boundary lines of other forms of discourse, neither surrendering to their superior political force nor fetishising its own purity. Apologetic and defiant at once, its closing 'half a hint' conjures horizons well beyond its modest confines.

Ecopoetics and the Site-Specific

Site-specificity is a concept more often encountered in the visual arts than in poetry, but the work of Ian Hamilton Finlay (1925–2006) constitutes a special case. Finlay is among the most important figures in contemporary landscape writing; not just a writer, he was also an artist, sculptor, concrete poet and 'avant-gardener'. His work overcomes the anxieties of its relationship to nature by, in many cases, becoming a physical part of it, most famously in the garden he created in Little Sparta in the Scottish Pentland Hills. Finlay's relations with the avant-garde and cultural nationalism expose important conflicts in modern and contemporary poetics, leaving many critics ill-equipped to respond. As Alec Finlay and Ken Cockburn have written: 'The Concrete Poetry movement [represented by Finlay] is a late episode in Modernism which [...] suggests alternative routes through the landscape of Scottish poetry as a whole.'[44] He forged connections with American poets such as Robert Creeley, Lorine Niedecker, and Cid Corman, whom he published in his journal *Poor. Old. Tired. Horse* (1962–68). As Richard Price observes: 'It is a classic example of how a little magazine [...] can operate effectively as a networking node, establishing a nub of contact' whose importance is not immediately apparent when judged against its 'longevity or circulation'.[45] Another tool against marginality (especially in the absence of an academic bailiwick, that frequent life-support system for more recent avant-gardes) is controversy, and Finlay was a ferocious polemicist who launched numerous campaigns against the Scottish arts establishment, even if – as Andrew Duncan has noted – he encountered an 'obscurantist and obstructive stance' from within Scottish avant-garde circles, in the form of Hugh MacDiarmid.[46] Finlay's work abounds in violent imagery (tanks, battleships, guillotines), and when commissioned by the French government to mark the bicentenary of the French Revolution his designs made use of the Waffen-SS lightning symbol (the commission was controversially dropped). If nothing else, this side of Finlay's imagination is a rebuff to those who would equate ecopoetics with well-behaved liberal politics. Where gardens as pastoral spaces have traditionally been equated with retreats, for Finlay 'they are really attacks',[47] dynamic and provocative spaces in which to bring his poetics to life.

Mallarmé famously informed Degas that poems are made out of words, not ideas, but Finlay frequently goes one step further and celebrates the individual letters from which words are made in acrostics, paronomasia and other word-games. Frequently, he transforms banal text to reveal the presence of the mythic in the everyday, as when the sequence 'Fishing News' turns a newspaper headline, 'Shetland Boats Turn to Scallops', into what might be a scenario from Ovid, or extracts a cosmic poetry from a fishing boat's name ('Ocean Starlight Towed Off Rocks').[48] Finlay is fascinated by pre-Socratic philosophy, and its sense of a world in which thoughts are actions rather than abstractions, as reflected in his compulsion to give his work the site-specificity of sculptural installation. The pre-Socratics are known to us chiefly through fragments, and Finlay delighted in ultra-short (one-word) poems, taking Pound's insistence that the natural object is always the adequate symbol to an impossible extreme. Frequently, the title of these short poems will be longer than the poem itself, but even so there will be space for the two to interact in a way that lifts the natural world into the realm of the *makar* (in the antique Scottish word for a poet) and of artistic creation. 'The Boat's Blueprint', for instance, reads, simply: 'water',[49] which is to say both the element for which the boat is designed and the mark it will leave on the sea. To spell the poem out in this manner is already to do it a form of violence (where his concrete poems were concerned, Finlay was adamant that they could not and should not be read aloud); these objects display extreme resistance to interpretation or appropriative repackaging. This resistance extends to Little Sparta, which remains a living entity rather than a frozen monument to its creator. Finlay's installations aspire to be merely *there*, in Heideggerian *Dasein*, supremely themselves and nothing besides. The difference between this vision and Jonathan Bate's, however, is that the violence of politics is paradoxically at the centre of the classical stillness Finlay's art inhabits. For Nicholas Zurbrugg, the '"exact" ideogrammatic structures' of Finlay's visual poems 'could not be more distant from the studied subjective intensity' in which the Beats or Confessional poets announced themselves to the world, carving out instead a space that is revolutionary but neo-classical too (the French Revolution again).[50]

Finlay's legacy is lively but problematic within Scottish and *avant-garde* critical debate. For a writer normally happy to scourge the *avant-garde*, Don Paterson possesses a Zen-like side whose shorter (and in some cases wordless) poems are heavily indebted to Finlay, while the work of an 'Informationist' poet such as Richard Price synthesises Finlay and his American contemporaries. Yet the relationship between the theory and practice of ecopoetics is significantly different from other fields in which practitioners are shadowed by theorists. While conventionally, as in American Language poetry, this doubling-up can be a sign of institutionalisation, with ecopoetics in its more dynamic manifestations practice and theory alike move out of the academy and into the field. For all its classical poise, Finlay's art is one of furious energy, synthesising the full panoply of activities from which ecopoetics is made – doing, making, writing, thinking, being. As Zurbrugg observes, in an age when most literary theory has argued for the demise of 'master narratives', 'the death of authorial originality and the disappearance of all authenticity', Finlay's work 'repeatedly demonstrate[s] that metaphorical meditations upon the conflict between order and disorder may still have considerable social, historical, political, spiritual, and aesthetic impact'.[51]

Water Music: Alice Oswald

Among the finest British poets to have emerged in recent years, Alice Oswald has provided startling new impetus to the tradition of English landscape writing. While her first collection, *The Thing in the Gap-Stone Stile* (1996), was well received, it was with her second, *Dart* (2002), that Oswald made her real breakthrough. Described as 'a sort of poetic census', *Dart* arose from several years of conversations with people who live by or make their living on the river Dart in Devon. Oswald has worked with Ian Hamilton Finlay, and Oswald's work too seems not just to arise out of, but to return bodily to its sources. So closely does Oswald work with her thoughts that the act of labelling her in any way seems wrong: 'She writes taut poems about nature but refuses to call them "nature poems"', as Aingeal Clare has written.[52] The intensity of Oswald's response to the natural world marks her out as a successor to Ted Hughes, but the structure of *Dart* as a poetic *roman fleuve*, its wordplay, and ecstatic immersion in its aqueous element, all suggest continuities with the Joyce of *Anna Livia Plurabelle* or its poetic recension in Hugh MacDiarmid's 'Water Music'. A series of marginal annotations supply our location throughout the poem and the identities of the speakers, while acknowledging Oswald's role as a writer in the field and insisting on the mediating framework through which we encounter the river's stories (Coleridge's 'Rime of the Ancient Mariner' (1798) too came with marginal annotations). Deryn Rees-Jones reads these various speakers as subsumed in the poet's 'unifying voice', a voice that 'creates the self' as it goes along,[53] when the poem might instead be seen as subtly resistant to the usual narrative underpinnings of voice and self. The poem constantly plays on its own forward movement ('all I know is walking / [...] What I love is one foot in front of another'),[54] but switches rapidly between quasi-blank verse, short prose paragraphs and ultra-short lines ('listen, / a / lark / spinning / around / one / note / splitting / and / mending / it'), refusing any settled form. Roy Fisher has spoken of a 'polytheism with-out gods',[55] and Oswald re-enchants her landscapes with all the force of paganism but none of the pseudo-shamanism we encounter in the work of the psychogeographers: here is no blighted urbanism to be overlaid with Hawksmoor pentagrams and ley lines, but an ability to switch from the perspective of a forester to a wood nymph or an oak tree with Protean skill, minus any gothic accompaniments. Tensions bubble under throughout between the desire to let the river speak for itself and the human uses to which we put it, whether in industry and fishing or the flights of fancy of Romantic tradition. Rees-Jones registers this in finding both 'harmony and disunity' in the poem's vision of England and its equation of the river with a space in which 'myth and modern technology coalesce'.[56] English dialect speech can appear twee in written form, but Oswald's solution, in a passage spoken by the river, is to invent a dialect speech and syntax of her own ('come falleth in my push-you where it hurts').[57] In a passage reminiscent of Hughes's *Remains of Elmet*, a description of harnessing the river for the manufacture of dye culminates in a (blank) page of silence, marking the river's desire for privacy but also our erosion of its voice. Hughes was a passionate environmentalist, as we have seen, and the tension identified by Rees-Jones may point towards the ambivalent aspects of his legacy for Oswald. Foraging and scavenging are opposed to the more destructive modes of industrial exploitation, and form implied metaphors for Oswald's artistic process ('I'm a gatherer, an amateur, a scavenger [...] my whole style's a stone wall, just wedging together what happens to be lying about at the time.')[58] They are also opposed to the mythic master narratives that attracted Hughes, presenting themselves instead as a form of inspired *bricolage*.

In her subsequent work, such as *Woods etc.* (2005) and *Weeds and Wild Flowers* (2009), Oswald has continued to re-orient landscape writing towards a style of creaturely intensity owing much to William Blake. The poem titles of *Woods etc.* are defiantly elemental and lacking in displays of local colour: 'Autobiography of a Stone', 'Field', 'River'. Here again there are Hughesian precedents (Hughes's *River*), but with a self-consciously philosophical density, half 'Auguries of Innocence', half Martin Heidegger, decentring the poems' apparent simplicity and making of the shortest lyrics gestures of epistemology, interrogations of our forms of knowing through the medium of verse. Finding residues of literary Anglicanism in Oswald's style, Aingeal Clare wonders about its spirituality:

■ the words read like the lyrics of a hymn whose organ accompaniment has been lost. As prayer it has no spirit, and as poetry its icy tidiness fails to live up to the watermark left by *Dart*. [...] Geoffrey Hill, in answer to critics complaining that he was incapable of grasping true religious experience, said that he was 'trying to make lyrical poetry out of a much more common situation – the sense of *not* being able to grasp true religious experience'.[59] □

One answer to Clare's anxieties is Oswald's reluctance to provide those organ-notes of the spiritual sublime. Trying to account for the difference between modern English and French poetry, Michael Hamburger contends that French poetry 'begins with "essences"' whereas English poetry 'begins with "aspects" or appearances', his example being a poem by Yves Bonnefoy about a lizard. Anglophone readers, he suggests, would find the poem too transparently a 'pretext' for the poet's mood, with its meditation on consciousness and solitude, to be convincing;[60] Oswald's achievement, repeatedly, is to find a style that does full philosophical justice to these themes, without any need to place the first-person pronoun centre-stage, leaving the poem a 'pretext' for nothing but its own occasion, with an absence where public gestures towards the 'spirit' might be. When a narrative 'I' obtrudes, as in 'Walking past a Rose this June Morning', an almost-comically insistent use of repetition repels its claims on our attention:

> ■ is my heart a rose?   how unspeakable
> is my heart folded to dismantle?   how unspeakable
> is a rose folded in its nerves?   how unspeakable[61] □

The entirety of *Woods etc.* is marked by incantatory repetitions and anaphoric syntax, lightly punctuated: describing birdsong as 'A song that assembles the earth'[62], Oswald reasserts the poet's role as a visionary but impersonal maker as much as a simple observer. For Carol Rumens, the questing nature of these poems means that Oswald 'disrupts syntax and opens up her stanzas in an almost mimetic way'.[63] In performance Oswald typically reads (or recites) her poems twice, once for the sound and once for the sense, and in her most recent work, *Memorial* (2011), a litany of death scenes from Homer, she reproduces the similes twice on the page too. As the author of a half-dozen books, Oswald is at the transitional point between a prize-winning newcomer and a poet who seems assured of canonical status. Like Finlay before her, she has channelled the pastoral tradition back to classical roots, but also into new and audacious forms (the book-length sequence, subsuming her individually exquisite lyrics). Oswald also shows affinities with Canadian poet Anne Carson, whose books have novelistic ambitions of their own, with heavily signalled debts to the Graeco-Roman classics.

'A Fragile and Usually Over-Written Map': Peter Riley's Palimpsests

As the joke puts it, archaeology is a load of old rubbish. Many of the writers considered here have engaged in poetic excavations of the past,

but one writer whose uncoverings of the distant past have done much
to bring British poetry into new environments is Peter Riley. Despite
his Cambridge affiliations, his work can be read in relation to any
number of other contexts, from 1940s poetry (he has championed the
work of the neglected Nicholas Moore) to the prose of John Cowper
Powys and the landscape art of Richard Long. He is also a poet of frank
emotional directness, whose vocabulary of 'Trust, Love and Kindness' is
'systematised within an ontological framework derived from Merleau-
Ponty and Heidegger'.[64] Riley has written travelogues of Romania
(*The Dance at Mociu*, 2003), a meditation on the Peak District that ranks
among the more ambitious long poems of recent years (*Alstonefield*,
1995), and explorations of his personal Celtic fringe (*The Llŷn Writings*,
2007), but in his 2004 sequence *Excavations* he most fully interro-
gates the question of landscape as palimpsest, a permanently written
and over-written field. *Excavations* addresses the Saxon burial mounds
of East Yorkshire, drawing on the work of Edwardian archaeologist
J. R. Mortimer, and internalises its subject matter in the time capsules,
or chambers, in which the text is arranged. The book's 175 fragments
mix Riley's own words with italicised and bold-face quotations from
Mortimer, Elizabethan lyrics, and a '10% anarchic principle' of mock
quotation. As Riley, or Mortimer, or the anarchic ghost in the machine,
writes: *'I conceived the idea that in this art of funerary ceremonial the opportunity of a death was taken as the occasion of a total theatre, of which the final
disposition left in the earth was the dénouement, of which the excavator finds a
fragile and usually over-written map.'*[65] As Jon Thompson has argued, *Excavations* can be read as a disguised elegy for the present.[66] Its form elegises
a collage-based modernist style that texts as diverse as David Jones's
The Anathémata (1952), Hugh MacDiarmid's *In Memoriam James Joyce*
(1955) and Lynette Roberts's *Gods with stainless ears* (1951) should have,
but have not, naturalised for readers of contemporary poetry; Geoffrey
Hill's *Mercian Hymns* is another obvious intertext. The book's own archaeology is not irrelevant here, part one appearing as *Distant Points* in 1995,
before being reinterred in expanded form a decade later. The long poem
Alstonefield too has had a peregrine existence from original ('unfinished')
version to a later revision to the further layer of topsoil we find in *The
Day's Final Balance: Uncollected Writings 1965–2006* (2007). Riley's texts
have also flitted from publisher to publisher, between British small press
stalwarts Reality Street, Shearsman and West House Books, to Carcanet,
and beyond to the US. 'Making a work is not thinking thoughts but
accomplishing an actual journey', David Jones wrote in *The Anathémata*,[67]
a principle Riley's work has honoured in all manner of ways down
the decades. A telling difference between Wordsworth and Coleridge,
on their shared walks in the Lake District, was Wordsworth's keeping
to the straight and narrow, while Coleridge habitually veered at an

unpredictable zig-zag across the path, much to the inconvenience of his walking companions. With Riley, there is often no discernible path or destination, but his journeys are among the most urgent and rewarding in the gazetteer of contemporary ecopoetics. In these works, place, movement and habitation are imagined anew, laying down paths and palimpsests for future excavation.

Lost Worlds and New Territories

The Peter Reading touted by Tom Paulin as the 'laureate of grot' was also, in his unusual way, an ecopoet. Isabel Martin's study, *Reading Peter Reading* (2000), pays little attention to Reading as a poet of the natural world, locating his bleak consolations instead in classical Latin, Greek and Chinese poetry, though in a 1994 appreciation Dennis O'Driscoll found Reading 'a poet concerned about environmental issues long before it became fashionable' but at odds with sentimental and anthropomorphic nature poetry.[68] In the final phase of his career, however, corresponding roughly to the third volume of his *Collected Poems* (2003) and the two collections that followed it, ecological poems achieved a new prominence in the Reading *oeuvre*. In collections such as *Marfan* (2000), *Faunal* (2002) and *–273.15* (2005), he writes poignantly of the natural world, especially birds, and with a hard-edged insistence on avoiding anthropomorphism. A Reading poem about a bird will typically describe the sighting (often mentioning his binoculars), give the bird's scientific name, and then the alcoholic beverage with which he later salutes it. Anything more, he implies, is anthropomorphism and not to be countenanced. Like Longley's child whose possessions amounted only to a list of possessions, the world of eco-catastrophe drawn in *–273.15* is one in which biodiversity is shrinking alarmingly to a list of names for species that may soon have vanished forever.

A paradox of the writing studied here is that so many of its environments find poetic expression just at the moment when they seem on the point of disappearance. The disappearance or blurring of the urban–rural divide is visible in the work of contemporary poetry's most distinguished chronicler of the city, Roy Fisher, principally in the sequences *City* and *A Furnace*. The work of other urban poets, from Peter Didsbury and Sean O'Brien to Ciaran Carson, grapples with the same dilemma. While the poetry of urban experience has been closely read for lessons on the theme of class, it has just as much to offer to ecopoetical readings. This too is an expanding field in search of a critical vocabulary: in his *Contemporary British Poetry and the City* (2001) Peter Barry is forced to ask, shamefacedly, where all the women poets of the city are, his answer being that women and men configure urban space differently ('Undoubtedly there is a book to be written about the city and contemporary women's poetry, but I had to conclude that tackling the topic adequately is beyond my range').[69]

In Carson's *Belfast Confetti* (1993) and *The Irish for No* (1987), the poet addresses an environment that strongly resists representation: the map may refuse to show it for security reasons, it may have been destroyed in rioting or explosions, or the poet may have drifted off on the currents of a shaggy dog tale of times past, walking historic or mythic landscapes whose overlap with present reality is tangential. While Carson remains an exponent of the Northern Irish lyric, his engagement with themes of political violence and the use of found texts have pushed his work in the direction of experimental writing in recent years, as critics have noted.[70] In Didsbury and O'Brien's cityscapes, the templates are chiefly the Northern locales of Hull and Newcastle, whose post-industrial dereliction seems to create a second-order natural landscape of railway sidings and Victorian warehouses. Do these poems look backwards or forwards? Michael Hofmann captures this ambivalence superbly in his 'Eclogue', normally a classical poem on a pastoral subject, but in this case a poem on a worked-out industrial landscape. Hofmann reaches for myth to dignify the ugliness, imagining his Victorian industrialist as Pluto abducting Proserpina to live in the underworld with him, before ending with an image of the inverted sublime:

> ■ A quarry is an inverted cathedral: witchcraft,
> a steeple of air sharpened and buried in the ground.[71] □

In the films of Russian Andrei Tarkovsky, dystopian visions find expression in scenes of abandoned factories and churches, yet – as in *Stalker* (1979), with its voyage to a mysterious forbidden 'zone' – these spaces conceal the secrets of renewal and wisdom too; it is on the far side of dereliction, rather than in our nostalgic dreams of unsullied nature, that we must look for sites of imaginary freedom.

An article of faith among some neo-Romantics is the hostility of poetry and science. The examples we have considered so far share an aversion to narrowly-prescribed precepts of nature writing, and the use of scientific material is another way in which contemporary poets have refused the discursive quarantine of poetry as a less than all-encompassing language. The recycling of un- or semi-digested scientific language is a central part of Prynne's aesthetic, but a more concentrated use of scientific responses to the environment can be found in the work of Helen Macdonald. Macdonald is a historian of conservation and ecology, and the author of *Shaler's Fish* (2001). Macdonald writes out of the Cambridge tradition: 'The excision of familiar teleologies, poetic or personal, has been fairly thorough', as Andrew Duncan notes.[72] But where the Cambridge poem stereotypically prefers to be, not mean (to paraphrase Archibald MacLeish), the objective correlative of her work – to use Eliot's term for the series of images or the *mise-en-scène* by which a work delivers its deeper meaning – is always hugely if mysteriously there, in the form of her birds:

> ■ inspiration like dry skin in its diminution silence
> and the sky is as motionless as the heart
> its hook to tie it from[73] □

Macdonald is a falconer and has written a fine prose book on the falcon, but as anyone who has flown a bird of prey knows, captive-bred birds allow us to get close to them at the cost of a certain denaturing; an imprinted bird will consider its handler not just a parent but also a sexual partner. The hook in these lines from 'Noar Hill' represents both the ties of affection and the bird's captivity on a leash: a double-bind indeed. Falconer and falcon commune across the species divide, but subject to these denaturing convergences, the human equivalent being the shamanistic melancholy we find in a great, but yearningly elegiac poem such as Macdonald's 'letter to america'. Dialogue across species becomes the basis of self-identification: 'I am a conversation across oceans', the poet declares, experiencing 'uncertainty or surprise // surviving precisely as a desire for redundancy'. The bird's approach to its handler induces dizziness wrapped in a double negative: 'as if / it weren't in fact anything other than the imaginary / front sight of one index pressed to your brow / which held you to a name and its willing execution'. The writing is painstakingly detailed: if the Romantics' exaltation of nature depended on the relegation of science, these poems are proof enough that a technical vocabulary has its magical aura too. Yet Macdonald stops short of claiming outright intimacy with her subject, falling back on reverent guesswork: the hawk 'rous[es] one's mind from safety and tameable illness / to beautiful comprehension in the form of a hunch'. Duncan lists some of the ways in which Macdonald's poems achieve these effects ('the avoidance of "functional" awareness, the use of simultaneity, the jumps between disparate ideas, the staging of complex fields of intellectual enquiry inviting long-term attention, the reliance on personal consciousness, the preference for conjecture over stabilised facts'), but ascribes her poems' success to the unique cluster of 'internal relationships' of which they are composed, just as the pattern formed by a flock of birds represents the sum of collective behavioural patterns for which no one bird is responsible.[74]

A distinctly Cambridge aspect of Macdonald's style is its sudden ninety-degree syntactic turns away from what we think is coming next, and which in context can be read as imitating the falcon's feints, banks and plunges: 'a static click breaking into small worlds / where death has music in a vice-like // I think not'. A prose classic of British nature writing, J. A. Baker's *The Peregrine (1967)*, ends by rewarding its author's obsessive pursuit of that bird with a drowsy peregrine on a branch, its usual instincts of suspicion and flight suspended, but the last lines of 'letter to america' unite author and bird in an epiphany of joint scattering into the air, a conclusion no less powerful for seeming to leave us with nothing but 'the pure suburban heavens'. Macdonald's is difficult but powerfully rewarding poetry. Here is not merely a bird poem, but poetry as a bird, sleek, effortless, difficult, cruel, unknowable and lovely:

> ■ looking for a small world in the uninhabitable air
> trying to extinguish some deeper desire for fire
> with something as cold and as hard and as temporary as flight[75] □

Conclusion: Criticism Today

In December 2011, citing her 'unease about a system that puts profit before ethics and makes protest a criminal act',[1] Alice Oswald withdrew from the shortlist for the T. S. Eliot Prize in protest at the sponsorship of the Poetry Book Society (PBS) by Aurum. An investment firm that manages hedge funds, Aurum had stepped in after a cut to the PBS's funding from the Arts Council. Replying to Oswald, one of the prize judges, Gillian Clarke, made a case for enlightened patronage of the arts, even if the money behind it comes from less than fragrantly ethical sources: 'Take it from the rich, give it to a poet and reader. The T. S. Eliot prize cleans the money.'[2] With its unfortunate overtones of money-laundering, Clarke's argument makes a poor job of bridging the worlds of poetry and corporate finance. The controversy serves to remind us of the difficult pact poetry must strike with the larger culture in which it functions. It can maintain its integrity at a protective distance from the world of hedge funds, or aspire to the wealth and prestige of other arts forms at the expense of its virtuous self-image. The equation of poetry and virtue is by no means beyond debate, just as the idea of the autonomy of poetry (rather than its dependence on a wealthy patron) is a post-Romantic innovation. Few of Aurum's detractors would claim that poetry is above all considerations of finance and *Realpolitik*, and as we have seen throughout this book the encounter of poetry and politics – whether class, gender, or postcolonial – rarely finds successful expression in absolutist positions. Poetry is not free to select the conditions under which it is made today, but must explore the experience of brushing up against (or being mauled by) politics and the public sphere.

The public face of poetry in the United Kingdom is the poet laureate, a job whose holders have ranged from the august to the forgotten. When Wordsworth accepted the post in 1843, it was on condition that he not be expected to produce any verse for state occasions, and later holders of the office have also struggled with their duties as court bard to the royal family. Ted Hughes, laureate from 1984 to 1998, was an anomaly: the laureate poems collected in *Rain-Charm for the Duchy* (1992) display an almost mystical belief in the crown and the mythic-divine status of the royal family. Appointed by Tony Blair, Andrew Motion was a consummate moderniser, altering the term of office to a decade and producing large amounts of undistinguished work on topical themes.

As the first woman laureate Carol Ann Duffy attracted controversy, but whether writing on celebrity culture, a royal wedding or the murder of Stephen Lawrence, Duffy has embraced an aesthetic of accessibility, cheerily recycling the language of the mass media. The vocabulary of Orwell's Newspeak is famously shrunken, but while the degraded language of today's media is a fitting subject for poetic scrutiny, there is a problematic line between satirical scrutiny of, and unwitting surrender to its reductiveness.

The only post in Britain comparable to that of laureate for its public profile is the Oxford Professorship of Poetry. Geoffrey Hill, its holder since 2010, has followed a different route of public engagement from that of Duffy. Hill used a lecture of 2011, 'Poetry, Policing and Public Order' – its title playing on his father's profession of village constable, and implying that he was 'policing' his poetic patch – to attack the shortcomings of Duffy's aesthetic. Hill's intervention is intriguing for a number of reasons: first, for his willingness in his late seventies to be publicly querulous but, second, for his refusal to accept his assigned role in this debate of disapproving elitist. On the contrary, and echoing Eliot's rallying cry that poetry 'must be *difficult*',[3] he strongly contends that only difficult poems are truly democratic, since in difficult poetry 'you are doing your audience the honour of supposing they are intelligent human beings', whereas 'so much of the popular poetry of today treats people as if they were fools'.[4] Reading a poem of Duffy's, he disputes its air of inclusiveness: 'my response is this is not democratic English but cast-off bits of oligarchical commodity English'. This is not a view designed to endear Hill to the larger public, but even making allowance for an element of the *provocateur* in Hill's public persona, the charge remains in need of a more comprehensive rebuttal than the catch-all accusation of elitism. Nevertheless, this was the form taken by many of the responses to Hill, such as that of Don Paterson: 'If you think the point you're making is a moral or ethical one ... it strikes me as plainly *un*ethical to present it in language likely to confound the reader.'[5] The unconfounded reader is value-neutral, and possessed of 'intrinsic virtue', in Paterson's words, in a way that a Geoffrey Hill poem is not. In his recent criticism Hill has frequently turned to Gerard Manley Hopkins's prose and his theories of Parnassian verse and the concept of 'bidding' in poetry. In debates such as these, however, Hill's apparently imperious manner shows its deeply democratic commitment to routing the cant and self-deceptions of our age, in language scarcely less powerful or moving than that of Hopkins himself. (It is no surprise that Pound's 'Hugh Selwyn Mauberley', with its equally surgical response to what 'the age demanded', should have been the repeated object of Hill's critical attention.)

Poets who contest the allotted role of their art form as dramatically as Geoffrey Hill, do so at their peril. Beyond the journalistic controversies generated by Hill's pronouncements, however, the public life of poetry in Britain remains in many ways one of subservience and abjection. Awarding Kathleen Jamie's *The Overhaul* (2012) the Costa Prize, its judges praised the book as 'the collection that will convert you to poetry'[6] – the implied default position for book-readers being one of resistance to poetry. If a best-selling novelist publishes a poetry collection and is interviewed on Radio 4, the interviewer asks how we make poetry 'relevant' for today's audience, and rather than reject the question the novelist agrees that poetry has 'lost the common touch'.[7] These problems are not unique to poetry: other specialised art forms such as classical music and opera are also problematic for the mass media. Too often, the airtime allowed to the minority art form becomes a circular debate about the existence of the art form at all, especially when the trigger word 'elitist' is used, stalling all meaningful debate. An episode of *Match of the Day*, by contrast, that quizzed Premiership footballers on the 'relevance' of football and the elitism of ticket prices rather than showing any footage of actual games would not strike most viewers as a good use of broadcasting time.

According to Kurt Gödel's 'incompleteness theorem', no internally consistent set of axioms can be used to prove something beyond their own system. Were the visiting alien of Craig Raine's *A Martian Sends a Postcard Home* to scan the list of recent prize-winning poets, he would absorb the canon of a certain kind of taste but not what lies beyond it. He would not encounter the work of Geoffrey Hill – to select only one of the similarly excluded poets studied in this book – since none of the remarkable series of books that began with *Canaan* in 1996 has been rewarded with a Forward or T. S. Eliot Prize. Conversely, it would mean little a generation or two from now to argue for Hill's worth on the basis of the prizes he attracted. In the sociology of fame, prizes are racing tips, punts on posterity, but, like racing tips, are heavily prone to error. Who could tell in the 1970s that Scottish poet W. S. Graham, so obscure that Faber & Faber mistakenly believed him to have died, would come to seem hardly less important than Philip Larkin? As with the anthologies considered in Chapter 1, prizes occupy the threshold between the trading floor of reviews, group membership and public visibility, and the unknown territory of the literary afterlife. Reputation is not double-entry book-keeping, and no amount of entries in the first column can guarantee a healthy surplus in the second. In his essay 'Pen Pals: Insider Trading in Poetry Futures' (2001), Dennis O'Driscoll describes with a mixture of anger and fatalism the cronyism to which poetry criticism (and prize-giving) is chronically prone. 'Poetry', he writes, 'is an increasingly parthenogenic art in which poets earn their living by producing new poets.'[8] There are many reasons why this should be. Poetry critics, much more so than with critics of other art forms, tend to be practising poets themselves. O'Driscoll, an Irish civil servant, was already distinctive by not working in a university English department or as a teacher of creative writing. Yet for all his indignation, O'Driscoll was also among the most unfailingly generous of critics. The genuinely savage is a rarity: perhaps the closest British poetry comes to this is Michael Hofmann, whose *Behind the Lines* (2001) shows the enduring power of the maverick, standing outside current orthodoxies or crashing into them with explosive force.

The problem with prizes as a form of poetry marketing goes beyond objections to the sullying of an ethereal art with the language of commerce. Rather, the marketing of poetry can be seen as closely related to the forces which threaten its existence in that very marketplace. A survey of the first twenty years of the Forward Prize for Best First Collection shows an overwhelming identification of the first-time poet with youth. Woe betide the first-time pensioner poet, not to mention the mid-career and middle-aged writer, their youthful splash long behind them and, in most cases, the never-to-be-reached promised land of a *Collected Poems* a flickering, mirage-like, on the horizon. A basic distinction between poetry presses such as Carcanet and Bloodaxe and poetry imprints within larger conglomerates such as Cape and Picador is the answerability of the poetry editor within the latter to company accountants, whereas in the first case the editor and the accountant are often the same person. The presence of unprofitable poets on a commercial list can add critical lustre but the poetry loss leader is a fragile entity, and not a few low-selling poets have been unceremoniously jettisoned from the lists of commercial presses, mid-career refugees washed up once more on the quieter shores of small-press publishing or, in some cases, disappearing altogether.

If the study and reception of poetry has been marked by one change above all others in the contemporary period, it is arguably the rise of creative writing. An anthology of younger American poets such as *Legitimate Dangers* (2006) displays a near-uniform profile, among its younger writers, of MFA degrees and teaching affiliation,[9] a trend that induces much soul-searching about the ghettoisation of poetry within higher education. 'The short story as a medium is in danger of dying of competence', wrote Flannery O'Connor,[10] and chief among the dangers of Creative Writing MA courses is a culture which, however unconsciously, rewards professionalised competence over unruly brilliance. Peter Reading's *Ob.* contains a number of satirical poems on an unsuccessful stint as a writer in residence at the University of East Anglia, an experience Reading did not repeat, but more common are the satirical poems on creative writing (such as Sean O'Brien's 'In Residence: A Worst Case View') written by poets who occupy university chairs in that very subject. A deal of confusion and bad faith clings to the interaction of poetry and the academy: it is noticeable how readily Don Paterson (himself a professor at St Andrews) reaches for the word 'academic' as a term of abuse in his assault on postmodernist poets. Yet of the twenty poets chosen for the Next Generation Poets in 2004, none of whom is likely to call down Paterson's ire, an overwhelming majority are academics, engaged in the teaching of creative writing at university level. This is an uneasy halfway house between the genuine collapse of poetry into institutionalisation and the old-style genteel autonomy of Larkin or Roy Fuller, unassuming nine-to-five men by day and poets by night.

The rise of creative writing has overlapped (coincidentally or not) with a sharp decline in old-fashioned print reviewing and the small magazine, in printed rather than online form at least. Whereas in the past the slaying of one generation of poets by their juniors has been an essential rite of passage, and the small magazine the natural arena for such joustings, the internet age has brought proliferation but loss of focus too, especially where criticism is concerned. A paradox of the internet is the ease of access and publication it allows, but the difficulties it poses for meaningful archiving. A posting on a poetry blog or listserv can attract heated debate, but many internet forums vanish without warning or trace. Uniquely among newspapers *The Guardian* maintains a huge archive of free (for the moment) online content, but other journals have retreated behind paywalls. A related problem is the disappearance of authors' manuscripts and correspondence. Collections of the letters of Ted Hughes and Philip Larkin may be among the last of their kind. The archival and publishing challenges represented by the *Collected Emails* of Simon Armitage or Don Paterson have yet to be fully addressed.

As mainstream and fringe, traditional form and free verse continue to do battle, the truly interesting developments are those which refuse pre-programmed oppositions and terms of debate. Formalist verse is often touted as undergoing revivals, but at no point in recent poetic history has it ever really gone away. Tom Chivers's anthology *Adventures in Form* (2012), subtitled *Rules and Constraints*, shows that the formalist impulse in contemporary poetry is as likely to come from playfulness *à la* Oulipo (the French movement for 'potential literature', founded in 1960, in which texts are generated from self-imposed stylistic constraints) as from strait-laced conservatism. An unexpected example of critical thinking across established categories in recent times is Nathan Hamilton's anthology *Dear World and Everyone In It*, which replaces the introduction with a mock-manifesto owing much to the Frank O'Hara of 'Personism' ('I don't want to be a poet. It is too complicated and too vague and the rewards are too small').[11] Beneath the playful tone, Hamilton is impatient with existing rites of passage for the debutant poet, and makes much of small-press publishing and the (not uncritical) use of new media as alternatives. Traditionally, an anthology might try to hoover up these developments with talk of 'hybridisation', but Hamilton rejects co-option and the appeal to the 'General Reader' in whose name the new is packaged and made safe. Instead he calls for a 'consideration of text as performative and participatory, involving interaction between reader and text',[12] a stance that involved engagement with the poets selected over who else should be in the book ('crowd-sourcing', in the current terminology). Other forms of modishness are treated more sceptically: Hamilton rejects the opposition of 'product' and 'process' as a metonymy for mainstream and experimental, and condemns the refusal of other media to discuss poetry on its own terms. Hamilton's choice of featured poets includes Keston Sutherland, Sam Riviere, and Frances Leviston, but his anthology is also distinguished by collaborations with the visual arts on a scale not seen since the 1960s and 1970s. *Dear World* has not gone unchallenged – to Michael Schmidt the O'Hara-style playfulness is a sign of creative writing in-speak and not an overcoming of it[13] – but it is a venturesome example of the direction British poetry may now take. Sam Riviere's 'Crisis Poem' (from his collection *81 Austerities*, 2012) captures perfectly its mood of cynicism but the aftermath of cynicism too, as a generation of poets who have lingered too long at art college or university wake up to the point, or pointlessness, of lyric art in the age of austerity Britain. Beginning by listing the grants he has been awarded for his poetry, the speaker then veers from empty generalisations ('capital is the index of meaning')[14] to fears of being reduced to shoplifting from the Co-op. His, we sense, is a precarious position in the cultural firmament. The anthology as genre, with which we began in Chapter 1, may have a final paradoxical insight for us into literary futurity. Many anthologies achieve influence through controversy and trend-spotting without possessing the contents, or actual poems, to match. Other anthologies do a better job of selection without making a polemical mark, and are passed over.[15] While the polemical stuff of anthology introductions draws critical debate off in one direction, the real life of poems may be taking place somewhere else entirely.

In 'Musée des Beaux Arts', Auden captures wisely the coexistence of crisis and banality in his description of Bruegel's *Landscape with The Fall of Icarus*. In the painting, Icarus falling into the sea is relegated to the background while the foreground is occupied by an unconcerned peasant ploughing his field. Critical debate about poetry thrives on crisis or the appearance of crisis, which it then becomes the business of criticism to stage-manage, but the state of crisis is not how most poetry lives from day to day. Seamus Heaney captures this poignantly in his poem 'Keeping Going', in which he compares his life as a professional meditator on the crisis of the Northern Irish Troubles with that of his brother, who has remained on the family farm in Co. Derry. 'You have good stamina,' he tells his brother, 'you keep / Old roads open by driving on the new ones.'[16] Stamina is a quality required in abundance for the critic of contemporary poetry hoping to last the pace from one generation to another. Revisiting his classic 1932 study *New Bearings in English Poetry* in 1950, F. R. Leavis tried to find something to say about developments in the intervening years. The best he could do was that 'Yeats has died, and Eliot has gone on.'[17] As a believer in the 'great tradition', Leavis was painfully sceptical of any figures (including Auden) who failed to match these Olympian masters. At the other extreme from Leavis's critical housekeeping, in 2012 poet and editor Todd Swift performed an online census of the poetic generation born since 1970 and found over 130 names to list.[18] This is to raise once more the spectre of Anthony Thwaite's 'On Consulting "Contemporary Poets of the English Language"', with its endlessly fecund present-day generation. Once an Arnoldian watchword, 'discrimination' is now more redolent of the employment tribunal – a comparison not so far-fetched in the current university research climate, where creative writers are forced to justify their presence with ever more utilitarian yardsticks of career success and 'impact' on the wider public.

Among the few constants in discussions of contemporary poetry is anxiety about its readership. Without a readership, it will die. A whole sub-genre of critical essays exists devoted to arguing that this has, in fact, already happened. In 2011, however, the realities of the poetry publishing market (or 'sector') in an era of economic austerity were grimly spelt out in significant cuts to the Arts Council's budget, resulting in severe cuts to the funding of smaller publishers such as Enitharmon and Anvil, followed in 2013 by the closure of the Salt poetry list. Having begun as a publisher of experimental poetry with strong Cambridge connections, Salt expanded into the wider market with encouragement from the Arts Council of England. Ultimately its embrace of the market and commitment to a growth-model proved unsustainable, despite vigorous campaigns to translate its large following on social networking websites into a book-buying public. Writing about Salt's demise on her blog, Clare Pollard commented on the disconnection between the support systems in place for 'emerging' writers, in the form of bursaries, mentorships and residencies, and the absence of a market for the basic unit of currency in poetry publishing, the slim volume. Where is the support, she wondered, for the 'emerged' writer?

■ It seems to me there are choices to be made. One option is for arts bodies to start supporting 'emerged' poets as actively as those who are 'emerging'. Another might be to accept that the days of the physical, 60-page collection are over and find a different model of poetic success.[19] □

Pollard's plea highlights the elusiveness of the connection between contemporary poetry and the nebulous entity we designate as 'posterity'. 'In his more curmudgeonly mode', Michael Longley has observed, 'John Hewitt once said to me: "If you write poetry, it's your own fault."'[20] The writing of poetry by apprentice writers as a vocational exercise is one that grant-aiding bodies may wish to subsidise, but the underwriting of a poet's fortunes once we reach the afterlife of literary history is beyond the power of any Arts Council. It is the awkward stage of 'emergence', midway between these poles, that is the problem.

In 1961 the composer György Ligeti was asked to give a lecture on 'The Future of Music'. Finding himself with nothing to say on the subject, he stood silently on stage. As the audience grew restive, Ligeti began to write musical instructions on a blackboard – *crescendo, più forte* – transforming himself from the butt of their displeasure into a conductor, manipulating and performing the noises they produced.[21] Predictions on the future of any art form are the preserve of prophets or confidence tricksters, and Ligeti's dramatisation of his helplessness is a fitting riposte to an unrealistic burden of expectation. Yet the atmosphere of Ligeti's performance was one of comic affirmation rather than sullen non-cooperation. Facing the future, poets and critics are truest to the art when they embrace the uncertainties, mysteries and doubts from which poems are born. The intelligent poet and critic helps cultivate the responsiveness through which we will know the genuine when we see it, and in search of which the art continues not in a state of desolate crisis but of sturdy, Heaneyesque 'keeping going'.

Notes

INTRODUCTION

1. Theodor Adorno, *Minima Moralia*, trans. E. F. N. Jephcott (London: Verso, 1978), p. 49.
2. Philip Larkin, *Complete Poems*, ed. Archie Burnett (London: Faber & Faber, 2012), p. 90.
3. Seamus Heaney, 'An Open Letter' (Derry: Field Day Company, 1983).
4. E. P. Thompson, *The Making of the English Working Class* (London: Gollancz, 1980), p. 12.
5. T. S. Eliot, *Selected Prose*, ed. John Hayward (Harmondsworth: Penguin, 1953), p. 25.
6. Ezra Pound, *An ABC of Reading* (London: Faber & Faber, 1961), p. 40.
7. John Carey, review of *Meeting the British*, *Sunday Times*, 21 June 1987, p. 56.
8. 'Peter Riley in Conversation with Keith Tuma', *Jacket*, 11, April 2000 (http://jacketmagazine.com/11/riley-iv-by-tuma.html).
9. Blake Morrison and Andrew Motion (eds), *The Penguin Book of Contemporary British Poetry* (Harmondsworth: Penguin, 1982), p. 11.
10. Graeme Richardson, 'Saving Peter Redgrove from Oblivion', review of Neil Roberts, *A Lucid Dreamer*, and Peter Redgrove, *Collected Poems*, *Times Literary Supplement*, 20 April 2012, p. 21.
11. Anthony Thwaite, *Collected Poems* (London: Enitharmon, 2007), p. 157.
12. John Redmond, *Poetry and Privacy: Questioning Public Interpretations of Contemporary British and Irish Poetry* (Bridgend: Seren, 2013), pp. 9–10.
13. Keith Tuma, *Fishing by Obstinate Isles: Modern and Postmodern British Poetry and American Readers* (Evanston, IL: Northwestern University Press, 1998), p. 1.
14. Roy Fisher, *The Long and the Short of It: Poems 1955–2005* (Tarset: Bloodaxe Books, 2005), p. 156.

CHAPTER ONE: ANTHOLOGIES AND CANON FORMATION

1. Edna Longley, *Poetry and Posterity* (Tarset: Bloodaxe, 2000), p. 203.
2. Cf. Blake Morrison, *The Movement: English Poetry and Fiction of the 1950s* (Oxford: Oxford University Press, 1980).
3. Michael Donaghy, 'On Being a New Generation Poet', in *The Shape of the Dance: Essays, Interviews and Digressions*, ed. Adam O'Riordan and Maddy Paxman (London: Picador, 2009), pp. 98–100 (99).
4. Fiona Sampson, *Beyond the Lyric: A Map of Contemporary British Poetry* (London: Chatto & Windus, 2012), p. 280.
5. Tim Kendall, *Thumbscrew*, 20–1 (2002), 3.
6. Fiona Sampson, *A Century of Poetry Review* (Manchester: Carcanet, 2009), p. xi.
7. Cf. Peter Barry, *Poetry Wars: British Poetry of the 1970s and the Battle of Earls Court* (Cambridge: Salt, 2006).
8. Sampson (2009), p. xxiii.
9. Cf. David Miller and Richard Price, *British Poetry Magazines 1914–2000: A History and Bibliography of 'Little Magazines'* (London: British Library and Oak Knoll, 2006).
10. Peter Forbes, 'Talking About the New Generation', *Poetry Review*, 84(1) (Spring 1994), 6.
11. David Harsent, *Another Round at the Pillars: Essays, Poems and Reflections on Ian Hamilton* (St Austell: Cargo Press, 1999).

12. Forbes (1994), 6.
13. Quoted in Dennis O'Driscoll (ed.), *Quote Poet Unquote: Contemporary Quotations on Poets and Poetry* (Washington DC: Copper Canyon Press, 2008), p. 258.
14. For an account of the influence of creative writing teaching on contemporary poetry, see Peter Carpenter, 'Singing Schools and Beyond: The Roles of Creative Writing', in Peter Robinson (ed.), *The Penguin Handbook of Contemporary British and Irish Poetry* (Oxford: Oxford University Press, 2013), pp. 322–37.
15. Patrick McGuinness, review of Sean O'Brien, *The Firebox*, and Simon Armitage and Robert Crawford, *The Penguin Book of Poetry from Britain and Ireland since 1945*, *London Review of Books*, 21(7), 1 April 1999 (accessed online).
16. Mark Ford, review of Neil Astley, *Staying Alive*, *The Guardian*, 7 September 2002 (accessed online).
17. August Kleinzahler, 'No Antonin Artaud with the Flapjacks Please', review of Garrison Keillor, *Good Poems*, *Poetry*, April 2004 (accessed online).
18. Quoted in Dennis O'Driscoll, *Troubled Thoughts, Majestic Dreams: Selected Prose Writings* (Loughcrew: Gallery Press, 2001), p. 158.
19. James Byrne and Clare Pollard (eds), *Voice Recognition: 21 Poets for the 21st Century* (Tarset: Bloodaxe Books, 2009), p. 10.
20. Simon Armitage, 'Life on the Line', *The Guardian*, 5 June 2004 (accessed online).
21. Christopher Ricks (ed.), *The Oxford Book of English Verse* (Oxford: Oxford University Press, 1999), p. xxxiv.
22. Ricks (1999), p. xxxiv.
23. Helen Vendler, review of *The Penguin Anthology of Twentieth-Century American Poetry*, *New York Review of Books*, LVIII(18) (24 November–7 December 2011), 19–22.
24. McGuinness (1999).
25. Matthew Sweeney and Jo Shapcott (eds), *Emergency Kit: Poems for Strange Times* (London: Faber & Faber, 1996); Maura Dooley (ed.), *Making for Planet Alice: New Women Poets* (Newcastle upon Tyne: Bloodaxe Books, 1997), cover blurbs.
26. Peter Howarth, 'Degree of Famousness etc.', review of Don Paterson, *Selected Poems*, *London Review of Books*, 35(6) (21 March 2013), 31.
27. Longley (2000), 210–11.
28. Cf. Carol Rumen's introduction to the anthology's second edition: *Making for the Open: Post-Feminist Poetry* (London: Chatto & Windus, 1987).
29. Michael Hulse, David Kennedy and David Morley (eds), *The New Poetry* (Newcastle upon Tyne: Bloodaxe Books, 1993), p. 16.
30. David Kennedy, *New Relations: The Refashioning of British Poetry 1980–1994* (Bridgend: Seren, 1998), pp. 247–9.
31. Sean O'Brien, *The Deregulated Muse: Essays on Contemporary British and Irish Poetry* (Newcastle upon Tyne: Bloodaxe Books, 1998), p. 250.
32. Roddy Lumsden, *Identity Parade: New British and Irish Poets* (Tarset: Bloodaxe Books, 2010), p. 20.
33. Michael Schmidt, *The Harvill Book of Twentieth-Century Poetry in English* (London: Harvill, 1999), p. xxvii.
34. Schmidt (1999), p. xxviii.
35. Schmidt (1999), p. xxxvii.
36. Schmidt (1999), p. xxxviii.
37. Longley (2000), p. 222.
38. Sampson (2012), p. 186.
39. Sean O'Brien, *The Firebox: Poetry in Britain and Ireland after 1945* (London: Picador, 1999), p. xxxv.
40. Simon Armitage and Robert Crawford, *The Penguin Book of Poetry from Britain and Ireland since 1945* (London: Penguin, 1999), p. xxvi.
41. McGuinness (1999).

42. Sean O'Brien, review of Keith Tuma, *Anthology of Twentieth-Century British and Irish Poetry*, *Poetry Review*, 91(2) (Summer 2001).
43. Keith Tuma, *Anthology of Twentieth-Century British and Irish Poetry* (New York: Oxford University Press, 2001), p. xxiii.
44. Tuma (2001), p. xx.
45. Tuma (2001), pp. xxii, xxviii.
46. William Wootten, 'To answer an appetite', *Times Literary Supplement*, 27 April 2012, 14–15 (15).
47. Edward Mendelson (ed.), *The English Auden: Poems, Essays and Dramatic Writings 1927–1939* (London: Faber & Faber, 1977), p. 246.
48. Tim Kendall, *Modern English War Poetry* (Oxford: Oxford University Press, 2006), p. 238.
49. Kendall (2006), p. 240.
50. Kendall (2006), p. 241.
51. Harold Pinter, 'American Football', in *Various Voices: Prose, Poetry, Politics 1948–2005* (London: Faber & Faber, 1998), p. 260.
52. Kendall (2006), p. 247.
53. For more on poetry as, or versus, political activism, see my 'Between "Helpless Right" and "Forc'd Power": The Political Poem Today', *Edinburgh Review*, 135 (2012), 7–18.
54. For more on Harrison's '*v*.', see my '"Dispatched Dark Regions Far Afield and Farther": Contemporary Poetry and Victorianism', in Matthew Bevis (ed.), *The Oxford Handbook of Victorian Poetry* (Oxford: Oxford University Press, 2012).
55. Tony Harrison, *A Cold Coming* (Newcastle upon Tyne: Bloodaxe Books, 1991), p. 12.
56. Todd Swift, 'Kendall Polemical', available at: http://toddswift.blogspot.co.uk/2008/10/kendall-polemical.html (accessed 23 February 2013).
57. W. B. Yeats, *Collected Poems* (London: Macmillan, 1978), p. 175.
58. Longley (2000), p. 203.

CHAPTER TWO: APPROACHES TO CONTEMPORARY BRITISH POETRY

1. Peter McDonald, 'Appreciating Assets' (review of *Finders Keepers*), *Poetry Review*, 92(2) (Summer 2002), p. 79.
2. Cf. my 'Professing Poetry: Seamus Heaney as Critic', in Bernard O'Donoghue (ed.), *The Cambridge Companion to Seamus Heaney* (Cambridge: Cambridge University Press, 2009), pp. 122–35.
3. Robert Conquest, introduction to *New Lines* (London: Macmillan, 1962), pp. xi, xv.
4. Cf. Antony Easthope and John Thompson (eds), *Contemporary Poetry Meets Modern Theory* (Hemel Hempstead: Harvester Wheatsheaf, 1991), *passim*.
5. Geoffrey Hill, *Collected Critical Writings*, ed. Kenneth Haynes (Oxford: Oxford University Press, 2008), p. 566.
6. Hill (2008), p. 566.
7. T. S. Eliot, *Selected Prose*, ed. John Hayward (Harmondsworth: Penguin, 1953), p. 118.
8. Geoffrey Hill, interview with Carl Phillips, *The Paris Review*, 154 (Spring 2000), accessed online at http://www.theparisreview.org/interviews/730/the-art-of-poetry-no-80-geoffrey-hill.
9. Hill (2008), p. 3.
10. Hill (2008), p. 4.
11. Hill (2008), p. 5.
12. Hill (2008), pp. 6–7.
13. Hill (2008), p. 566.
14. Hill (2008), p. 565.
15. Hill (2008), p. 565.
16. Hill (2008), pp. 567–8.
17. Hill (2008), pp. 572–3.

18. Hill (2008), p. 578.
19. Hill (2008), p. 579.
20. Hill (2008), p. 163.
21. Hill (2008), p. 579.
22. Hill (2008), p. 580.
23. Hill (2008), p. 580.
24. Cf. Terry Eagleton, *Literary Theory: An Introduction* (Oxford: Blackwell, 1996).
25. Peter McDonald, *Mistaken Identities: Poetry and Northern Ireland* (Oxford: Oxford University Press, 1997), p. 19.
26. Christopher Ricks, *Essays in Appreciation* (Oxford: Oxford University Press, 1998), p. 312.
27. Quoted in Michael Hamburger, *The Truth of Poetry: Tensions in Modern Poetry from Baudelaire to the 1960s* (Manchester: Carcanet, 1982), p. 243.
28. Ricks (1998), p. 317.
29. Quoted in Ricks (1998), p. 324.
30. Ricks (1998), p. 324.
31. Marilyn Butler, 'The Verity of Verity', review of Christopher Ricks, *Essays in Appreciation*, *London Review of Books*, 18(15), 1 August 1996.
32. Paul Muldoon, 'Ireland', in *Poems 1968–1998* (London: Faber & Faber, 2001), pp. 82–3.
33. Paul Muldoon, 'A Trifle', in *Poems 1968–1998* (London: Faber & Faber, 2001), p. 121.
34. Sean O'Brien, *The Deregulated Muse: Essays on Contemporary British and Irish Poetry* (Newcastle upon Tyne: Bloodaxe, 1998), p. 172.
35. Quoted in Alec Reid, *All I Could Manage, More Than I Could: An Approach to the Plays of Samuel Beckett* (Dublin: Dolmen Press, 1968), p. 11.
36. Neil Corcoran, 'Paul Muldoon in Conversation with Neil Corcoran', in Elmer Kennedy-Andrews (ed.), *Paul Muldoon: Poetry, Prose & Drama, A Collection of Critical Essays* (Gerrards Cross: Colin Smythe, 2008), pp. 165–88 (172).
37. Corcoran (2008), p. 172.
38. Samuel Johnson, 'The Life of Cowley', in *Johnson's Lives of the Poets: A Selection*, ed. J. P. Hardy (Oxford: Clarendon Press, 1971), p. 12.
39. Paul Muldoon, 'Getting Round: Notes Towards an *Ars Poetica*', *Essays in Criticism*, 48(2) (April 1998), 107–28 (110); and *The End of the Poem: Oxford Lectures on Poetry* (London: Faber & Faber, 2006).
40. Robert Frost, *Collected Poems, Prose, and Plays*, ed. Richard Poirier and Mark Richardson (New York: Library of America, 1995), p. 342.
41. Paul Muldoon (1998), 127.
42. Muldoon (1998), 120.
43. Muldoon (1998), 127.
44. Fiona Sampson, *Beyond the Lyric: A Map of Contemporary British Poetry* (London: Chatto & Windus, 2012), p. 283.
45. Eliot (1953), p. 23, and quoted in William Wootten, 'In the Community Halls', review of Glyn Maxwell, *On Poetry*, and Fiona Sampson, *Beyond the Lyric*, *Times Literary Supplement*, 23 November 2012, 10–11 (11).
46. David Gervais, *Literary Englands: Versions of 'Englishness' in Modern Writing* (Cambridge: Cambridge University Press, 1993), p. 202.
47. Don Paterson, *God's Gift to Women* (London: Faber & Faber, 1993), p. 1.
48. Sampson (2012), pp. 77, 63, 280, 283.
49. Fran Brearton, *Reading Michael Longley* (Tarset: Bloodaxe Books, 2006); Heather Clark, *The Ulster Renaissance: Poetry in Belfast 1962–1972* (Oxford: Oxford University Press, 2006).
50. Quoted in Clark (2006), p. 187.
51. Sampson (2012), p. 283.
52. Tom Paulin, *Minotaur: Poetry and the Nation State* (London: Faber & Faber, 1992), p. 281.
53. Hill (2008), 375.
54. Hill (2008), p. 379.

55. Christopher Ricks, *True Friendship: Geoffrey Hill, Anthony Hecht, and Robert Lowell Under the Sign of Eliot and Pound* (New Haven, CT: Yale University Press, 2010), p. 33.
56. Ricks (2010), pp. 33–4.
57. Geoffrey Hill, *The Triumph of Love* (New York: Houghton Mifflin, 1998), p. 82.
58. Quoted in John Haffenden (ed.), *W. H. Auden: Collected Critical Heritage* (London: Routledge, 1997), p. 72.
59. Quoted in Peter McDonald, *Serious Poetry: Form and Authority from Yeats to Hill* (Oxford: Clarendon Press, 2002), p. 2.
60. Philip Larkin, *All What Jazz* (London: Faber & Faber, 1985), p. 27.
61. Quoted in McDonald (2002), p. 4.
62. Philip Larkin, *Complete Poems*, ed. Archie Burnett (London: Faber & Faber, 2012), pp. 35–6.
63. McDonald (2002), p. 7.
64. Cf. John Osborne, *Larkin, Ideology and Critical Violence: A Case of Wrongful Conviction* (Basingstoke: Palgrave Macmillan, 2007).
65. McDonald (2002), p. 15.
66. Ezra Pound, *Literary Essays of Ezra Pound*, ed. T. S. Eliot (London: Faber & Faber, 1954), p. 9.
67. Quoted in Angela Leighton, *On Form: Poetry, Aestheticism, and the Legacy of a Word* (Oxford: Oxford University Press, 2007), p. 7.
68. Leighton (2007), pp. 7–8.
69. Quoted in Leighton (2007), p. 20.
70. Leighton (2007), p. 232.
71. Roy Fisher, *The Long and the Short of It: Poems 1955–2005* (Tarset: Bloodaxe Books, 2005), p. 310.
72. Clair Wills, 'A Furnace and the Life of the Dead', in John Kerrigan and Peter Robinson (eds), *The Thing About Roy Fisher: Critical Studies* (Liverpool: Liverpool University Press, 2000), pp. 257–74 (259).
73. Fisher (2005), p. 53.
74. Cf. Kerrigan and Robinson (2000), and Peter Robinson and Robert Sheppard (eds), *News for the Ear: A Homage to Roy Fisher* (Exeter: Stride Publications, 2000).
75. Leighton (2007), p. 241.

CHAPTER THREE: POSTCOLONIALISM

1. 'British tag is "coded racism"', *The Guardian*, 11 October 2000, 1.
2. Cf. Robert Crawford, *Devolving English Literature*, 2nd edn (Edinburgh: Edinburgh University Press, 2000), and *The Modern Poet: Poetry, Academia and Knowledge since the 1750s* (Oxford: Oxford University Press, 2001).
3. Donald Davie, *With the Grain: Essays on Thomas Hardy and Modern British Poetry*, ed. Clive Wilmer (Manchester: Carcanet, 1998), p. 270.
4. Crawford, *Devolving English Literature* (2000), p. 14.
5. Cf. Gilles Deleuze and Félix Guattari, *Anti-Oedipus*, trans. Robert Hurley, Mark Seem and Helen R. Lane (London and New York: Continuum, 2004), and *Kafka: Towards a Minor Literature*, trans. Dana Polan (Minneapolis: Minnesota University Press, 1986).
6. Robert Crawford, 'Cosmopolibackofbeyondism', in W. N. Herbert and Matthew Hollis (eds), *Strong Words: Modern Poets on Modern Poetry* (Tarset: Bloodaxe Books, 2000), pp. 262–4.
7. Jahan Ramazani, 'Black British Poetry and the Translocal', in Neil Corcoran (ed.), *The Cambridge Companion to Twentieth-Century English Poetry* (Cambridge: Cambridge University Press, 2007), pp. 200–14 (200).
8. Jahan Ramazani, *A Transnational Poetics* (London: University of Chicago Press, 2009), p. 5.
9. Crawford, *Devolving English Literature* (2000), p. 261.
10. Craig Raine, 'Barbarous Dialects', in *Haydn and the Valve Trumpet: Literary Essays* (London: Faber & Faber, 1990), p. 89.
11. Helen Vendler, *Seamus Heaney* (London: Harper Collins, 1998), p. 49.

12. Vendler (1998), p. 51.
13. Edna Longley, *Poetry in the Wars* (Newcastle upon Tyne: Bloodaxe Books, 1986), p. 185.
14. Edna Longley, *Poetry and Posterity* (Tarset: Bloodaxe Books, 2000), p. 248.
15. Longley (1986), p. 154.
16. Mark Patrick Hederman, 'Poetry and the Fifth Province', *The Crane Bag*, 9(1) (1985), 112.
17. David Lloyd, *Anomalous States: Irish Writing and the Post-Colonial Moment* (Dublin: Lilliput Press, 1993), p. 37.
18. Thomas Kinsella, *The New Oxford Book of Irish Verse* (Oxford: Oxford University Press, 1986), p. xxx.
19. Geoffrey Hill, *The Triumph of Love* (New York: Houghton Mifflin, 1998), p. 40.
20. Tom Paulin, letter to the *Times Literary Supplement*, 7 November 1992, p. 15.
21. Philip Larkin, *Complete Poems*, ed. Archie Burnett (London: Faber & Faber, 2012), p. 64.
22. David Gervais, *Literary Englands: Versions of 'Englishness' in Modern Writing* (Cambridge: Cambridge University Press, 1993), p. 274.
23. Sean O'Brien, *The Deregulated Muse: Essays on Contemporary British and Irish Poetry* (Newcastle upon Tyne: Bloodaxe Books, 1998), p. 41.
24. Larkin (2012), p. 64.
25. James Booth, 'Larkin, Heaney and the Poetry of Place', in James Booth (ed.), *New Larkins for Old: Critical Essays* (Basingstoke: Macmillan, 2000), pp. 190–212 (208).
26. George Orwell, 'The Lion and the Unicorn', in Sonia Orwell and Ian Angus (eds), *The Collected Essays, Journalism and Letters of George Orwell* (New York: Harcourt, 1968), II, 67–8.
27. Jo Shapcott, *Her Book: Poems 1988–1998* (London: Faber & Faber, 2000), pp. 65–6.
28. Sean O'Brien (1998), p. 254.
29. Keith Tuma, *Fishing by Obstinate Isles: Modern and Postmodern British Poetry and American Readers* (Evanston, IL: Northwestern University Press, 1998), 199.
30. Shapcott (2000), p. 124.
31. Roy Fisher, *The Long and the Short of It: Poems 1955–2005* (Tarset: Bloodaxe Books, 2010), p. 157.
32. Simon Armitage, *The Universal Home Doctor* (London: Faber & Faber, 2002), p. 17.
33. Michael Hofmann, *Behind the Lines: Pieces on Writing and Pictures* (London: Faber & Faber, 2001), p. 91.
34. Hofmann (2001), p. xii.
35. Hofmann, *Nights in the Iron Hotel* (London: Faber & Faber, 1983), p. 45.
36. Hofmann, *Acrimony* (London: Faber & Faber, 1986), p. 34.
37. O'Brien (1998), p. 236.
38. Hofmann (1986), p. 45.
39. John Bull and John Barrell (eds), *The Penguin Book of Pastoral Verse* (Harmondsworth: Penguin, 1974), p. 432.
40. Hofmann (1986), p. 28.
41. O'Brien (1998), p. 237.
42. Fred D'Aguiar, 'Metaphors for England: Michael Hofmann's *Nights in the Iron Hotel*', in André Naffis-Sahely and Julian Stannard (eds), *The Palm Beach Effect: Reflections on Michael Hofmann* (London: CB Editions, 2013), pp. 6–17 (16).
43. Hofmann, *Approximately Nowhere* (London: Faber & Faber, 1999), p. 36.
44. D'Aguiar (2013), 14.
45. E. A. Markham, *Looking Out, Looking In: New and Selected Poems* (London: Anvil Press, 2009), p. 21.
46. E. A. Markham, *A Rough Climate* (London: Anvil Press, 2002), p. 99; and Omaar Hena, 'Multi-Ethnic British Poetries', in Peter Robinson (ed.), *The Oxford Handbook of Contemporary British and Irish Poetry* (Oxford: Oxford University Press, 2013), pp. 517–37 (524).
47. David Dabydeen, quoted in Christopher Ricks and Leonard Michael (eds), *The State of the Language* (London: Faber & Faber, 1990), p. 12.

48. Fred D'Aguiar, 'Have You Been Here Long? Black Poetry in Britain', in *New British Poetries: The Scope of the Possible*, ed. Robert Hampson and Peter Barry (Manchester: Manchester University Press, 1993), pp. 51–71 (70).

49. Bernardine Evaristo and Daljit Nagra (eds), *Ten New Poets* (Tarset: Bloodaxe Books, 2010).

50. Sarah Broom, *Contemporary British and Irish Poetry: An Introduction* (Basingstoke: Palgrave Macmillan, 2006), p. 48.

51. Quoted in Robert Burchfield, *The English Language* (Oxford: Oxford University Press, 1985), p. 34.

52. David Dabydeen, *Slave Song* (Sydney: Dangaroo Press, 1984), p. 42.

53. Dabydeen (1984), p. 9.

54. Dabydeen (1984), p. 9.

55. Quoted in Broom (2006), p. 50.

56. Blake Morrison, review of *Bill of Rights*, *London Review of Books*, 5 December 1985 (accessed online).

57. Fred D'Aguiar, *Bill of Rights* (London: Chatto & Windus, 1998), p. 133.

58. Cf. Tim Kendall, *Paul Muldoon* (Bridgend: Seren, 1996); and Clair Wills, *Reading Paul Muldoon* (Newcastle upon Tyne: Bloodaxe Books, 1998).

59. Paul Muldoon, *Poems 1968–1998* (London: Faber & Faber, 2001), p. 291.

60. Kendall (1996), p. 163.

61. Muldoon (2001), p. 309.

62. Patrick McGuinness, review of *Zero Gravity*, *London Review of Books*, 5 October 2000 (accessed online).

63. Deryn Rees-Jones, *Consorting with Angels: Essays on Modern Women Poets* (Tarset: Bloodaxe Books, 2005), p. 188.

64. Gwyneth Lewis, 'Whose Coat is that Jacket? Whose Hat is that Cap?' *Poetry Review*, 85(4) (Winter 1995–6), pp. 12–17.

65. Rees-Jones (2005), p. 189.

66. M. Wynn Thomas, 'R. S. Thomas and Modern Welsh Poetry', in Neil Corcoran (ed.), *Twentieth-Century English Poetry* (Cambridge: Cambridge University Press, 2007), p. 163.

67. Gwyneth Lewis, *Parables & Faxes* (Newcastle upon Tyne: Bloodaxe Books, 1995), p. 42.

68. Rees-Jones (2005), p. 190.

69. Gwyneth Lewis, *Keeping Mum* (Tarset: Bloodaxe Books, 2003), p. 14.

70. Lewis (2003), p. 13.

71. Lewis (2003), p. 15.

72. Daljit Nagra, *Look We Have Coming to Dover!* (London: Faber & Faber, 2007), pp. 42–3.

73. Derek Walcott, *Collected Poems* (London: Faber & Faber, 1992), p. 346.

74. Fredric Jameson, 'Third World-Literature in the Era of Multinational Capitalism', *Social Text*, 15 (1985), p. 66.

75. Kamau Brathwaite, *Middle Passage* (New York: New Directions, 1993), p. 106.

76. Don Wellman, 'Cultural Cannibalism and the Intercultural Text', in Romana Huk, *Assembling Alternatives: Reading Postmodern Poetries Transnationally* (Middletown, CT: Wesleyan University Press, 2003), pp. 207–18 (210).

77. Quoted in Jahan Ramazani, *The Hybrid Muse: Postcolonial Poetry in English* (Chicago, IL: University of Chicago Press, 2001), p. 56.

78. Vahni Capildeo, *Undraining Sea* (Norwich: Eggbox, 2009), p. 73.

79. Capildeo (2009), p. 7.

80. Capildeo (2009), p. 67.

81. Vahni Capildeo, *No Traveller Returns* (Cambridge: Salt, 2003), p. 53.

82. Homi Bhabha, *The Location of Culture* (London: Routledge, 1986), p. 86.

83. Virginia Woolf, *Three Guineas* (New York: Harcourt Brace, 1966), p. 166.

84. Moniza Alvi, 'The Least International Shop in the World', in Alison Mark and Deryn Rees-Jones (eds), *Contemporary Women's Poetry: Reading/Writing/Practice* (Basingstoke: Macmillan, 2000), p. 36.

85. Elizabeth Bishop, *Collected Poems* (London: Chatto & Windus, 1991), p. 3.
86. Moniza Alvi, *Split World: Poems 1990–2005* (Tarset: Bloodaxe Books, 2008), p. 40.
87. Ruth Padel, *The Poem and the Journey, And Sixty Poems to Read Along the Way* (London: Vintage, 2008), pp. 293–6.
88. Alvi (2008), p. 30.
89. Rees-Jones (2005), p. 207.
90. Cf. my 'Changing the Story: Eavan Boland and Literary History', *Irish Review*, 31 (2004), 103–20.
91. Alvi (2008), p. 254.
92. Wallace Stevens, *Collected Poems* (London: Faber & Faber, 1954), p. 10.
93. Alvi (2008), p. 252.
94. Patience Agbabi, *Bloodshot Monochrome* (Edinburgh: Canongate, 2008), p. 20.
95. Broom (2006), p. 256.
96. Capildeo (2009), p. 19.
97. Philip Larkin, *Further Requirements: Interviews, Broadcasts, Statements and Book Reviews*, ed. Anthony Thwaite (London: Faber & Faber, 2001), p. 25.
98. Ivan Blatný, *The Drug of Art*, trans. Matthew Sweney, Justin Quinn et al. (New York: Ugly Duckling Presse, 2007), p. 117.
99. Jacques Derrida, *Shibboleth* (Paris: Galilée, 1986); and in Geoffrey H. Hartman and Sanford Budick (eds), *Midrash and Literature* (New Haven, CT: Yale University Press, 1986), pp. 307–47.
100. Quoted in Bradley Woodworth and Constance Richards, *St Petersburg* (New York: Chelsea House, 2005), p. 85.
101. W. N. Herbert, *The Big Bumper Book of Troy* (Tarset: Bloodaxe Books, 2002), p. 87.
102. Hugh MacDiarmid, *The Ugly Birds With No Wings* (Edinburgh: A. Donaldson, 1962).
103. Iain Galbraith, 'Scottish Poetry in the Wider World', in Peter Robinson (ed.), *The Oxford Handbook of Contemporary British and Irish Poetry* (Oxford: Oxford University Press, 2013), pp. 558–75 (570).
104. O'Brien (1998), p. 262.
105. W. N. Herbert, back cover text of *Forked Tongue* (Newcastle upon Tyne: Bloodaxe Books, 1990).
106. Herbert (1990), p. 10.
107. W. N. Herbert, *Omnesia: Remix* (Tarset: Bloodaxe Books, 2013), p. 169; and *Omnesia: Alternative Text* (Tarset: Bloodaxe Books, 2013), p. 13.
108. Herbert, *Omnesia: Remix* (2013), pp. 102, 70, 68.
109. Herbert (2002), p. 94.
110. Justin Quinn, 'Irish and Scottish Poetry in the East', in Peter Mackay, Edna Longley and Fran Brearton (eds), *Modern Irish and Scottish Poetry* (Cambridge: Cambridge University Press, 2011), pp. 199–200.
111. Hena (2013), p. 517.
112. Tuma (1998), p. 264.
113. Geoffrey Hill, *Speech! Speech!* (Washington: Counterpoint, 2000), pp. 10, 25.
114. Hill (2000), p. 44.
115. Hill (2000), p. 50.

CHAPTER FOUR: GENDER, SEXUALITY AND CLASS

1. Vicki Bertram, *Gendering Poetry* (London: Pandora, 2005), p. 137.
2. Quoted in Tim Kendall, review of *Birthday Letters*, *Oxford Poetry* X(1), 1998 (accessed online).
3. For an account of this moment in American poetry, see Lucy Collins, 'Confessionalism', in Neil Roberts (ed.), *A Companion to Twentieth-Century Poetry* (Oxford: Blackwell, 2001), pp. 197–208.

4. Deryn Rees-Jones, 'Consorting with Angels: Anne Sexton and the Art of Confession', *Women: A Cultural Reader*, 10(3) (Winter 1999), 285.
5. Bertram (2005), p. 146.
6. Ian Sansom, review of *Birthday Letters*, *London Review of Books*, 20(4), 19 February 1998 (accessed online).
7. For a detailed intertextual account of Plath and Hughes's work, see Heather Clark, *The Grief of Influence: Sylvia Plath and Ted Hughes* (Oxford: Oxford University Press, 2011).
8. Jane Dowson and Alice Entwistle, *A History of Twentieth-Century British Women's Poetry* (Cambridge: Cambridge University Press, 2005), p. 254.
9. Elizabeth Lowry, 'Dream On', review of Medbh McGuckian, *Selected Poems*, *Metre*, 4 (1998), 46–53 (46).
10. Medbh McGuckian, epigraph to *Captain Lavender* (Loughcrew: Gallery Press, 1994).
11. Medbh McGuckian, *The Flower Master and Other Poems* (Loughcrew: Gallery Press, 1993), p. 54.
12. Clair Wills, *Improprieties: Politics and Sexuality in Northern Irish Poetry* (Oxford: Clarendon Press, 1993), pp. 165–6.
13. Paul Muldoon, introduction to Medbh McGuckian, *Single Ladies: Sixteen Poems* (Budleigh Salterton: Interim Press, 1980), p. 21.
14. Wills (1993), p. 169.
15. Fiona Sampson, *Beyond the Lyric: A Map of Contemporary British Poetry* (London: Chatto & Windus, 2012), p. 211.
16. Wills (1993), pp. 187–8.
17. Shane Alcobia-Murphy, *Sympathetic Ink: Intertextual Relations in Northern Irish Poetry* (Liverpool: Liverpool University Press, 2006), pp. 81–2. Cf. also Shane Alcobia-Murphy, *Medbh McGuckian: The Poetics of Exemplarity* (Aberdeen: AHRC Centre for Irish and Scottish Studies, 2013).
18. Quoted in Leontia Flynn, 'Domestic Violences: Medbh McGuckian and Irish Women's Writing in the 1980s', in Fran Brearton and Alan Gillis (eds), *The Oxford Handbook of Modern Irish Poetry* (Oxford: Oxford University Press, 2013), pp. 419–34 (434). Cf. also Leontia Flynn, *Reading Medbh McGuckian* (Dublin: Irish Academic Press, 2014).
19. Brearton and Gillis (2013), p. 434.
20. Cf. Clair Wills, *Reading Paul Muldoon* (Newcastle upon Tyne: Bloodaxe Books, 1998).
21. McGuckian (1994), p. 69.
22. Peter Forbes, 'Winning Lines', *The Guardian*, 31 August 2002 (accessed online).
23. Angelica Michelis and Antony Rowland, *Choosing Tough Words: The Poetry of Carol Ann Duffy* (Manchester: Manchester University Press, 2003), p. 1.
24. Michelis and Rowland (2003), p. 1.
25. John Redmond, 'Lyric Adaptations: James Fenton, Craig Raine, Christopher Reid, Simon Armitage, Carol Ann Duffy', in Neil Corcoran (ed.), *The Cambridge Companion to Twentieth-Century English Poetry* (Cambridge: Cambridge University Press, 2007), pp. 245–58 (253).
26. Carol Ann Duffy, *Selected Poems* (Harmondsworth: Penguin, 1994), p. 66.
27. Redmond (2007), p. 254.
28. Sarah Broom, *Contemporary British and Irish Poetry* (Basingstoke: Palgrave Macmillan, 2006), p. 87.
29. Duffy (1994), p. 95.
30. Duffy (1994), p. 94.
31. David Kennedy, *New Relations: The Refashioning of British Poetry 1980–1994* (Bridgend: Seren, 1996), p. 230.
32. Dowson and Entwistle (2005), p. 255.
33. Redmond (2007), p. 253.
34. Peter Forbes, 'Profile: Carol Ann Duffy', *The Guardian*, 31 August 2002 (accessed online).
35. Sean O'Brien, *The Deregulated Muse: Essays on Contemporary British and Irish Poetry* (Newcastle upon Tyne: Bloodaxe Books, 1998), p. 167.

36. O'Brien (1998), p. 168.
37. Carol Ann Duffy, *The Feminine Gospels* (London: Picador, 2002), p. 12.
38. Stephen Burt, review of Carol Ann Duffy, *The Feminine Gospels, Times Literary Supplement*, 27 September 2002 (accessed online).
39. Deryn Rees-Jones, *Consorting with Angels: Essays on Modern Women Poets* (Tarset: Bloodaxe Books, 2005), p. 163.
40. Pascale Petit, 'Do Women Poets Write Differently to Men?' *Poetry Review*, 102(4) (Winter 2012) (accessed online).
41. Petit (2012).
42. Moynagh Sullivan, 'Irish Poetry After Feminism: In Search of "Male Poets"', in Justin Quinn (ed.), *Irish Poetry After Feminism* (Gerrards Cross: Colin Smythe, 2008), p. 16.
43. Seamus Heaney, quoted in Selina Guinness, 'The Annotated House: Feminism and Form', in Quinn (2008), p. 69.
44. Vona Groarke, *Juniper Street* (Loughcrew: Gallery Press, 2006), p. 55.
45. Guinness, in Quinn (2008), p. 74.
46. John Osborne, *Larkin, Ideology and Critical Violence: A Case of Wrongful Conviction* (Basingstoke: Palgrave Macmillan, 2008), pp. 159–86.
47. Guinness, in Quinn (2008), p. 74.
48. Guinness, in Quinn (2008), p. 78.
49. John Redmond, *Poetry and Privacy: Questioning Public Interpretations of Contemporary British and Irish Poetry* (Bridgend: Seren, 2013), p. 179.
50. Guinness, in Quinn (2008), p. 71.
51. Andy Brown (ed.), *Binary Myths: Conversations with Contemporary Poets* (Exeter: Stride, 1998), p. 18.
52. Don Paterson, *God's Gift to Women* (London: Faber & Faber, 1997), p. 51.
53. Paterson (1997), p. 53.
54. Bertram (2005), p. 189.
55. Cf. Patricia Coughlan, '"Bog Queens": The Representation of Women in the Poetry of John Montague and Seamus Heaney', in David Cairns and Toni O'Brien Johnson (eds), *Gender in Irish Writing* (Milton Keynes: Open University Press, 1991), pp. 88–111.
56. Eavan Boland, 'Compact and Compromise: Derek Mahon as a Young Poet', *Irish University Review*, 24(1) (Spring/Summer 1994), 66.
57. James Campbell, *Thom Gunn in Conversation* (London: Between the Lines, 2000), p. 54.
58. Thom Gunn, *Boss Cupid* (London: Faber & Faber, 2000), p. 87.
59. Stephen Burt, 'Thom Gunn: Kinetic Aesthetics', in *Close Calls with Nonsense: Reading New Poetry* (Saint Paul, MN: Graywolf, 2009), pp. 199–214 (206).
60. Thom Gunn, *Collected Poems* (London: Faber & Faber, 1993), p. 39.
61. Burt (2009), p. 214.
62. Gunn (1993), p. 463.
63. Gunn (1993), p. 464.
64. Roy Fisher, *The Long and the Short of It: Poems 1955–2005* (Tarset: Bloodaxe Books, 2005), p. 170.
65. Kennedy (1996), p. 52.
66. Broom (2006), p. 10.
67. Tony Harrison, *Selected Poems* (London: Penguin, 1984), p. 123.
68. Robert Potts, 'Bathetic Fallacies', review of *Laureate's Block, The Guardian*, 26 February 2000 (accessed online).
69. Douglas Dunn, *Love or Nothing* (London: Faber & Faber, 1974), p. 41.
70. Sean O'Brien, 'Dunn and Politics', in Robert Crawford and David Kinloch (eds), *Reading Douglas Dunn* (Edinburgh: Edinburgh University Press, 1992), pp. 66–79 (68); David Kennedy, *Douglas Dunn* (Tavistock: Northcote House, 2007), p. 10.

71. Quoted in Neil Astley (ed.), *Bloodaxe Critical Anthologies 1: Tony Harrison* (Newcastle upon Tyne: Bloodaxe Books, 1991), pp. 129–32.
72. Douglas Dunn, *Terry Street* (London: Faber & Faber, 1969), p. 17. For more on the conflict between Dunn's Scottishness and his North of England milieu, see my '"Dafter than we care to own": Some Poets of the North of England', in Peter Robinson (ed.), *The Oxford Handbook of Contemporary British and Irish Poetry* (Oxford: Oxford University Press), pp. 407–23.
73. Dunn (1969), p. 18.
74. Dunn (1969), pp. 24, 26.
75. Kennedy (2007), p. 16.
76. Douglas Dunn, *New Selected Poems* (London: Faber & Faber, 2003), p. 45.
77. Kennedy (2007), p. 40.
78. Dunn (2003), p. 46.
79. Kennedy (1996), p. 31.
80. Kennedy (1996), p. 51.
81. Sean O'Brien, *The Frighteners* (Newcastle upon Tyne: Bloodaxe, 1987), p. 22.
82. Adam Newey, review of Sean O'Brien, *Cousin Coat: Selected Poems*, *The Guardian*, 1 February 2003 (accessed online).
83. Peter Davidson, *The Idea of North* (London: Reaktion Books, 2005), p. 226.
84. Sean O'Brien, *Ghost Train* (Oxford: Oxford University Press, 1995), p. 17.
85. Sean O'Brien, *Downriver* (London: Picador, 2001), p. 9.
86. Quoted in John Goodby, *Irish Poetry since 1950: From Stillness into History* (Manchester: Manchester University Press, 2000), p. 225.
87. Maria Johnston, review of Sean O'Brien, *November*, *Poetry Matters*, 2011 (http://www.tower poetry.org.uk/poetry-matters/reviews/reviews-archive/453-november-by-seanobrien-reviewed-by-maria-johnston).
88. Don Paterson, *Nil Nil* (London: Faber & Faber, 1993), p. 21.
89. Peter Howarth, review of Don Paterson, *Selected Poems*, *London Review of Books*, 21 March 2013 (accessed online).
90. Sampson (2012), p. 128.
91. Georgia Graham, 'Working class children must learn to be middle class to get on in life, government advisor says', *Daily Telegraph*, 3 March 2014 (accessed online).
92. Tom Leonard, *Intimate Voices: Selected Work 1963–1983* (London: Vintage, 1995), p. 9.
93. Leonard (1995), p. 140.
94. Broom (2006), p. 24.
95. Tom Paulin, 'Peter Reading: Junk Britain', in *Minotaur: Poetry and the Nation State* (London: Faber & Faber, 1992), pp. 285–94.
96. O'Brien (1998), p. 131.
97. Isabel Martin, introduction to Peter Reading, *Collected Poems 1: Poems 1970–1984* (Newcastle upon Tyne: Bloodaxe Books, 1995), p. 17.
98. Peter Reading, 'Shropshire Lads', in *Collected Poems 3: Poems 1997–2003* (Tarset: Bloodaxe Books, 2003), p. 62.
99. Anne Stevenson, 'Inside and Outside History', in *Between the Iceberg and the Ship: Selected Essays* (Ann Arbor, MI: University of Michigan Press, 1998), pp. 82–3.
100. Nuala Ní Dhomhnaill, 'What Foremothers?' *P.N. Review*, 91 (May–June 1993), quoted in Anne Stevenson, 'Outside Histrionics: Answering Nuala Ní Dhomhnaill', in *Between the Iceberg and the Ship*, pp. 85–9 (86).
101. Stevenson (1998), pp. 87, 89.
102. Mary O'Malley, 'Credo', in *The Boning Hall* (Manchester: Carcanet, 2002), p. 59.
103. Kit Fryatt, review of Paula Meehan, *Painting Rain*, *The Stinging Fly*, 13(2) (Summer 2009), 117–19 (119).
104. Burt (2002, accessed online).
105. Marianne Moore, *Complete Poems* (London: Faber & Faber, 1968), p. 36.

CHAPTER FIVE: EXPERIMENT AND LANGUAGE

1. Veronica Forrest-Thomson, *Collected Poems*, ed. Anthony Barnett (Exeter: Shearsman, in association with Allardyce, 2008), p. 58.
2. Peter Robinson and Robert Sheppard (eds), *News for the Ear: A Homage to Roy Fisher* (Exeter: Stride, 2000), p. 119.
3. Ian Gregson, *Contemporary Poetry and Postmodernism: Dialogue and Estrangement* (Basingstoke: Macmillan, 1996), p. 106.
4. Peter Howarth, *The Cambridge Introduction to Modernist Poetry* (Cambridge: Cambridge University Press, 2012), p. 5.
5. Gregson (1996), p. 198. Cf. also Forrest-Thomson's poem on the duck–rabbit illusion, 'Zettel', in Forrest-Thomson (2008), pp. 77–9.
6. John Wilkinson, *The Lyric Touch: Essays on the Poetry of Excess* (Cambridge: Salt Publishing, 2007), p. 5.
7. Wilkinson (2007), p. 6.
8. Wilkinson (2007), p. 20.
9. Sean O'Brien, *Journeys to the Interior: Ideas of England in Contemporary Poetry* (Newcastle upon Tyne: Bloodaxe Books, 2012), p. 41.
10. Michael Donaghy, *The Shape of the Dance: Essays, Interviews and Digressions* (London: Picador, 2009), p. 70.
11. J. H. Prynne, *Poems* (Tarset: Bloodaxe Books, 2005 [1999]), p. 162.
12. Natalie Pollard, '"Is a chat with me your fancy?": Address in Contemporary British Poetry', in Peter Robinson (ed.), *The Oxford Handbook of Contemporary British and Irish Poetry* (Oxford: Oxford University Press, 2013), pp. 638–56 (651–2).
13. See Robert Potts, review of *Poems*, *The Guardian*, 10 April 2004 (accessed online).
14. Anthony Thwaite, *Poetry Today, 1960–1973* (London: Longman, 1973), p. 69. For a survey of twentieth-century small press activity, see David Miller and Richard Price (eds), *British Poetry Magazines 1914–2000: A History and Bibliography* (New Castle, DE, and London: Oak Knoll Press and The British Library, 2006).
15. Howarth (2012), p. 220.
16. Michel Foucault, 'What is an author?' in Paul Rabinow (ed.), *The Foucault Reader* (Harmondsworth: Penguin, 1984), pp. 101–20 (101).
17. Keith Tuma, *Fishing by Obstinate Isles: Modern and Postmodern British Poetry and American Readers* (Evanston, IL: Northwestern University Press, 1998), p. 196.
18. Steve Clark, 'Prynne and the Movement', *Jacket*, 24, November 2003 (http://jacket magazine.com/24/clark-s.html). Clark's thesis provoked a furious rebuttal from Andrew Duncan in the same issue of *Jacket* ('Response to Steve Clark's "Prynne and the Movement"', *Jacket*, 24 (http://jacketmagazine.com/24/duncan.html).
19. Emily Critchley, 'When I say I believe women ...', in Carrie Etter (ed.), *Infinite Difference: Other Poetries by U.K. Women Poets* (Exeter: Shearsman, 2010), p. 177.
20. Linda Kinahan, 'Feminist Experimentalism, Literary History, and Subjectivity: "this lyric forever error" of Kathleen Fraser and Denise Riley', in Romana Huk (ed.), *Assembling Alternatives: Reading Postmodern Poetries Transnationally* (Middletown, CT: Wesleyan University Press, 2003), pp. 275–83 (275).
21. Kinahan (2003), p. 275.
22. Maggie O'Sullivan, *out of everywhere: linguistically innovative poetry by women in North America & the UK* (London: Reality Street Editions, 1996); and Carrie Etter, *Infinite Difference: Other Poetries by UK Women Poets* (Exeter: Shearsman, 2010).
23. David Kennedy and Christine Kennedy, *Women's Experimental Poetry in Britain 1970–2010* (Liverpool: Liverpool University Press, 2013), p. 84.
24. Denise Riley, *Selected Poems* (London: Reality Street Editions, 2000), p. 52.
25. John Wilkinson, 'Illyrian Places', *Parataxis*, 6 (1994), 58–69 (68).
26. Denise Riley (2000), pp. 30–1.

27. Kennedy and Kennedy (2013), p. 96.
28. Wilkinson, 'Illyrian Places' (1994), 58–69; quoted in Kennedy and Kennedy (2013), p. 97.
29. Fiona Sampson, *Beyond the Lyric: A Map of Contemporary British Poetry* (London: Chatto & Windus, 2012), p. 267.
30. Denise Riley (2000), p. 11.
31. Cf. Peter Riley, 'Denise Riley and the Force of Bereavement', *Fortnightly Review*, March 2012 (http://fortnightlyreview.co.uk/2012/03/denise-riley-force-bereavement/). Peter Riley suggests the term 'lament', with its classical and Eastern European overtones, as a more appropriate description of 'A Part Song'.
32. Denise Riley, 'A Part Song', *London Review of Books*, 34(3), 9 February 2012 (accessed online).
33. Donaghy (2009), p. 159.
34. Andy Brown (ed.), *Binary Myths: Conversations with Contemporary Poets* (Exeter: Stride Publications, 1998), p. 59.
35. Barry MacSweeney, *Wolf Tongue: Selected Poems 1965–2000* (Tarset: Bloodaxe Books, 2003), p. 196.
36. 'An Interview with Don Paterson', *The Harlequin*, 2 (http://www.theharlequin.org/paterson1/).
37. Cf. Jeremy Noel-Tod, 'Much Ado About Poets', review of Randall Stevenson, *The Last of England? The Oxford English Literary History*, vol. 12, *Daily Telegraph*, 14 March 2004.
38. Iain Sinclair (ed.), *Conductors of Chaos* (London: Picador, 1996), p. xiii.
39. Trevor Joyce, 'Irish Terrain: Alternate Plains of Cleavage', in Romana Huk (ed.), *Assembling Alternatives* (2003), pp. 156–68.
40. Drew Milne, 'David Jones: A Charter for Philistines', in Sinclair (1996), p. 263.
41. Sinclair (1996), p. xv.
42. Sinclair (1996), p. xviii.
43. Richard Caddel and Peter Quartermain (eds), *Other: British and Irish Poetry since 1970* (London: Wesleyan University Press, 1999), p. xx.
44. Andrew Duncan, *The Failure of Conservatism in Modern British Poetry* (Cambridge: Salt Publishing, 2003), p. 1.
45. Duncan (2003), p. 15.
46. Duncan is a prolific commentator, whose other work can be found in *Centre and Periphery in Modern British Poetry* (Liverpool: Liverpool University Press, 2005); *Origins of the Underground: British Poetry Between Apocryphon and Incident Light, 1933–1979* (Cambridge: Salt Publishing, 2008); and *The Council of Heresy: A Primer of Poetry in a Balkanized Terrain* (Exeter: Shearsman, 2009).
47. Geoffrey Hill, *Collected Poems* (Harmondsworth: Penguin, 1985), p. 97.
48. Peter Manson, *Stéphane Mallarmé: The Poems in Verse* (Oxford, OH: University of Miami Press, 2012), p. 281.
49. Peter Manson, *Between Cup and Lip* (Oxford, OH: Miami University Press, 2008), p. 57.
50. Dónal Moriarty, *The Art of Brian Coffey* (Dublin: University College Dublin Press, 2000), p. 57.
51. Moriarty (2000), p. 57.
52. Manson (2012), p. 169.
53. Wilkinson (2007), p. 134.
54. Keston Sutherland, *The Odes to TL61P* (London: Enitharmon, 2013), p. 7.
55. Wilkinson (2007), p. 134.
56. Sutherland (2013), p. 33.
57. Sutherland (2013), p. 58.
58. Keston Sutherland, *Stupefaction: A Radical Anatomy of Phantoms* (London: Seagull, 2011), p. 242.
59. Ian Hamilton and Jeremy Noel-Tod (eds), *The Oxford Companion to Modern Poetry*, 2nd edn (Oxford: Oxford University Press, 2013), p. 603.

60. Jeremy Noel-Tod, 'Walking the Yellow Brick Road: A Pedestrian Account of J. H. Prynne's *Poems'*, in David Kennedy (ed.), *Necessary Steps: Poetry, Elegy, Walking, Spirit* (Exeter: Shearsman, 2007), p. 90.

61. Ben Watson, *The Negative Dialectics of Poodle Play* (London: Quartet, 1995).

62. Noel-Tod, quoting 'The Ideal Star-Fighter' (2007), p. 95.

63. Cited in Marjorie Perloff, *Unoriginal Genius: Poetry by Other Means in the New Century* (London: University of Chicago Press, 2012), p. 149.

64. Cited in Perloff (2012), p. 9.

65. Robert Crawford, *The Modern Poet: Poetry, Academia and Knowledge since the 1750s* (Oxford: Oxford University Press, 2001), p. 221.

66. *Private Eye*, 1343 (28 June–11 July 2013), 28.

CHAPTER SIX: NEW ENVIRONMENTS

1. John Redmond, *Poetry and Privacy: Questioning Public Interpretations of Contemporary British and Irish Poetry* (Bridgend: Seren, 2013), p. 16.

2. Sam Adams, 'Interview with Robert Minhinnick' (http://www.carcanet.co.uk/cgi-bin/scribe?showdoc=14;doctype=interview).

3. Other poets to have written ecological prose of note include R. F. Langley in his *Journals* (Exeter: Shearsman, 2006), and Iain Sinclair, best known for his urban landscapes, in his *Edge of the Orison: In the Traces of John Clare's 'Journey Out of Essex'* (London: Hamish Hamilton, 2005).

4. Kathleen Jamie, 'A Lone Enraptured Male', review of Robert Macfarlane, *The Wild Places*, *London Review of Books*, 30(5) (6 March 2008).

5. Redmond (2013), p. 106.

6. Redmond (2013), pp. 106, 108.

7. Sylvia Plath, *Collected Poems*, ed. Ted Hughes (London: Faber & Faber, 1981), p. 191.

8. Samuel Beckett, *Complete Dramatic Works* (London: Faber & Faber, 1990), p. 97.

9. For an intriguing investigation of the ethical dimension of ecopoetics, see Randy Malamud, *Poetic Animals and Animal Souls* (Basingstoke: Palgrave Macmillan, 2002).

10. For a survey of early responses to Heaney, see Michael Allen (ed.). *New Casebooks: Seamus Heaney* (Basingstoke: Macmillan, 1997).

11. Sarah Broom, *Contemporary British and Irish Poetry* (Basingstoke: Palgrave Macmillan, 2006), p. 33.

12. Kathleen Jamie, *The Overhaul* (London: Picador, 2012), p. 16.

13. Peter Mackay, '*The Tree House* and *Findings*: The Tilt from One Parish to Another', in Rachel Falconer (ed.), *Kathleen Jamie: Essays and Poems on Her Work* (Edinburgh: Edinburgh University Press, forthcoming).

14. Maria Johnston, review of *The Overhaul*, *The Guardian*, 9 November 2012.

15. Peter Riley, *The Glacial Stairway* (Manchester: Carcanet, 2011), p. 88.

16. Kathleen Jamie, *Sightlines* (London: Sort Of Books, 2012), p. 176.

17. Derek Mahon, *Collected Poems* (Loughcrew: Gallery Press, 1999), p. 89.

18. Mahon, *An Autumn Wind* (Loughcrew: Gallery Press, 2010), 23.

19. Mahon, *Life on Earth* (Loughcrew: Gallery Press, 2008), p. 44.

20. Christopher Reid, *Expanded Universes* (London: Faber & Faber, 1996), p. 16.

21. For the historical evolution of the term 'nature', see Raymond Williams, *Keywords: A Vocabulary of Culture and Society* (London: Fontana, 1976).

22. Jonathan Bate, *The Song of the Earth* (London: Picador, 2000), p. 266.

23. Tom Paulin, *The Secret Life of Poems* (London: Faber & Faber, 2008), pp. 79–86.

24. Bate (2000), p. 107.

25. Bate (2000), p. 199.

26. Bate (2000), p. 202.

27. Bate (2000), p. 204.

28. Bate (2000), p. 283.

29. Fran Brearton, *Reading Michael Longley* (Tarset: Bloodaxe Books, 2006), p. 72.
30. Edna Longley, *Poetry and Posterity* (Tarset: Bloodaxe Books, 2000), p. 131.
31. Michael Longley, *Collected Poems* (London: Jonathan Cape, 2006), p. 59.
32. Brearton (2006), pp. 89–90.
33. Michael Longley (2006), p. 61.
34. Brearton (2006), p. 86.
35. George Oppen, *New Collected Poems*, ed. Michael Davidson (Manchester: Carcanet, 2003), p. 99.
36. Christopher Ricks, 'Andrew Marvell: "Its Own Resemblance"', in *The Force of Poetry* (Oxford: Clarendon Press, 1984), pp. 34–5.
37. Michael Longley (2006), p. 186.
38. Michael Longley (2006), p. 197.
39. Neil Astley (ed.), *Earth Shattering: Ecopoems* (Tarset: Bloodaxe Books, 2007), p. 66.
40. Harriet Tarlo (ed.), *The Ground Aslant: An Anthology of Radical Landscape Poetry* (Exeter: Shearsman, 2011), pp. 11–12.
41. Jeremy Noel-Tod, 'A Bird That Isn't There', review of R. F. Langley, *Collected Poems*, *London Review of Books*, 23(3), 23 February 2001 (accessed online).
42. R. F. Langley, *Collected Poems* (Manchester: Carcanet, 2000), p. 24.
43. Gianni Vattimo et al. (eds), *Weak Thought* (New York: State University of New York Press, 2013).
44. Ken Cockburn and Alec Finlay (eds), *The Order of Things: An Anthology of Scottish Sound, Pattern and Concrete Poems* (Edinburgh: Morning Star Publications, 2001), p. 13. Cf. also Eleanor Bell, '"The ugly burds without wings?": reaction to tradition since the 1960s', in Peter Mackay, Edna Longley and Fran Brearton (eds), *Modern Irish and Scottish Poetry* (Cambridge: Cambridge University Press, 2011), pp. 238–50.
45. Richard Price, 'Cat-Scanning the Little Magazine', in Peter Robinson (ed.), *The Oxford Handbook of Contemporary British and Irish Poetry* (Oxford: Oxford University Press, 2013), pp. 173–90 (179).
46. Andrew Duncan, *The Failure of Conservatism in Modern British Poetry* (Cambridge: Salt Publishing, 2003), p. 103.
47. Ian Hamilton Finlay, '*from* Detached Sentences on Gardening', in *Selections*, ed. Alec Finlay (Berkeley: University of California Press, 2012), p. 179.
48. Ian Hamilton Finlay, *Selections*, ed. Alec Finlay (London: University of California Press, 2012), p. 153.
49. Ian Hamilton Finlay (2012), p. 157.
50. Nicholas Zurbrugg, 'Ian Hamilton Finlay and Concrete Poetry', in James Acheson and Romana Huk, *Contemporary British Poetry: Essays in Theory and Criticism* (Albany, NY: State University of New York Press, 1996), pp. 113–41 (124).
51. Zurbrugg (1996), p. 134.
52. Aingeal Clare, review of Alice Oswald, *Woods etc.*, *London Review of Books*, 23 March 2006 (accessed online).
53. Deryn Rees-Jones, *Consorting with Angels: Essays on Modern Women Poets* (Tarset: Bloodaxe Books, 2005), p. 234.
54. Alice Oswald, *Dart* (London: Faber & Faber, 2002), p. 2.
55. Roy Fisher, *The Long and the Short of It: Poems 1955–2005* (Tarset: Bloodaxe Books, 2005), p. 43.
56. Rees-Jones (2005), pp. 234–5.
57. Oswald (2002), p. 15.
58. Oswald (2002), p. 33.
59. Clare (2006).
60. Michael Hamburger, *The Truth of Poetry: Tensions in Modern Poetry from Baudelaire to the 1960s* (Manchester: Carcanet, 1982), pp. 244–5.
61. Alice Oswald, *Woods etc.* (London: Faber & Faber, 2005), p. 20.

62. Oswald (2005), p. 5.
63. Carol Rumens, review of Alice Oswald, *Woods etc.*, *The Guardian*, 24 September 2005 (accessed online).
64. John Wilkinson, *The Lyric Touch: Essays on the Poetry of Excess* (Cambridge: Salt Publishing, 2007), pp. 98–9.
65. Peter Riley, *Excavations* (Hastings: Reality Street, 2004), p. 131.
66. Jon Thompson, review of Peter Riley, *Excavations*, *Free Verse*, 7 (Winter 2004) (http://english.chass.ncsu.edu/freeverse/Archives/Winter_2004/reviews/J_Thompson_on_P_Riley.htm).
67. David Jones, *The Anathémata* (London: Faber & Faber, 1952), p. 33.
68. Dennis O'Driscoll, 'Peter Reading: *No-God and Species Decline Stuff*', in *Troubled Thoughts, Majestic Dreams* (Loughcrew: Gallery Press, 2001), pp. 278–96 (281).
69. Peter Barry, *Contemporary British Poetry and the City* (Manchester: Manchester University Press, 2000), pp. 19–20. For an answer to Barry's question, see Zoë Skoulding, *Contemporary Women's Poetry and Urban Space: Experimental Cities* (Basingstoke: Palgrave Macmillan, 2013), which studies the work of Geraldine Monk, Ágnes Lehóczky, Fiona Templeton and other poets in an international context.
70. Cf. Alex Houen, *Terrorism and Modern Literature: From Joseph Conrad to Ciaran Carson* (Oxford: Oxford University Press, 2002), and David Wheatley, '"Pushed Next to Nothing": Ciaran Carson's Breaking News', in Elmer Kennedy-Andrews (ed.), *Ciaran Carson: Critical Essays (Dublin:* Four Courts Press, 2009) pp. 45–65.
71. Michael Hofmann, *Acrimony* (London: Faber & Faber, 1986), p. 29.
72. Andrew Duncan, review of Helen Macdonald, *Shaler's Fish*, *Jacket*, 20 (December 2002) (accessed online).
73. Helen Macdonald, *Shaler's Fish* (Buckfastleigh: Etruscan Books, 2001), p. 57.
74. Duncan (2002).
75. Macdonald (2001), p. 62.

CONCLUSION

1. Alice Oswald, 'Why I Pulled Out of the T. S. Eliot Poetry Prize', *The Guardian: Comment Is Free*, 12 December 2011 (accessed online).
2. Gillian Clarke, 'The T. S. Eliot Prize Cannot Survive without Sponsorship at a Time of Cuts', *The Guardian: Comment is Free*, 13 December 2011 (accessed online).
3. T. S. Eliot, 'The Metaphysical Poets', in *Selected Prose*, ed. John Hayward (Harmondsworth: Penguin, 1953), p. 118.
4. Alison Flood, 'Carol Ann Duffy is "Wrong" about Poetry, Says Geoffrey Hill', *The Guardian*, 31 January 2012 (accessed online).
5. Ahren Warner, interview with Don Paterson, *Poetry London*, Spring 2013, 35–8 (35).
6. Mark Brown, 'Costa Awards 2012: Graphic Biography Wins Category Prize', *The Guardian*, 3 January 2013 (accessed online).
7. Interview with Louis de Bernières, *Front Row*, Radio 4, 2 August 2013.
8. Dennis O'Driscoll, 'Pen Pals: Insider Trading in Poetry Futures', in *Troubled Thoughts, Majestic Dreams* (Loughcrew: Gallery Press, 2001), p. 57; cf. also 'Blurbonic Plague' in Dennis O'Driscoll, *The Outnumbered Poet: Critical and Autobiographical Essays* (Loughcrew: Gallery Press, 2013), pp. 37–44.
9. Michael Dumanis and Cate Marvin (eds), *Legitimate Dangers: American Poets of the New Century* (New York: Sarabande Books, 2006).
10. Quoted in R. Neil Scott and Irwin H. Streight (eds), *Flannery O'Connor: The Contemporary Reviews* (Cambridge: Cambridge University Press), p. 363.
11. Nathan Hamilton (ed.), *Dear World and Everyone In It* (Tarset: Bloodaxe Books, 2012), p. 15.
12. Hamilton (2012), p. 16.
13. Michael Schmidt, editorial, *P. N. Review* 212, 39(6) (July–August 2013), 3.

14. Hamilton (2012), p. 245.
15. Cf. John Redmond, review of *Dear World and Everyone In It*, *Edinburgh Review*, 138 (2013), 113–19.
16. Seamus Heaney, *The Spirit Level* (London: Faber & Faber, 1996), p. 12.
17. F. R. Leavis, *New Bearings in English Poetry* (Harmondsworth: Pelican, 1972), p. 166.
18. Todd Swift, 'Are You On the Eyewear Young UK Poets List?' (http://toddswift.blogspot.co.uk/2013/02/are-you-on-eyewear-young-uk-poets-list.html') (accessed February 2012).
19. Clare Pollard, 'The Health of Poetry' (http://clarepollard.wordpress.com/2013/05/20/the-health-of-poetry/) (accessed 4 July 2013).
20. Dennis O'Driscoll (ed.), *Quote Poet Unquote: Contemporary Quotations on Poets and Poetry* (Washington DC: Copper Canyon Press, 2008), p. 157.
21. Cf. Richard Steinitz, *György Ligeti: Music of the Imagination* (London: Faber & Faber, 2003), p. 119.

Bibliography

INTRODUCTION
Critical Reading
Adorno, Theodor, *Minima Moralia*, trans. E. F. N. Jephcott (London: Verso, 1978).

Pound, Ezra, *An ABC of Reading* (London: Faber & Faber, 1961).

Redmond, John, *Poetry and Privacy: Questioning Public Interpretations of Contemporary British and Irish Poetry* (Bridgend: Seren, 2013).

Tuma, Keith, *Fishing by Obstinate Isles: Modern and Postmodern British Poetry and American Readers* (Evanston, IL: Northwestern University Press, 1998).

Poetry Texts
Fisher, Roy, *The Long and the Short of It: Poems 1955–2005* (Tarset: Bloodaxe Books, 2005).

Morrison, Blake and Andrew Motion (eds), *The Penguin Book of Contemporary British Poetry* (Harmondsworth: Penguin, 1982).

Thwaite, Antony, *Collected Poems* (London: Enitharmon, 2007).

CHAPTER ONE: ANTHOLOGIES AND CANON FORMATION
Critical Reading
Barry, Peter, *Poetry Wars: British Poetry of the 1970s and the Battle of Earls Court* (Cambridge: Salt, 2006).

Hamilton, Ian and Jeremy Noel-Tod (eds), *The Oxford Companion to Twentieth-Century Poetry*, 2nd edn (Oxford: Oxford University Press, 2013).

Kendall, Tim, *Modern English War Poetry* (Oxford: Oxford University Press, 2006).

Longley, Edna, *Poetry and Posterity* (Tarset: Bloodaxe Books, 2000).

Miller, David and Richard Price (eds), *British Poetry Magazines 1914–2000: A History and Bibliography* (New Castle, DE, and London: Oak Knoll Press and The British Library, 2006).

O'Brien, Sean, *The Deregulated Muse: Essays on Contemporary British and Irish Poetry* (Newcastle upon Tyne: Bloodaxe Books, 1998).

O'Driscoll, Dennis, *Troubled Thoughts, Majestic Dreams* (Loughcrew: Gallery Press, 2001).

Poetry Texts and Anthologies of British and Irish Poetry
Allott, Kenneth (ed.), *The Penguin Book of Contemporary Verse*, 2nd edn (Harmondsworth: Penguin, 1962).

Armitage, Simon and Robert Crawford (eds), *The Penguin Book of Poetry from Britain and Ireland since 1945* (Harmondsworth: Penguin, 1998).

Astley, Neil, *Staying Alive* (Tarset: Bloodaxe Books, 2002).

Astley, Neil, *Being Alive* (Tarset: Bloodaxe Books, 2004).

Astley, Neil, *Being Human* (Tarset: Bloodaxe Books, 2011).

Baker, Kenneth (ed.), *The Faber Book of Landscape Poetry* (London: Faber & Faber, 2000).

Bull, John and John Barrell (eds), *The Penguin Book of Pastoral Verse* (Harmondsworth: Penguin, 1974).

Byrne, James and Clare Pollard (eds), *Voice Recognition: 21 Poets for the 21st Century* (Tarset: Bloodaxe Books, 2009).

Caddel, Richard and Peter Quartermain (eds), *Other: British and Irish Poetry since 1970* (Hanover: Wesleyan University Press, 1999).

Conquest, Robert, *New Lines* (London: Macmillan, 1956).

Crawford, Robert and Mick Imlah (eds), *The New Penguin Book of Scottish Verse* (Harmondsworth: Penguin, 2000).

Crozier, Andrew and Tim Longville, *A Various Art* (London: Paladin, 1990).

Dooley, Maura, *Making for Planet Alice: New Women Poets* (Newcastle upon Tyne: Bloodaxe Books, 1997).

Dunn, Douglas (ed.), *The Faber Book of Twentieth-Century Scottish Poetry* (London: Faber & Faber, 1992).

Elfyn, Menna and John Rowlands (eds), *The Bloodaxe Book of Modern Welsh Poetry: Twentieth-Century Welsh Poetry in Translation* (Tarset: Bloodaxe Books, 2003).

Etter, Carrie, *Infinite Difference: Other Poetries by UK Women Poets* (Exeter: Shearsman, 2010).

Evaristo, Bernardine and Daljit Nagra, *Ten New Poets Spread the Word* (Tarset: Bloodaxe Books, 2010).

Hamilton, Nathan, *Dear World and Everyone In It* (Tarset: Bloodaxe Books, 2012).

Hulse, Michael, David Kennedy and David Morley, *The New Poetry* (Newcastle upon Tyne: Bloodaxe Books, 1993).

Keegan, Paul (ed.), *The New Penguin Book of English Verse* (Harmondsworth: Penguin, 2000).

Kinsella, Thomas (ed.), *The New Oxford Book of Irish Verse* (Oxford: Oxford University Press, 1986).

Larkin, Philip (ed.), *The Oxford Book of Twentieth-Century English Verse* (Oxford: Oxford University Press, 1973).

Longley, Edna (ed.), *The Bloodaxe Book of 20th Century Poetry* (Tarset: Bloodaxe Books, 2000).

Lumsden, Roddy, *Identity Parade: New British and Irish Poets* (Tarset: Bloodaxe Books, 2010).

MacAulay, Donald, *Nua-Bhardachd Ghaidhlig / Modern Scottish Gaelic Poems*, 2nd edn (Edinburgh: Canongate, 1987).

Markham, E. A. *Hinterland: Caribbean Poetry from the West Indies and Britain* (Newcastle-upon-Tyne: Bloodaxe Books, 1989).

Morrison, Blake and Andrew Motion (eds), *The Penguin Book of Contemporary British Poetry* (Harmondsworth: Penguin, 1982).

O'Brien, Peggy (ed.), *The Wake Forest Book of Irish Women's Poetry 1967–2000* (Winston-Salem, NC: Wake Forest University Press, 2000).

O'Brien, Sean, *The Firebox: Poetry in Britain and Ireland after 1945* (London: Picador, 1998).

Ormsby, Frank, *A Rage for Order: Poetry of the Northern Ireland Troubles* (Belfast: Blackstaff, 1992).

O'Sullivan, Maggie, *out of everywhere: linguistically innovative poetry by women in North America and the UK* (London: Reality Street Editions, 1996).

Pinter, Harold, *Various Voices: Prose, Poetry, Politics 1948–2005* (London: Faber & Faber, 1998).

Ricks, Christopher (ed.), *The Oxford Book of English Verse* (Oxford: Oxford University Press, 1999).

Rumens, Carol, *Making for the Open: Post-feminist Poetry* (London: Chatto & Windus, 1985; 2nd edn, 1987).

Salzman, Eva and Amy Wack, *Women's Work: Modern Women Poets Writing in English* (Bridgend: Seren, 2008).

Schmidt, Michael (ed.), *Some Contemporary Poets of Britain and Ireland* (Manchester: Carcanet, 1983).

Schmidt, Michael (ed.), *The Harvill Book of Twentieth-Century Poetry in English* (London: Harvill, 1999).

Shapcott, Jo and Matthew Sweeney (eds), *Emergency Kit: Poems for Strange Times* (London: Faber & Faber, 1996).

Sheers, Owen, *A Poet's Guide to Britain* (Harmondsworth: Penguin, 2010).

Sinclair, Iain (ed.), *Conductors of Chaos: A Poetry Anthology* (London: Picador, 1996).

Tarlo, Harriet (ed.), *The Ground Aslant: An Anthology of Radical Landscape Poetry* (Exeter: Shearsman, 2011).

Tuma, Keith (ed.), *An Anthology of Twentieth-Century British and Irish Poetry* (New York: Oxford University Press, 2001).

CHAPTER TWO: APPROACHES TO CONTEMPORARY BRITISH POETRY
Critical Reading

Brearton, Fran, *Reading Michael Longley* (Tarset: Bloodaxe Books, 2006).

Clark, Heather, *The Ulster Renaissance: Poetry in Belfast 1962–1972* (Oxford: Oxford University Press, 2006).

Eagleton, Terry, *Literary Theory: An Introduction*, 2nd revd edn (Oxford: Blackwell, 1996).

Easthope, Antony and John Thompson (eds), *Contemporary Poetry Meets Modern Theory* (Hemel Hempstead: Harvester Wheatsheaf, 1991).

Eliot, T. S., *Selected Prose*, ed. John Hayward (Harmondsworth: Penguin, 1953).

Everett, Barbara, *Poets in Their Time: Essays on English Poetry from Donne to Larkin* (Oxford: Clarendon Press, 1991).

Ford, Mark, *A Driftwood Altar: Essays and Reviews* (London: Waywiser, 2005).

Gervais, David, *Literary Englands: Versions of 'Englishness' in Modern Writing* (Cambridge: Cambridge University Press, 1993).

Hamburger, Michael, *The Truth of Poetry: Tensions in Modern Poetry from Baudelaire to the 1960s* (London: Weidenfeld & Nicolson, 1969).

Heaney, Seamus, *Finders Keepers: Selected Prose 1971–2001* (London: Faber & Faber, 2002).

Hill, Geoffrey Hill, *Collected Critical Writings*, ed. Kenneth Haynes (Oxford: Oxford University Press, 2008).

Kennedy-Andrews, Elmer (ed.), *Paul Muldoon: Poetry, Prose and Drama, A Collection of Critical Essays* (Gerrards Cross: Colin Smythe, 2008).

Kerrigan, John and Peter Robinson (eds), *The Thing About Roy Fisher: Critical Studies* (Liverpool: Liverpool University Press, 2000).

Leighton, Angela, *On Form: Poetry, Aestheticism, and the Legacy of a Word* (Cambridge: Cambridge University Press, 2007).

McDonald, Peter, *Mistaken Identities: Poetry and Northern Ireland* (Oxford: Clarendon Press, 1997).

McDonald, Peter, *Serious Poetry: Form and Authority from Yeats to Hill* (Oxford: Clarendon Press, 2002).

Muldoon, Paul, 'Getting Round: Notes Towards an *Ars Poetica*'. *Essays in Criticism*, 48(2) (April 1998).

Muldoon, Paul, *The End of the Poem: Oxford Lectures on Poetry* (London: Faber & Faber, 2006).

O'Donoghue, Bernard (ed.), *The Cambridge Companion to Seamus Heaney* (Cambridge: Cambridge University Press, 2009).

Osborne, John, *Larkin, Ideology and Critical Violence: A Case of Wrongful Conviction* (Basingstoke: Palgrave Macmillan, 2007).

Paulin, Tom, *Minotaur: Poetry and the Nation State* (London: Faber & Faber, 1992).

Pound, Ezra, *Literary Essays of Ezra Pound*, ed. T. S. Eliot (London: Faber & Faber, 1954).

Ricks, Christopher, *Essays in Appreciation* (Oxford: Oxford University Press, 1998).

Ricks, Christopher, *True Friendship: Geoffrey Hill, Anthony Hecht, and Robert Lowell Under the Sign of Eliot and Pound* (New Haven, CT: Yale University Press, 2010).

Robinson, Peter and Robert Sheppard (eds), *News for the Ear: A Homage to Roy Fisher* (Exeter: Stride Publications, 2000).

Sampson, Fiona, *Beyond the Lyric: A Map of Contemporary British Poetry* (London: Chatto & Windus, 2012).

Poetry Texts

Fisher, Roy, *The Long and the Short Of It, Poems 1955–2005* (Tarset: Bloodaxe Books, 2005).

Larkin, Philip, *Complete Poems*, ed. Archie Burnett (London: Faber & Faber, 2012).

Muldoon, Paul, *Poems 1968–1998* (London: Faber & Faber, 2001).

Paterson, Don, *God's Gift to Women* (London: Faber & Faber, 1997).

CHAPTER THREE: POSTCOLONIALISM
Critical Reading
Bhabha, Homi, *The Location of Culture* (London: Routledge, 1986).

Booth, James (ed.), *New Larkins for Old: Critical Essays* (Basingstoke: Macmillan, 2000).

Brathwaite, Kamau, *History of the Voice: The Development of Nation Language in Anglophone Caribbean Poetry* (London: New Beacon Books, 1984).

Corcoran, Neil (ed.), *The Chosen Ground: Essays on the Contemporary Poetry of Northern Ireland* (Bridgend: Seren, 1992).

Corcoran, Neil, *Poets of Modern Ireland* (Cardiff: University of Wales Press, 1999).

Corcoran, Neil (ed.), *The Cambridge Companion to Twentieth-Century English Poetry* (Cambridge: Cambridge University Press, 2007).

Crawford, Robert, *Identifying Poets: Self and Territory in Twentieth-Century Poetry* (Edinburgh: Edinburgh University Press, 1993).

Crawford, Robert, *Devolving English Literature*, 2nd edn (Edinburgh: Edinburgh University Press: 2000).

Crawford, Robert, *The Modern Poet: Poetry, Academia and Knowledge since the 1750s* (Oxford: Oxford University Press, 2001).

Dabydeen, David, *The Black Presence in English Literature* (Manchester: Manchester University Press, 1985).

Davie, Donald, *With the Grain: Essays on Thomas Hardy and Modern British Poetry*, ed. Clive Wilmer (Manchester: Carcanet, 1998).

Deleuze, Gilles and Félix Guattari, *Kafka: Towards a Minor Literature*, trans. Dana Polan (Minneapolis: Minnesota University Press, 1986).

Deleuze, Gilles and Félix Guattari, *Anti-Oedipus*, trans. Robert Hurley, Mark Seem and Helen R. Lane (London and New York: Continuum, 2004).

Derrida, Jacques, 'Shibboleth', trans. Joshua Wilner, in Geoffrey H. Hartman and Sanford Budick (eds), *Midrash and Literature* (New Haven, CT: Yale University Press, 1986), pp. 307–47.

Hart, Matthew, *Nations of Nothing but Poetry: Modernism, Transnationalism, and Synthetic Vernacular Writing* (Oxford: Oxford University Press, 2010).

Hofmann, Michael, *Behind the Lines: Pieces on Writing and Pictures* (London: Faber & Faber, 2001).

Lloyd, David, *Anomalous States: Irish Writing and the Postcolonial Moment* (Dublin: Lilliput Press, 1993).

Longley, Edna, *Poetry in the Wars* (Newcastle upon Tyne: Bloodaxe Books, 1986).

Naffis-Sahely, André and Julian Stannard (eds), *The Palm Beach Effect: Reflections on Michael Hofmann* (London: CB Editions, 2013).

Padel, Ruth, *The Poem and the Journey, And Sixty Poems to Read Along the Way* (London: Vintage, 2008).

Quinn, Justin, *The Cambridge Introduction to Modern Irish Poetry, 1800–2000* (Cambridge: Cambridge University Press, 2008).

Raine, Craig, *Haydn and the Valve Trumpet: Literary Essays* (London: Faber & Faber, 1990).

Ramazani, Jahan, *The Hybrid Muse: Postcolonial Poetry in English* (Chicago: University of Chicago Press, 2001).

Ramazani, Jahan, *A Transnational Poetics* (London: University of Chicago Press, 2009).

Rees-Jones, Deryn, *Consorting with Angels: Essays on Modern Women Poets* (Tarset: Bloodaxe Books, 2005).

Tuma, Keith, *Fishing By Obstinate Isles: Modern and Postmodern British Poetry and American Readers* (Evanston, IL: Northwestern University Press, 1998).

Poetry Texts
Agbabi, Patience, *Bloodshot Monochrome* (Edinburgh: Canongate, 2008).

Alvi, Moniza, 'The Least International Shop in the World', in Alison Mark and Deryn Rees-Jones (eds), *Contemporary Women's Poetry: Reading/Writing/Practice* (Basingstoke: Macmillan, 2000).

Alvi, Moniza, *Split World: Poems 1990–2005* (Tarset: Bloodaxe Books, 2008).

Brathwaite, Kamau, *The Arrivants: A New World Trilogy* (Oxford: Oxford University Press, 1973).

Brathwaite, Kamau, *Middle Passage* (New York: New Directions, 1993).

Capildeo, Vahni, *No Traveller Returns* (Cambridge: Salt, 2003).

Capildeo, Vahni, *Undraining Sea* (Norwich: Egg Box, 2009).

Carson, Ciaran, *Collected Poems* (Loughcrew: Gallery Press, 2008).

Dabydeen, David, *Slave Song* (Sydney: Dangaroo Press, 1984).

D'Aguiar, Fred, *Mama Dot* (London: Chatto & Windus, 1985).

D'Aguiar, Fred, *Bill of Rights* (London: Chatto & Windus, 1998).

Herbert, W. N., *Forked Tongue* (Newcastle upon Tyne: Bloodaxe Books, 1990).

Herbert, W. N., *Cabaret McGonagall* (Newcastle upon Tyne: Bloodaxe Books, 1996).

Herbert, W. N., *The Big Bumper Book of Troy* (Tarset: Bloodaxe Books, 2002).

Herbert, W. N., *Omnesia*, 2 vols (Tarset: Bloodaxe Books, 2013).

Hill, Geoffrey, *Collected Poems* (Harmondsworth: Penguin, 1985).

Hill, Geoffrey, *Canaan* (Harmondsworth: Penguin, 1996).

Hill, Geoffrey, *The Triumph of Love* (Boston, MA: Houghton Mifflin, 1998).

Hill, Geoffrey, *Speech! Speech!* (Washington FC: Counterpoint, 2000).

Hill, Geoffrey, *Speech! Speech!* (Washington DC: Counterpoint, 2003).

Hofmann, Michael, *Nights in the Iron Hotel* (London: Faber & Faber, 1983).

Hofmann, Michael, *Acrimony* (London: Faber & Faber, 1986).

Hofmann, Michael, *Corona, Corona* (London: Faber & Faber, 1993).

Hofmann, Michael, *Approximately Nowhere* (London: Faber & Faber, 1999).

Lewis, Gwyneth, *Parables and Faxes* (Newcastle upon Tyne: Bloodaxe Books, 1995).

Lewis, Gwyneth, *Keeping Mum: Voices from Therapy* (Tarset: Bloodaxe Books, 2003).

Lewis, Gwyneth, *Chaotic Angels: Poems in English* (Tarset: Bloodaxe Books, 2005).

Nagra, Daljit, *Look We Have Coming to Dover!* (London: Faber & Faber, 2007).

Nagra, Daljit, *Tippoo Sultan's Incredible White-Man-Eating Tiger Toy-Machine!!!* (London: Faber & Faber, 2012).

Shapcott, Jo, *Her Book: Poems 1988–1998* (London: Faber & Faber, 2000).

Walcott, Derek, *Collected Poems* (London: Faber & Faber, 1992).

CHAPTER FOUR: GENDER, SEXUALITY AND CLASS
Critical Reading

Bertram, Vicki (ed.), *Kicking Daffodils: Twentieth-Century Women Poets* (Edinburgh: Edinburgh University Press, 1997).

Bertram, Vicki, *Gendering Poetry: Contemporary Women and Men Poets* (London: Pandora, 2005).

Boland, Eavan, *Object Lessons: The Life of the Woman and the Poet in Our Time* (Manchester: Carcanet, 1995).

Brearton, Fran and Alan Gillis (eds), *The Oxford Handbook of Modern Irish Poetry* (Oxford: Oxford University Press, 2012).

Brown, Andy (ed.), *Binary Myths: Conversations with Contemporary Poets* (Exeter: Stride, 1998).

Burt, Stephen, *Close Calls with Nonsense: Reading New Poetry* (Saint Paul, MN: Graywolf, 2009).

Cairns, David and Toni O'Brien Johnson (eds), *Gender in Irish Writing* (Milton Keynes: Open University Press, 1991).

Clark, Heather, *The Grief of Influence: Sylvia Plath and Ted Hughes* (Oxford: Oxford University Press, 2011).

Crawford, Robert and David Kinloch (eds), *Reading Douglas Dunn* (Edinburgh: Edinburgh University Press, 1992).

Davidson, Peter, *The Idea of North* (London: Reaktion Books, 2005).

Dowson, Jane, *The Cambridge Companion to Twentieth-Century British and Irish Women's Poetry* (Cambridge: Cambridge University Press, 2011).

Dowson, Jane and Alice Entwistle, *A History of Twentieth-Century British Women's Poetry* (Cambridge: Cambridge University Press, 2005).

Goodby, John, *Irish Poetry since 1950: From Stillness into History* (Manchester: Manchester University Press, 2000).

Jacobus, Mary (ed.), *Women Writing and Writing about Women* (London and Sydney: Croom Helm, 1979).

Kennedy, David, *New Relations: The Refashioning of British Poetry 1980–1994* (Bridgend: Seren, 1996).

Quinn, Justin (ed.), *Irish Poetry After Feminism* (Gerrards Cross: Colin Smythe, 2008).

Roberts, Neil (ed.), *A Companion to Twentieth-Century Poetry* (Oxford: Blackwell, 2001).

Wills, Clair, *Improprieties: Politics and Sexuality in Northern Irish Poetry* (Oxford: Oxford University Press, 1993).

Poetry Texts

Didsbury, Peter, *Scenes from a Long Sleep: New and Collected Poems* (Tarset: Bloodaxe Books, 2003).

Duffy, Carol Ann, *Selected Poems* (Harmondsworth: Penguin, 1994).

Duffy, Carol Ann, *The World's Wife* (London: Anvil, 1999).

Duffy, Carol Ann, *The Feminine Gospels* (London: Picador, 2002).

Dunn, Douglas, *Terry Street* (London: Faber & Faber, 1969).

Dunn, Douglas, *Dante's Drum Kit* (London: Faber & Faber, 1993).

Dunn, Douglas, *New Selected Poems* (London: Faber & Faber, 2003).

Groarke, Vona, *Juniper Street* (Loughcrew: Gallery Press, 2006).

Gunn, Thom, *Collected Poems* (London: Faber & Faber, 1994).

Gunn, Thom, *Boss Cupid* (London: Faber & Faber, 2000).

Leonard, Tom, *Intimate Voices: Selected Work 1965–1983* (Newcastle upon Tyne: Galloping Dog Press, 1984).

Leonard, Tom, *Intimate Voice: Selected Work 1963–1983* (London: Vintage, 1995).

McGuckian, Medbh, *Marconi's Cottage* (Loughcrew: Gallery Press, 1991).

McGuckian, Medbh, *The Flower Master and Other Poems* (Loughcrew: Gallery Press 1993).

McGuckian, Medbh, *Captain Lavender* (Loughcrew: Gallery Press, 1994).

McGuckian, Medbh, *Venus and the Rain* (Loughcrew: Gallery Press 1994).

O'Brien, Sean, *The Frighteners* (Newcastle upon Tyne: Bloodaxe Books, 1987).

O'Brien, Sean, *Ghost Train* (Oxford: Oxford University Press, 1995).

O'Brien, Sean, *Collected Poems* (London: Picador, 2012).

Paterson, Don, *Nil Nil* (London: Faber & Faber, 1993).

Paterson, Don, *The Eyes (After Machado)* (London: Faber & Faber, 1999).

Paterson, Don, *Landing Light* (London: Faber & Faber, 2003).

Paterson, Don, *Rain* (London: Faber & Faber, 2009).

Reading, Peter, *Collected Poems 1: Poems 1970–1984* (Newcastle upon Tyne: Bloodaxe Books, 1995).

Reading, Peter, *Collected Poems 2: Poems 1985–1996* (Newcastle upon Tyne: Bloodaxe Books, 1996).

Reading, Peter, *Collected Poems 3: Poems 1997–2003* (Tarset: Bloodaxe Books, 2003).

Reading, Peter, *−273.15* (Tarset: Bloodaxe Books, 2005).

Reading, Peter, *Vendange Tardive* (Tarset: Bloodaxe Books, 2010).

CHAPTER FIVE: EXPERIMENT AND LANGUAGE
Critical Reading

Acheson, James and Romana Huk (eds), *Contemporary British Poetry: Essays in Theory and Criticism* (Albany: State University of New York Press, 1996).

Donaghy, Michael, *The Shape of the Dance: Essays, Interviews and Digressions* (London: Picador, 2009).

Duncan, Andrew, *The Failure of Conservatism in Modern British Poetry* (Cambridge: Salt, 2003).

Duncan, Andrew, *Origins of the Underground: British Poetry between Apocryphon and Incident Light, 1933–79* (Cambridge: Salt, 2008).

Duncan, Andrew, *The Council of Heresy: A Primer of Poetry in a Balkanised Terrain* (Exeter: Shearsman, 2009).

Forrest-Thomson, Veronica, *Poetic Artifice: A Theory of Twentieth-Century Poetry* New York: St Martin's Press, 1978).

Gregson, Ian, *Contemporary Poetry and Postmodernism: Dialogue and Estrangement* (Basingstoke: Macmillan, 1996).

Gregson, Ian, *The Male Image: Representation of Masculinity in Postwar Poetry* (Basingstoke: Macmillan, 1999).

Howarth, Peter, *The Cambridge Introduction to Modernist Poetry* (Cambridge: Cambridge University Press, 2012).

Huk, Romana (ed.), *Assembling Alternatives: Reading Postmodern Poetries Transnationally* (Middletown, CT: Wesleyan University Press, 2003).

Kennedy, David (ed.), *Necessary Steps: Poetry, Elegy, Walking, Spirit* (Exeter: Shearsman, 2007).

Kennedy, David and Christine Kennedy, *Women's Experimental Poetry in Britain 1970–2010* (Liverpool: Liverpool University Press, 2013).

O'Brien, Sean, *Journeys to the Interior: Ideas of England in Contemporary Poetry* (Tarset: Bloodaxe Books, 2012).

Perloff, Marjorie, *Unoriginal Genius: Poetry by Other Means in the New Century* (London: University of Chicago Press, 2012).

Sutherland, Keston, *Stupefaction: A Radical Anatomy of Phantoms* (Chicago, IL: Chicago University Press, 2011).

Thwaite, Anthony, *Poetry Today, 1960–1973* (London: Longman, 1973).

Wilkinson, John, *The Lyric Touch: Essays on the Poetry of Excess* (Cambridge: Salt, 2007).

Poetic Texts

Forrest-Thomson, Veronica, *Collected Poems*, ed. Anthony Barnett (Exeter: Shearsman, in association with Allardyce, 2008).

MacSweeney, Barry, *Wolf Tongue: Selected Poems 1965–2000* (Tarset: Bloodaxe Books, 2003).

Manson, Peter, *Between Cup and Lip* (Oxford, OH: Miami University Press, 2008).

Manson, Peter, *Stéphane Mallarmé: The Poems in Verse* (Oxford, OH: University of Miami Press, 2012).

Prynne, J. H, *Poems* (Tarset: Bloodaxe Books, 2005).

Reid, Christopher, *Katerina Brac* (London: Faber & Faber, 1985).

Riley, Denise, *Selected Poems* (London: Reality Street Editions, 2000).

Sutherland, Keston, *The Odes to TL61P* (London: Enitharmon, 2013).

CHAPTER SIX: NEW ENVIRONMENTS
Critical Reading

Barry, Peter, *Contemporary British Poetry and the City* (Manchester: Manchester University Press, 2001).

Bate, Jonathan, *The Song of the Earth* (London: Picador, 2000).

Broom, Sarah, *Contemporary British and Irish Poetry* (Basingstoke: Palgrave Macmillan, 2006).

Bryson, J. Scott (ed.), *Ecopoetry: A Critical Introduction* (Salt Lake City: University of Utah Press, 2002).

Garrard, Greg, *Ecocriticism* (London: Routledge, 2004).

Jamie, Kathleen, *Findings* (London: Sort Of Books, 2005).

Jamie, Kathleen, *Sightlines* (London: Sort Of Books, 2012).

Malamud, Randy, *Poetic Animals and Animal Souls* (Basingstoke: Palgrave Macmillan, 2002).

Paulin, Tom, *The Secret Life of Poems* (London: Faber & Faber, 2008).
Ricks, Christopher, *The Force of Poetry* (Oxford: Oxford University Press, 1984).

Poetic Texts
Finlay, Ian Hamilton, *Selections*, ed. Alec Finlay (London: University of California Press, 2012).
Jamie, Kathleen, *Jizzen* (London: Picador, 1999).
Jamie, Kathleen, *Mr and Mrs Scotland Are Dead: Poems 1980–1994* (Tarset: Bloodaxe Books, 2002).
Jamie, Kathleen, *The Tree House* (London: Picador, 2004).
Jamie, Kathleen, *The Overhaul* (London: Picador: 2012).
Langley, R. F., *Collected Poems* (Manchester: Carcanet, 2000).
Langley, R. F., *Journals* (Exeter: Shearsman, 2006).
Langley, R. F., *The Face of It* (Manchester: Carcanet, 2007).
Macdonald, Helen, *Shaler's Fish* (Buckfastleigh: Etruscan Books, 2001).
Mahon, Derek, *Collected Poems* (Loughcrew: Gallery Press, 1999).
Mahon, Derek, *Life on Earth* (Loughcrew: Gallery Press, 2008).
Mahon, Derek, *An Autumn Wind* (Loughcrew: Gallery Press, 2010).
Oswald, Alice, *The Thing in the Gap-Stone Stile* (Oxford: Oxford University Press, 1996).
Oswald, Alice, *Dart* (London: Faber & Faber, 2002).
Oswald, Alice, *Woods etc.* (London: Faber & Faber, 2005).
Oswald, Alice, *A Sleepwalk on the Severn* (London: Faber & Faber, 2009).
Oswald, Alice, *Weeds and Wild Flowers* (London: Faber & Faber, 2009).
Oswald, Alice, *Memorial* (London: Faber & Faber, 2011).
Reid, Christopher, *Expanded Universes* (London: Faber & Faber, 1996).
Riley, Peter, *Passing Measures: A Collection of Poems* (Manchester: Carcanet, 2000).
Riley, Peter, *Alstonefield: A Poem* (Manchester: Carcanet, 2003).
Riley, Peter, *The Dance at Mociu* (Exeter: Shearsman Books, 2003).
Riley, Peter, *Excavations* (Hastings: Reality Street, 2004).
Riley, Peter, *The Day's Final Balance: Uncollected Writings 1965–2006* (Exeter: Shearsman, 2007).
Riley, Peter, *The Llŷn Writings* (Exeter: Shearsman, 2007).
Riley, Peter, *The Glacial Stairway* (Manchester: Carcanet, 2011).

CONCLUSION
Critical Reading
Brinton, Ian, *Contemporary Poetry: Poets and Poetry since 1990* (Cambridge: Cambridge University Press, 2009).
Leavis, F. R., *New Bearings in English Poetry* (Harmondsworth: Pelican, 1972).
O'Driscoll, Dennis, *The Outnumbered Poet: Critical and Autobiographical Essays* (Loughcrew: Gallery Press, 2013).

Poetic Texts
Hamilton, Nathan (ed.), *Dear World and Everyone In It* (Tarset: Bloodaxe Books, 2012).
Heaney, Seamus, *The Spirit Level* (London: Faber & Faber, 1996).
Heaney, Seamus, *Opened Ground: Poems 1966–1996* (London: Faber & Faber, 2002).

FURTHER READING: SINGLE-AUTHOR STUDIES
Alcobia-Murphy, Shane, *Medbh McGuckian: The Poetics of Exemplarity* (Aberdeen: AHRC Centre for Irish and Scottish Studies, 2012).
Alexander, Neal, *Ciaran Carson: Space, Place, Time* (Liverpool: Liverpool University Press, 2010).
Allen, Michael (ed.), *New Casebooks: Seamus Heaney* (Basingstoke: Macmillan, 1997).

Astley, Neil (ed.), *Bloodaxe Critical Anthologies 1: Tony Harrison* (Newcastle upon Tyne: Bloodaxe Books, 1991).

Booth, James (ed.), *New Larkins for Old: Critical Essays* (Basingstoke: Macmillan, 2000).

Corcoran, Neil, *The Poetry of Seamus Heaney*, 2nd edn (London: Faber & Faber, 1998).

Davies, Damian Walford, *Echoes to the Amen: Essays After R. S. Thomas* (Cardiff: University of Wales Press, 2003).

Haughton, Hugh, *The Poetry of Derek Mahon* (Oxford: Oxford University Press, 2007).

Herbert, W. N., *To Circumjack MacDiarmid: The Poetry and Prose of Hugh MacDiarmid* (Oxford: Clarendon Press, 1992).

Kendall, Tim, *Paul Muldoon* (Bridgend: Seren, 1996).

Kendall, Tim and Peter McDonald, *Paul Muldoon: Critical Essays* (Liverpool: Liverpool University Press, 2003).

Kennedy, David, *Douglas Dunn* (Tavistock: Northcote House, 2008).

Kennedy-Andrews, Elmer (ed.), *The Poetry of Derek Mahon* (Gerrards Cross: Colin Smythe, 2002).

Kennedy-Andrews, Elmer (ed.), *Ciaran Carson: Critical Essays* (Dublin: Four Courts Press, 2009).

Kerridge, Richard and Neil Reeve, *Nearly Too Much: The Poetry of J. H. Prynne* (Liverpool: Liverpool University Press, 1996).

Lyon, John and Peter McDonald, *Geoffrey Hill: Essays on His Later Work* (Oxford: Oxford University Press, 2012).

Mark, Alison, *Veronica Forrest-Thomson and Language Poetry* (Tavistock: Northcote House, 2001).

Martin, Isabel, *Reading Peter Reading* (Newcastle upon Tyne: Bloodaxe Books, 2000).

Michaelis, Angelica and Antony Rowland (eds), *The Poetry of Carol Ann Duffy: 'Choosing Tough Words'* (Manchester: Manchester University Press, 2003).

Moriarty, Dónal, *The Art of Brian Coffey* (Dublin: University College Dublin Press, 2000).

Peacock, Alan J. and Kathleen Devine, *The Poetry of Michael Longley* (Gerrards Cross: Colin Smythe, 2000).

Robinson, Peter and Robert Sheppard (eds), *News for the Ear: A Homage to Roy Fisher* (Exeter: Stride Publications, 2000).

Vendler, Helen, *Seamus Heaney* (London: Harper Collins, 1998).

Wills, Clair, *Reading Paul Muldoon* (Newcastle upon Tyne: Bloodaxe Books, 1997).

Wintle, Justin, *Furious Interiors: Wales, R. S. Thomas and God* (London: Harper Collins, 1996).

OTHER STUDIES

Alcobia-Murphy, Shane, *Sympathetic Ink: Intertextual Relations in Northern Irish Poetry* (Liverpool: Liverpool University Press, 2006).

Alderman, Nigel and C. D. Blanton, *A Concise Companion to Postwar British and Irish Poetry* (Oxford: Wiley-Blackwell, 2009).

Archambeau, Robert, *The Poet Resigns: Poetry in a Difficult World* (Akron, OH: The University of Akron Press, 2013).

Bedient, Calvin, *Eight Contemporary Poets* (Oxford: Oxford University Press, 1974).

Brearton, Fran, Edna Longley and Peter Mackay (eds), *Modern Irish and Scottish Poetry* (Cambridge: Cambridge University Press, 2011).

Campbell, Matthew (ed.), *The Cambridge Companion to Contemporary Irish Poetry* (Cambridge: Cambridge University Press, 2003).

Corcoran, Neil, *English Poetry since 1940* (London: Longman, 1993).

Davie, Donald, *Under Briggflatts: A History of Poetry in Great Britain, 1960–1988* (Manchester: Carcanet, 1989).

Day, Gary and Brian Docherty (eds), *British Poetry from the 1950s to the 1990s* (Basingstoke: Macmillan, 1997).

Fisher, Roy, *Interviews Through Time, and Selected Prose* (Exeter: Shearsman, 2000).

Herbert, W. N. and Matthew Hollis (eds), *Strong Words: Modern Poets on Modern Poetry* (Tarset: Bloodaxe Books, 2000).

Jarrell, Randall, *Poetry and the Age* (London: Faber & Faber, 1996).

Johnston, Dillon, *The Poetic Economies of England and Ireland, 1912–2000* (Basingstoke: Macmillan, 2000).

Longley, Edna, *The Living Stream: Literature and Revisionism in Ireland* (Newcastle upon Tyne: Bloodaxe, 1994).

Longley, Edna, *Yeats and Modern Poetry* (Cambridge: Cambridge University Press, 2013).

Lucas, John, *Modern English Poetry from Hardy to Hughes* (London: B. T. Batsford, 1986).

Mark, Alison and Deryn Rees-Jones (eds), *Contemporary Women's Poetry: Reading/ Writing/ Practice* (Basingstoke: Macmillan, 2000).

Matthews, Steven, *Irish Poetry: Politics, History, Negotiation: The Evolving Debate, 1969 to the Present* (Basingstoke: Macmillan, 1997).

Maxwell, Glyn, *On Poetry* (London: Oberon, 2012).

Morrison, Blake, *The Movement: English Poetry and Fiction of the 1950s* (Oxford: Oxford University Press, 1980).

O'Neill, Michael and Madeleine Callaghan, *Twentieth-Century British and Irish Poetry: Hardy to Mahon* (Oxford: Wiley-Blackwell, 2011).

Raban, Jonathan, *The Society of the Poem* (London: Harrap, 1971).

Ricks, Christopher, *Allusion to the Poets* (Oxford: Oxford University Press, 2002).

Roberts, Neil, *Narrative and Voice in Postwar Poetry* (London: Longman, 1999).

Robinson, Alan, *Instabilities in Contemporary British Poetry* (Basingstoke: Macmillan, 1988).

Ryan, Ray, *Ireland and Scotland: Literature and Culture, State and Nation, 1966–2000* (Oxford: Clarendon Press, 2002).

Smith, Stan, *Inviolable Voice: History and Twentieth-Century Poetry* (Dublin: Gill & Macmillan, 1982).

Index